Five Years Behind
Hitler's Barbed Wire

Five Years Behind Hitler's Barbed Wire

A Diary of French Officers in a German Prison Camp, 1940–1945

HENRI NATTER *and*
ADAM RÉFRÉGIER

Translated and Edited by
Jacqueline Vautrain Collins

FOREWORD BY JOHN B. ROMEISER

McFarland & Company, Inc., Publishers
Jefferson, North Carolina

LIBRARY OF CONGRESS CATALOGUING-IN-PUBLICATION DATA

Natter, Henri, author.
[Six mille à l'Oflag XVII A. English]
    Five years behind Hitler's barbed wire : a diary of French officers in a German prison camp, 1940–1945 / Henri Natter and Adam Réfrégier ; translated and edited by Jacqueline Vautrain Collins ; foreword by John B. Romeiser.
        p. cm.
    Includes bibliographical references and index.

    ISBN 978-0-7864-9980-9 (softcover : acid free paper) ∞
    ISBN 978-1-4766-2220-0 (ebook)

    1. Natter, Henri—Diaries. 2. Réfrégier, Adam—Diaries. 3. World War, 1939–1945—Prisoners and prisons, German. 4. World War, 1939–1945—Personal narratives, French. 5. Oflag XVII A (Concentration camp) I. Réfrégier, Adam, author. II. Collins, Jacqueline Vautrain, 1935– translator, editor. III. Title.
D805.G3N3613 2015
940.54'7243612092341—dc23   2015031091

BRITISH LIBRARY CATALOGUING DATA ARE AVAILABLE

© 2015 Jacqueline Vautrain Collins. All rights reserved

No part of this book may be reproduced or transmitted in any form or by any means, electronic or mechanical, including photocopying or recording, or by any information storage and retrieval system, without permission in writing from the publisher.

On the cover: Watchtower of German prison camp (photograph by Bruno Lutz)

Printed in the United States of America

McFarland & Company, Inc., Publishers
  Box 611, Jefferson, North Carolina 28640
  www.mcfarlandpub.com

Barbed wire on the left. Barbed wire on the right. Barbed wire in front.
Barbed wire behind.
Barbed wire everywhere at all times.
The only way to escape the obsession of this cursed grid,
When the earth is warm:
Lying down on one's back, following the moving changes of a cloud,
The whirling of the larks, the migration of birds
In full flight, or plunging into the infinity of the blue sky.
For they have not yet thought of putting a grid on the sky.

—Adaptation of diary entry, 12 June 1942

Contents

Foreword by John B. Romeiser   1
Preface by Jacqueline Vautrain Collins   5

1. Called to Serve Their Country
   1 September 1939–17 June 1940   13
2. Capture
   17 June–1 July 1940   18
3. Betrayal and Humiliation
   22 June–3 July 1940   25
4. Defiance
   4–20 July 1940   36
5. Settling In
   21 July–15 November 1940   47
6. Eight Months in Nuremberg
   September 1940–May 1941   65
7. Creating a Town Behind Barbed Wire
   16 November 1940–20 May 1941   76
8. La Semaine de France (the French Week)
   25 May–September 1941   100
9. Barbed Wire Blues
   October 1941–May 1942   118
10. Reaching Mid-Point
    June–December 1942   138
11. The Great Adventure
    January–14 October 1943   150

12. Wait: The Leitmotiv of the Prisoner
 Late October, 1943–15 April 1945   169
13. Trekking Eighty Miles to Freedom
 16 April–11 May/19 June 1945   191

Epilogue by Jacqueline Vautrain Collins   219
Background   231
Chapter Notes   241
Bibliography   250
Index   253

Foreword
by John B. Romeiser

Fresh stories and perspectives on historical events from World War II, a conflict which is now almost seventy years old, continue to arrive almost daily. Public fascination with what was truly a world war of the first and worst order, culminating in over sixty million civilian and military dead, has not waned with the passing of time, but instead has steadily climbed. Films, historical novels, popular and scholarly histories, conferences and colloquia, reenactments, television channels, public memorials, museums, monuments, and Internet-based sites are now legion and steadily draw viewers, participants, and scholars. The public, both internationally and within the United States, cannot seem to get enough of World War II, including the events leading up to it, its prosecution and major personalities, and the aftermath that redrew national borders, led to the first international war crimes tribunals in Nuremberg, Germany, for the newly coined term of "genocide," the explosion of the atomic bomb, Bretton Woods, the United Nations Charter, the Marshall Plan to rebuild Europe, the fall of the Iron Curtain, the cold war, and much of the world as we know it today.

One of the more notable and searing events of World War II was the unexpected and sudden fall of France in 1940, a major liberal democracy with a glorious military past, the *débâcle* as it quickly became known. Swiftly and efficiently overrun by the Wehrmacht in late spring 1940 in only a matter of weeks, France suffered a crushing blow to its morale and national pride that just several decades before had been uplifted by difficult and costly victories at Verdun and the first and second battles of the Marne. The German Army and military government occupied the northern zone of the country with Paris as its command and control center. A large area to the south was carved out for the so-called "free" zone with the resort town of Vichy as the capital for the collaborationist government of Marshal Philippe Pétain, the World I hero. In November 1942 as Allied forces began landing in North Africa as part of Operation Torch, the initial campaign to free Europe from Nazi oppression, the German Army occupied all of France until Liberation in fall 1944.

Of the many stories about World War II there have been countless prisoner of war accounts from both the European and Pacific theaters with one of the most famous being the one that inspired the 1963 film *The Great Escape*, which was based on the 1950 book. The plight of prisoners of war on all sides varied greatly. For instance, many German and Italian soldiers who were taken prisoner early in the war were shipped to internment camps in the United States where food was relatively plentiful and appropriate clothing, health care, and living conditions were provided. These prisoners were given a fair amount of freedom in that escape on the other side of the Atlantic was not very likely. Prisoner of war camps in the Pacific for British and Commonwealth POWs as well as U.S. military personnel were uniformly grim and often brutal. The humane treatments of POWs prescribed by 1929 Geneva Convention on Prisoners of War were all too often breached or ignored in the Pacific by the Japanese and by Axis forces in Europe, along with erstwhile ally Russia near the end of the war.

The story of captured French soldiers at the outset of the Battle for France has not figured prominently in World War II historical accounts for a number of reasons. First, the German blitzkrieg was so rapid and overwhelming that the French army barely knew what had happened. Outmaneuvered and in some respects outgunned, French soldiers who had not shed their uniforms and melted back into the civilian population were quickly herded into makeshift camps in their homeland. Public intellectuals and writers like André Malraux and Jean-Paul Sartre, who had been conscripted into the French army, both recorded their mixed emotions upon being confined to these camps. There is a second consideration perhaps accounting for the dearth of studies of French POWs in World War II, i.e., the impression that the French, with the exception of the lonely crusader Charles de Gaulle and a ragtag Resistance, all but abandoned the fight against Nazi aggression and chose the easier path of collaboration with the enemy.

Jacqueline Vautrain Collins' impressive new translation of Henri Natter and Adam Réfrégier's diary dispels many of these myths and offers a rich and well-textured account of a group of French officers who not only stayed the course, but who suffered emotionally and physically while being separated from their families during the entire duration of the war. The diary that two of the French POWs kept, and which her father published in 1946 for the 5,000 officers interned with him near Edelbach, Austria, chronicles the hardships, the challenges, the privation, and yet, at the same time, the countless ways in which the prisoners triumphed over adversity in trying to maintain an orderly life and preserve their dignity and cultural traditions. All of these activities and undertakings are tributes to the courage of these men and to the resilience of the human spirit.

John B. Romeiser is a professor of French and Francophone studies at the University of Tennessee, Knoxville. His book *Beachhead Don: Reporting the War from the European Theater, 1942–1945* (2004), is an edited compilation of Don Whitehead's World War II reporting for the Associated Press; and he edited *Combat Reporter: Don Whitehead's World War II Diary and Memoirs* (2006).

Preface
by Jacqueline Vautrain Collins

This is the story of French officers, prisoners of war in an Oflag in the Third Reich. Many books and stories have been written about the numerous German prison camps during World War II, but very little has been told about Oflags, camps specifically for Allied officers, who by international convention were not required to work. Non-commissioned officers and enlisted men were sent to stalags, from where they generally went to work for the Germans. Yet, when the dust settled at the end of the battle for France in 1940, of the two million men prisoners of war (mostly French: 1,800,000) 36,000 were officers. The majority remained prisoners for as much as five years.

Five thousand French officers were sent to Oflag XVIIA, located in a mountainous area northwest of Vienna, Austria. These men who had held leading positions, either in the military or as civilians, were thrown together at random in deplorable living conditions with nothing to do, leaving them idle all day except for meals and roll calls. The curse of idle time became an opportunity. Setting up their own administrative structure, and over the years utilizing their wide-ranging knowledge and know-how, they created a small town with its own university, library, newspaper, theater, and orchestra.

My father, Jacques Vautrain, was a prisoner in that camp, and upon his return published the original form of this diary written by two fellow prisoners, Henri Natter and Adam Réfrégier—a day-by-day account of the community's activities and events. Printed in its original form of daily notes, the diary portrays all aspects of the collective life of the camp, engaging the reader in the life of the officer POWs with candid musings, cries of despair, some wry humor, detailed observations, and descriptions of the community's remarkable achievements. Yet, its innuendoes, code words, allusions, and recording of activities that seem well beyond the known resources of the camp invite deeper inspection.

About the English Edition

I began to translate the diary and prepare it for publication shortly after I retired, partly as a means to renew my interest in languages, my field of study in college, and partly to portray for an American audience a little known but important facet of World War II in Europe. Growing up in France and spending my entire adulthood in the United States has given me insight into both countries.

I lived in Paris with my mother during World War II while my father was a prisoner of war, a four-year-old when my father left for the war and ten when he came back. Upon his return my father made only a few comments about the camp, but when he did, it was so heartfelt that I still remember them today and will mention them as the story unfolds. He wrote, "We endured in our way, obscure and without glory, but knowing that each day we persevered would affirm that we had served our country with honor."[1]

I immigrated to the United States in my early twenties, leaving much behind in France, yet the diary and some of the books about the camp, published by my father, made the voyage with me more by default than by design. Perhaps my father insisted that I take them with me, confident that I would read them later and would some day understand these men's unrelenting tenacity to survive with self-respect and reclaim their dignity. Amazingly, these books remained in my possession despite all my peregrinations over the next fifty years.

At that time, I had just a general idea that the book was about the camp where my father was for five years during the war. Reading the diary, however, kept me up late that night. It is sprightly, descriptive, witty, occasionally lyrical, and mostly positive, candidly capturing the changing mood of the community and noting its events and activities. With dry humor it describes the indignities of lengthy roll calls, the searches of barracks by the Gestapo destroying personal possessions: documentation in real time of the life of the officer POWs.

But there were also coded language, allusions, and unusual statements. The commentaries fill in the unstated incidents, experiences, undercurrents in the camp, the cultural background, and the specific clandestine activities, which could not be revealed in the diary. And then, there were truly mysterious entries. One such occurred on the occasion of the dedication of the camp's church/chapel, when the diarist mentioned acquiring the old crucifix from the church in Edelbach. Would the Austrians really give their crucifix to the officer POWs?

Edelbach, a village one mile from the camp, was officially marking the location of the camp. A lover of maps, I went to the atlas, Google and other places to find its geographical location. Nowhere could I find it until I discovered the book *Die Entweihte Heimat*[2] (*The Desecrated Homeland*), telling the tragic story of this area of Austria called Der Waldviertel. When Hitler entered Austria in 1938, he emptied forty villages of their seven thousand inhabitants to use the area as a maneuver ground. In 1940 these villages stood mostly unoccupied until the Russian troops, taking over the maneuver grounds, reduced them to piles of stones, using them as targets during their occupation of Austria. Edelbach, which like that entire area was settled in the thirteenth century, did not exist on maps after World War II, and thus the location of the camp was erased, at least until found later, as will be shown.

There were more personal discoveries. I saw the name of my father's publishing company in a footnote, mentioning illustrations for a planned publication. It led me, a few years ago, to the special pleasure of speaking with one of my father's comrades just before his death.

When I began working on the diary, there were very few records to go on: a couple of memoirs and a few books my father had published about the camp. Fortunately, my queries coincided with the time the Internet became a means for people to tell their stories and post documents. This was the beginning of an exciting journey, connecting one clue to another, discovering from other sources the actions of the resistance group within the camp and the specifics of how they planned the largest escape of the war. Small details led to unusual discoveries: an email to a stranger produced copies of the clandestine pictures of the camp and another resulted in my joining a group of French families visiting the actual site of the camp near Vienna, Austria, in 2010, which led me to the invaluable copies of the original camp newspaper in the archives of the Austrian National Library (Österreichische Nationalbibliotek). The newspaper published a wealth of articles, written by the officers, and many columns conveyed a good sense of the life of the camp. In addition, major German records of the 1940 campaign came to light changing the conventional wisdom of the 1940 campaign. I conducted my research in English, French, and German.

Extensive commentaries accompany the diary, bringing to light the clandestine activities, behind-the-scene events, good-humored pranks at the expense of the Germans, and the essential role of the resistance group as well as the cultural, historical, and political contexts. The commentaries shed light on the means by which these men obtained supplies to pursue remarkable activities. The commentaries also note some of the community's original dissension, which was overcome by the men's tight solidarity in the last two and a half years of their captivity.

My family background made the political events of the war particularly thought-provoking. My grandfather on my father's side was a Major on Philippe Pétain's staff—at that time Colonel Pétain—in the 33rd Infantry Regiment, which Charles de Gaulle joined as a young Lieutenant. After my grandfather was killed in the early days of the Battle of the Marne, under tragic circumstances, General Pétain—later Marshal Pétain—kept in touch with my family. There was also some connection with General de Gaulle. In pre-war maneuvers my father and General de Lattre became friends.

As it became evident that by 1942 the men were well aware of the French troops' involvement in the war, it seemed that a brief review of the battles would provide a context to their discussions, and so I added the Background as a supplement to the notes. Starting with the Middle East and Africa and after the landing of U.S. troops in Algiers at the end of 1942, the Background presents a brief review of the subsequent occupation of France's free zone by the Germans. This marked a complete change in the situation in France, increasing the prominence of the Free French in North Africa and the political power of General de Gaulle. The Background ends with a short description of the French Army's role in the battles of the summer and fall of 1944, led by General de Lattre.

The Prisoners' Experience

> *The cannons are silent and so is the rattle of machine gun fire. A few thumping explosions rumble and echo in the deep valleys of Les Vosges. Our munitions are exploding. A light mist rises from the earth. Here and there, the golden dots of a few small lights disclose the presence of isolated farms. Night falls. It's all over.* —Diary, 22 June 1940

These few lines, written seventy-five years ago on the fateful day France and Germany signed an armistice, immediately brought back to me the ever-present feeling of sadness I experienced as a young child during World War II. The Germans occupied over half of France in the early summer of 1940 after an unforeseen offensive and a campaign which lasted less than six weeks. Close to two million men were taken prisoners of war in a country of forty million. People were stunned. Everyone had expected a protracted war.

In 1945 the returning prisoners shared very few of their experiences.

One officer wrote: "The physical distress was hard enough: hunger, freezing during lengthy roll calls, and one crowded room for all aspects of living. Yet, the emotional scars were deeper: loss of control, humiliation, and exile far from families and friends. We hid this suffering at the bottom of our hearts like intimate secrets that could be confided only to our comrades in misery."[3]

Five Years Behind Hitler's Barbed Wire starts with a short background from the declaration of war in September 1939 to the signature of an armistice in June 1940 and moves on to the circumstances of the capture of the officers. The diary itself begins with the journey to Oflag XVIIA.

The Germans observed the Geneva Convention's provision that officers as prisoners of war should not be required to work, but they totally disregarded the other requirements of the Convention, notably for housing, food, and hygiene. Oflag XVIIA at Edelbach consisted of primitive 5,400 squarefoot barracks, housing 220 men for all aspects of life, with fields in the back. The entire camp, twenty-eight barracks in blocks of four, each block separated by barbed wire, was enclosed in a double row of barbed wire, dotted at intervals with watchtowers. The officers would see a wide open countryside on the other side of the open mesh of the wires, a barrier they could not cross without risking their lives, so the barbed wire became an obsession, prompting the officers to compare their lives to fluttering birds in a cage.

Despite the chaos following their arrival, within days the officer POWs selected their senior colonel as their leader and established a chain of command, which gave them the ability to organize a functioning community. There were no material supplies when they entered the camp but what they wore and had carried on their back. A building site in the camp became a rich source of materials to improve their living space: wood, nails, screws, cardboard, newspapers. Stones became hammers. Recognizing that the strength of their community was in its abundant human resources, they turned to the richness of their human abilities. "We must establish at all cost the primacy of a spiritual life,"[4] wrote my father. Their motto: As captives our bodies are shackled, but our spirits are free.

They immediately started tapping into the vast knowledge, diverse skills and talents of the reservists of all professions, from well-known scientists to artists and athletes, and utilized the know-how of all military services, including the colonial officers. Teachers and professors in civilian life gave lectures and seminars and started foreign languages groups. They formed regional, professional, and hobby groups, and a choir, which, at first, harmonized wellknown folksongs, then sang new pieces composed in the camp. Some groups improvised plays, comedies and satires, and a library was started with the books the men had carried in the backpacks. For two years they published a fourteen-page tabloid-size newspaper.

As communications resumed with the outside world, they received some packages and letters. Librarians cataloged new books, the theater grew, and after the arrival of instruments and music scores an orchestra formed. The early individual seminars and speeches were organized into regular instruction, leading to the founding of the *Université de captivité Oflag XVIIA*, which included a renowned mathematician, a well-known biologist and a geologist. Architects embellished the camp, professional soccer and basketball players set up teams. By the fall of 1941, about a year after their arrival, they had created the activities of a small town.

Later, as they found ways to bypass the filtering of packages, they acquired forbidden items such as shortwave radios and organized a full news service informing them fully of the progression of the war, the French re-entry into the battles of 1943 to 1945, and the political events. That knowledge encouraged many to want to join the fight, leading to the building of an escape tunnel, from which one hundred thirty-two men escaped in September 1943, the largest escape of the war.

It is worth noting that they created the life of a small town within a miserable environment: 5,000 men in a small enclosed space, crowded living quarters, which remained the same for the entire five years, showers once a month, and scant medical care. Food, which was meager for the first eight months, improved after receiving packages, as the men formed small family groups to share the additional provisions. The situation became dire again in the last year and a half, when communications with the outside world stopped completely during the battles of 1944 and 1945.

The officer POWs' achievements in captivity, fortitude and perseverance to maintain their dignity and uphold their honor were a revelation, much at odds with the popular opinion that blamed the 1940 debacle on the lack of courage of the French Army. Fortuitously, an important recent study by a German historian, examining the field reports of the German officers during the Blitzkrieg, showed the Germans' great respect for the spirit of the French troops.[5] The reports from the front revealed that these men showed the same fortitude and resilience on the battlefields as demonstrated in the diary.

This discovery was particularly striking for me. I had heard throughout my childhood that the soldiers of 1940 did not measure up in any way to the Poilus, the soldiers of World War I, although it never occurred to me that this opinion applied also to my father. His attitude pointed to his belief that they reacted with a "fierce will" to sustain their dignity and honor. In one introduction he explicitly wrote, "If, after reading these essays, those, who are trying to understand and judge us, can perceive our energy and confidence, then we will know that our writing has accomplished our task, and we will be certain that we have been understood."[6] The diary and my research bear witness to their "fierce will" to sustain their honor and dignity.

Notes on the Diary

The original diary, *6000 à l'Oflag 17A ou cinq ans de captivité au fil des jours*, published in its raw form of daily entries kept as such in the translation, is a story of the camp community. Individual officers are identified by their initials and even in the printed edition after the war, the only indication of authorship is the appearance of the last names of the two diarists on the cover.

My father published the diary in 1946, specifically for the 5,000 officers in the camp. He registered a copyright to his publishing company (Editions Jacques Vautrain). After researching some information about the diarists, I found their first names and some other genealogical data, learning notably that Adam Réfrégier was born in 1892 and Henri Natter died in 1981. Then, over the course of eight months, I consulted an American copyright lawyer and a French copyright lawyer. She produced a detailed inconclusive legal memorandum, which prompted me to pursue a search for the heirs. Upon her recommendation, I consulted a specialist of a French literary society, who informed me that the book was listed in the World Catalog and it had not been republished, and the heirs were not listed in any registry of heirs of authors.

It seemed that I had exhausted any reasonable means of tracking down the heirs. As of today they are unknown.

Since H. Natter and A. Réfrégier were captured at the same place, it is likely they each contributed to the diary from the beginning. How, we do not know, as the diary was written in secret. By August 1941 the Vichy Regime (Marshall Pétain) obtained the repatriation of the officers (excluding generals) who were World War I veterans and born before January 1, 1900. I know from the military records that A. Réfrégier was born in 1892 and indeed I have his French repatriation record as of August 13, 1941. By the middle of August the sole diarist is H. Natter. The diary, however, was completed by both men as indicated by the signature at the end, showing both Paris (Natter's place of residence) and La Loupe (Réfrégier's home in retirement). They gathered information from some of their comrades who were in separate groups around the time of liberation, as detailed in the final chapter of this book, and combined the various recollections to complete the diary.

In the text of the diary that follows, any quotes originally in French are my translation, except when from a book already translated into English.

When the diary and commentaries intertwine, the diary is in roman, my commentaries in italics.

Because the diarists refer to themselves as officers, not as prisoners, I mention them in my text as officer POWs, in order to keep the self-respect they dearly upheld. POWs designate the French enlisted men. Generally, officers, if not qualified by an adjective, will denote German officers.

To differentiate between the Germans and the French: *K*ommandant with a K for the Germans, *C*ommandant with a C for the French.

Acknowledgments

I will always remember my excitement when, ushered in by the staff's warm welcome, I obtained access to the camp newspaper, *le Canard en KG*, in the ornate Augustinerlesesaal of the Österreichishe Nationalbibliothek (Austrian National Library) in Vienna. I appreciated their subsequent help.

I would like to particularly thank Dr. John Romeiser, professor of French and Francophone studies at the University of Tennessee, Knoxville, for his ready support and warm encouragement over a number of years. His work in French studies and World War II veterans is invaluable.

I am grateful for the editorial comments of my South Carolina WW's writers group, particularly Michael Robertson and James Nicholson. This book is much better as a result of their insightful criticism.

I have enjoyed and learned much from my discussions with friends and acquaintances, who always gave me perceptive feedback and encouragement, especially Paul Nelson, who followed the progress of the manuscript, reading all the sections as they were written, and Frances Hay for her steadfast encouragement and support.

Most of all, my four daughters—Danielle, Kathleen, Patricia, and Eileen—and grandchildren, specifically Katherine, sustained a keen interest in my research. They have been a comforting inspiration, each in their own ways. Their inquiries and use of 2014 technology for a few pictures done in the 1940s were invaluable.

My father died in 1981. The legacy he left in his multiple publications gave me an intimate understanding of the energy and spirit of the life of the camp and of the depth of the men's grief from five years of exile and absence far away from their families. It greatly influenced my writing.

1

Called to Serve Their Country
1 September 1939–17 June 1940

In the early days of September 1939, all roads and trains were crammed with men. Germany had invaded Poland on 1 September. It was the trigger for France and England to declare war on Germany. On 2 September the French woke up to the radio announcement of a general mobilization. Posters with crossed tricolor flags were glued to walls calling all men of all walks of life from twenty to forty-eight years old to report to their assigned posts.

Some traveled north toward the frontier with Belgium, where the British Expeditionary Force joined them. A great number headed east to the Maginot Line, a powerful system of fortifications[1] which defended the frontier with Germany. Others went a short distance to their base camps in the interior. Over half of the men were married, of whom two-thirds had children. My father, thirty-three years old, left for the Maginot Line in Alsace. Armand Oldra, married a few weeks before, left his new bride, pregnant with a son he would not see until he was five years old.

Memories of World War I weighed heavily on the spirit of the men going to the front, many of whom had lost their fathers twenty years earlier. They left in silence in sharp contrast to the 1914 soldiers, who were accompanied by bands, songs, and shouts of "On to Berlin." On their way to the front, there was no escaping the reminders of that war, as most men passed by its killing fields on the way east or northeast. Traveling to Metz in Lorraine, one soldier recalled a "huge cemetery laid out in lines left over from the war." Another "journeyed through villages, hills, and forts whose names he had often read as a child in the communiqués during the last war."[2] The memory of the ravages brought by World War I was deeply ingrained in my own family, as one of my grandfathers died in the Battle of the Marne (1914) and the other was killed at Verdun (1916).

Despite their somber attitude, however, these men "held a firm belief in doing their duty," wrote one observer.[3] Another officer remarked, "Morale is good. They are loyal, and like any good farmer, resigned to good and ill fortune, and one can be certain that they will bring honor to the regiment." A commander reported that for most, "fighting a war was accepted as a job to be done."[4] But feeling no strong overarching principles for fighting the war, the men gave the impression that they had little enthusiasm for it.

In fact, they reflected the general mood of the country. A member of the government summarized the general feeling when he said, "France could not afford the luxury of a Battle of the Marne [the devastating battle that stopped the Germans in 1914] every twenty years."[5] Nonetheless, after the signing of the Munich Pact in 1938 (Great Britain, France, and Italy endorsed Hitler's annexation of the Sudetenland, without even consulting with the Czechoslovakian government), polls showed that seventy percent of the French population was ready to resist Germany, and Hitler's invasion of Czechoslovakia in March 1939 convinced most people that he could not be trusted. In addition, Mussolini's saber rattling toward the French colonies in North Africa rallied a patriotic mood.

After reaching their posts the army stayed put. The French High Command had planned on a defensive war with the intention of mounting an offensive in 1941 or 1942. Concurrently, Hitler, who had planned an offensive in November, was delayed, partly because of the weather, and partly because his generals proposed a new plan. From September 1939 to April 1940 the troops sat waiting (the Phoney War). It was quiet in the north and in the east, so quiet that anticipating a long grueling war of attrition, students in the Montpellier Lycée stayed in school in the late spring to prepare for the admission exam to Saint Cyr (the French West Point). They planned to go to school for a couple of years and then join the army at the time of an expected offensive.[6]

By November letters from the front showed that the soldiers were either exhausted or bored. In the north, life consisted of long marches, strenuous digging, and intensive training for the front-line regiments. The reserve troops were forced to dig defenses with spades for lack of equipment. Adding to the misery, the winter of 1939-40 was one of the coldest winters on record. In January one soldier reported, "We are huddled around the stove. We are numb with apathy and cold."

The men on the Maginot Line, better equipped for daily life, filled their time with theater presentations, films, cards games, or reading books, sent in great numbers by the Red Cross. Some men painted frescoes on the walls of the Maginot Line's underground rooms and hallways. A Parisian reservist, writing home, declared in December, "The days pass, interminable, empty, and without the slightest obligation beyond presence at roll calls. The surprising tranquility of the front ought to reassure us and help us put up with our semi-captivity, which is at least without risk."[7]

Jean-Paul Sartre wrote that they were dying of boredom. Describing his daily life, he noted that he had plenty of time to read, reply to letters, and work on his war journal and novel, being interrupted only by roll calls, meals, and occasional guard duty.[8] The only bright spot was the possibility of going on leave. These stories of boredom in the winter contributed to the conventional wisdom that the troops were demoralized.

By early spring, however, things changed. As soon as the Germans invaded Holland in early May (the Blitzkrieg, May-June), morale began to improve. Many soldiers greeted the news with relief. Letters from the front attested that the dour assessments of the winter doldrums had quickly changed (surveys of correspondence in mid–April and in May indicated that army morale was excellent, or very good). "This time it's the real war; so much the better since at last we can see the end," wrote one soldier headed for Belgium. "If you just knew how confident and hopeful I am,"[9] wrote another, sentiments confirmed by the British Chief of General Staff inspecting the front. A couple of weeks later, a soldier in General de Gaulle's armored division wrote, "In fifteen days, we have carried out four attacks and we have always been successful, so we are going to pull together, and we will get that pig Hitler."[10]

It was, however, quite a different situation in the Ardennes. Attacked on 10 May by a new kind of motorized army, which changed the way of conducting warfare, the French infantry and artillery were subjected to massive bombardments no one expected. A rain of bombs, lasting eight hours, destroyed French positions, bunkers, gun emplacements, and telephone communications. Adding to the troops' woes was the lack of antiaircraft guns, and the slow response of the British and French airplanes allowed the Germans to be masters of the sky. Even more significant was the psychological impact of the shrieking of the diving Stukas, the German bombers. The German troops on the other side of the river reported, "We stand and watch what is happening as if hypnotized; down below all hell is let loose!"[11] As the pounding became more sporadic, some soldiers fled, mixing on the road with civilian refugees. By evening, the Germans crossed the Meuse River. With no French reserve troops ready to stop them, the way was open for the Germans to advance toward the Channel directly across from Great Britain.

The troops in Belgium, which had successfully kept the Germans at bay, were ordered to retreat, so they would not be encircled. Some established positions around Dunkirk on the coast facing England, where they held the Germans in check for ten days. In one of the most daring events of the war, it allowed the British Expeditionary Force and some French units to evacuate to England on an armada of every conceivable vessel. The final surrender of these troops for lack of ammunitions marked the collapse of the northern front.

The French Army regrouped in the northeast during the first two weeks of June. Letters from the front reflected a high morale. "We are really tired, but we have to be here. They will not pass and we will get them."[12] Even though facing a force three times their size, the French troops inflicted heavy losses on the advancing German Army. In the end, however, the French, lacking supplies, reserves, and ammunitions, could not stop the Germans and retreated south. Prepared for a war fought twenty years before, the French military lacked the equipment to stem the German motorized war.

The three French Armies on the Maginot line in the east, Lorraine, Alsace and the Vosges,[13] were still intact.

On 13 June the French Cabinet declared Paris an open city and left for Bordeaux in the south of France (they went later to Vichy). The Germans marched on the Champs Elysées the next day. A few days later, Marshal Pétain was named President du Conseil (Prime Minister). Eighty-four years old, Pétain was the revered military hero of World War I for his role as the defender of Verdun (Battle of Verdun, December 1915–December 1916, three hundred days with almost one million casualties) and for restoring morale after a mutiny in the army. On 17 June, the day after being named Prime Minister, he spoke to the nation and unexpectedly declared: "I come to you today with a heavy heart to say that it is necessary to stop fighting." He then intimated that he was asking the Germans "for a way to end the hostilities," a vague reference to the possibility of an armistice.

The speech was ambiguous; people heard different things. Some thought he had said, "*Try* to stop fighting," as was reported in the newspapers the following day. Others thought he simply said, "stop fighting," the phrase recorded in the official document. The British historian Richard Vinen, noting the reaction of a crowd in a restaurant, reported that someone asked, "What has the Marshal said? Did he mean that a state of armistice already exists?" and Vinen added, "Some maintained that hostilities had already ceased, and others that no armistice had even been asked for."[14] In fact, the negotiations for an armistice did not start until 20 June, and it was signed on 22 June.

The situation was particularly difficult for the troops. The regiments, who had previously fought in the north, had retreated south to the middle of France, taking positions around the Loire Valley with the intention of making a stand and blowing up the bridges. They clashed everywhere with the civilian bureaucracy. The French Minister of the Interior had sent a telegram the day after Pétain's speech to all the towns of over twenty thousand inhabitants, asking them to stop all fighting and to declare their towns open, in order to minimize expected reprisals.[15] In Nantes, for example, as the army was ready to blow up the bridges, the civilian authorities marched forward to present a white flag to the incoming German troops. In Chateauroux, the mayor put white flags at the entrances of the town and disarmed the French soldiers passing through. When the commanding officer of the unit arrived, outraged, he demanded that the soldiers patrol the streets with their weapons.[16]

The battle for France lasted six weeks.

The five thousand officers who eventually formed the community of Oflag XVIIA came to the camp in two main groups; the largest group to which the diarists belonged went to Oflag XVIIA directly after being taken prisoners. The men in the other group were taken prisoners in various places in France and sent to Oflag XIII B before going to Oflag XVIIA. Their capture is the focus of the next chapter. The diary starts in Chapter 3.

2

Capture
17 June–1 July 1940

One million eight hundred thousand men, of which thirty-six thousand were officers, were taken prisoners. According to an unofficial survey, over one million were taken between 17 June (Marshal Pétain's speech) and 25 June (the official end of hostilities). An additional ninety thousand were taken from 25 June to 1 July, many days after the signing of the armistice[1] (the armistice: 22 June, the cessation of hostilities: 25 June). The physical capture of the troops with a few exceptions took place in nonviolent ways, since the Geneva Convention dictated that troops surrendering after the signing of an armistice would be demobilized and sent home. Confused and yielding to reality, most units accepted the forced surrender and laid down their weapons without a fight, convinced that they would be quickly demobilized and sent home.

The Germans tried to capitalize on the confusion. Some came forward to French positions waving white flags, announcing that the war had ended and that the French troops would go home very soon. In another instance, to the surprise of a Cavalry Major in the center of France, a German motorized unit stopped to let his company of horse-drawn cannons cross the road before speeding on its way, seemingly more interested in reaching the Atlantic coast than to fight.[2] His unit decided to camp in the nearby forest to wait out the signing of the armistice.

A few days preceding the armistice a Cadet wrote, "I tried to find comfort in thinking that after all the Germans were not barbarians. If we were taken prisoners after the armistice, we would be sent home." He recalled how his captain, after hearing of the cease-fire speech, simply disassembled the breeches of the cannons and buried them. He continued, "It was not long until we were encircled by a host of German vehicles. Neither side firing a shot we were loosely led by some German troops toward a pass in the Vosges." It was disorganized enough that "at dusk, our captain, taking advantage of the forest on the side of the road, directed us to disappear under the trees. When we got into a clearing, he told us that we were going to wait here, until we could be certain that an armistice had been signed."[3]

Some commandants took the speech as an order. On 20 June a lieutenant, stationed not far from Nantes, noted in his diary, "A new order has arrived. We are not allowed to leave our encampment under penalty of War Council, even if the enemy were to surprise us and take us prisoners." The officers present, about forty, discussed whether they should leave or stay. Since it was an official order from their commandant, they decided to stay.[4]

Others continued to fight. The colonel leading the cadets of the Cavalry School of Saumur confronted the mayor of the town, who wanted to declare his town an open city, and told him that they would fight. They took their positions and for three days held fast in fierce combat, despite a German force much larger than their own. In the face of the possible destruction of the town of Saumur, the colonel relented and agreed to the surrender of the survivors. They were taken prisoners the next day, the day the armistice was signed. By that time the colonel, not able to bear the thought of the school standard falling into German hands, had left with a few cars and a machine-gun escort to make a mad dash south. He succeeded in getting to the free zone (that is the part of France which the Germans had not reached and did not occupy until 1942), and saved the standard.[5] Isolated fights and resistance continued for a few days until the munitions were exhausted.

In Lorraine, where the German offensive had started on 13 June and continued through 20 June, the units already engaged by the Germans resisted as long as they could. Some individual units went deeper into the Vosges, forming pockets of resistance; many lasted until 24 June, two days after the signing of the armistice. A few companies, knowing the backcountry paths, evaded the Germans and reached either Switzerland or the free zone in France. In the south of Alsace, the Germans crossed the Rhine and pushed the French back into the valleys of the Vosges with most units surrendering at the time of the armistice.

On the Maginot Line, where the French forces in the fortresses and bunkers could be self-sufficient for two to three weeks, Marshal Pétain's speech was particularly confusing. Generally, the officers did not hear the speech itself, but relied on hearsay. No official order came from their superiors, leaving the decision to the commandant of the sector. In the northern corner of Alsace, the heavily fortified sector of Haguenau, facing Germany both in the east and the north (my father was part of the infantry in that section), included large fortifications dominated by the fortress of Schoenenbourg. The commandant of the sector ordered his troops to stay put and to fight to the end.

After a few days of skirmishes the Germans began a major attack as late as 18 June. For the next five days the Germans bombed the forts and bunkers, but the guns of Schoenenbourg continued firing through the evening of 24 June. They stopped only when the formal call to cease all hostilities was announced the next morning.[6] After giving the order to stop firing, the Commandant sent a letter to his superior, in which "he protested the treatment inflicted on the officers, the noncommissioned officers and the troop, who have not been beaten but are asked to surrender." He continued, "I have kept all my forces, the enemy has not succeeded in piercing my defenses. I will surrender only upon the reception of a direct order of the Commander-in-Chief and not because of the exigencies of being encircled by enemy troops."[7]

The Germans, not anticipating such a large number of prisoners, requisitioned schools, public buildings, mansions, and chateaux, throwing out whoever occupied the premises in order to incarcerate the French troops which could not be marched directly into Germany. The conditions in these holding facilities were generally livable except for the lack of food; without constant oversight by the Germans or the humiliation of searches, the French were fairly autonomous, reinforcing their hope of being demobilized.

Four temporary camps housed officers who would be sent later to Oflag XVIIA.

The officers near Nantes saw the arrival of the Germans on 22 June. The French colonel immediately worked out an agreement with his German counterpart to be treated as *Prisonniers d'honneur*, a status which allowed them to go to town for meals three times a day, as long as they would come back to the encampment. Officers, in particular, did not feel it was appropriate to escape.

This condition did not last long, however. In early July, they were marched to the train station, destination unknown. The men were quick to notice that there were passenger cars for the officers and cattle cars for the troops. They traveled to the town of Laval about one hundred miles away. Upon arrival the twelve hundred officers of this unit were separated from their troops and incarcerated in the seminary building in town, the seminarians having been thrown out.[8] The colonel took it upon himself to organize the French officers into small groups with one officer leading each group. Trying to keep the officers' morale high, he established a strict routine and met every morning with the heads of each group. With nothing to do, they utilized the library of the seminary and gave lectures on a variety of subjects.

2. Capture

The unit of the Cavalry Major, who had camped out in the forest after meeting the Germans on the road, stayed in the forest for a few days without being noticed. Learning of the signing of the armistice, their leader sent two men to the nearby town to inquire about the text of the clauses concerning the army. They were told that the French Forces would be demobilized *after a time to be determined* (my emphasis) and that the units in the occupied zone would be sent to the free zone after leaving their materiel where they were stationed. Accordingly, they laid down their arms at the nearby town hall, believing that this would be the first step toward demobilization.

By 1 July, as no one had noticed the presence of their unit, they sent two representatives to the nearby German headquarters to tell them where they were. Surprised by the existence of a French unit, the Germans dispatched one of their companies to meet them. After the Germans arrived and perhaps not understanding each other's language, the French harnessed their horses and mounted them, ready to get on their way. But the Major recalled, "The German Kommandant ordered us to dismount. Their officers then gathered the best horses including my beautiful mare, Miquette. Giving her up was a most painful separation I will never forget. We were then quartered in a nearby farm."[9] They remained there for a couple of weeks before being transferred to another temporary camp.

In the Vosges columns after columns of men marched through the mountain passes before descending toward the Alsatian plain, prisoners going directly to Germany just on the other side of the Rhine River. For one unit, however, the destination was a military base close to the town of Neuf-Brisach in mid–Alsace near the Rhine River. One of its officers noted what he called the "poignant spectacle of this mass exodus of French prisoners." Yet, as he came down from a mountain pass into the valley, he took heart from the natural beauty of the environment and refusing to feel forlorn marched with his friends at the head of the column. Later he wrote, "On this summer evening, surrounded by magnificent mountains, my spirit was lifted by the blue-green forests and the prairies wreathed in a golden light. The air carried the good smell of the nearby pines. We were infused with the peace that comes at dusk."[10]

Being among the first officers to arrive, they were lodged in multilevel dorms, crowded but with some facilities. As more troops arrived, bringing the count to about forty thousand, many times the capacity of the base, most men had to camp outside in the fields under makeshift tents or rudimentary shelters. There was little food. The only relief came from a few Red Cross women from the nearby town, who obtained the permission to come once a day with one, sometimes two cars, full of foodstuff, paltry help for forty thousand men. The only other relief came from a dedicated young woman who took it upon herself to bike to the camp, as often as she could, with bags of bread, canned food, and clothes, passing them through the spaces in the fence away from the guards.

The base was well guarded, but they could move freely within it. It was, however, very chaotic, and discipline was lax with so many men crowded in an inadequate space, camping without decent quarters, nothing to do, and an uncertain future. To remedy some of this conundrum, the senior French General went to the German Kommandant and asked to be allowed to assume command over the French. The Germans agreed. Taking into consideration all the different military units and services mixed together, the general created a new chain of command, dividing the men into groups, each with an officer in charge; this semi-autonomy restored discipline.

Within a few days another disaster struck. A huge storm sent torrents of water, transforming the fields where the men were camping into a mud hole. During the day, the men walked in feet of slush and mud, sleeping at night in that muck. The camp became known as *Le camp de la misère* (the camp of wretchedness). Learning that the nearby town of Neuf-Brisach had been evacuated by the Alsatians at the beginning of the war, the French General decided to appeal to his German counterpart and asked for a transfer. The town of Neuf-Brisach, a perfect hexagon, was—and still is—completely surrounded by a wall and outer fortifications built in the early eighteenth century with three entrances, making it easy to guard.[11] The only drawback: it was a small town of four thousand. Could forty thousand men be housed there? How risky would it be to unleash all these men in civilian houses and buildings?

The general assured his counterpart that he would take responsibility for the troop's good behavior. As the two military men respected each other, the German Kommandant listened to the general and after consulting his staff authorized the move. Using a four-tier hierarchy, the General created a command, exclusively with French officers. The transfer to Neuf-Brisach was effected in an orderly manner with units occupying either a house or a designated part of a public building. When establishing their living spaces in the houses, the men moved all the furniture, wall hangings, and other objects into a separate room and used the rest of the house including, when necessary the attic and sometimes a shed. They were in very close quarters, but had a roof over their heads.[12]

Meanwhile in Haguenau, the Commandant of the sector had received

2. Capture

a direct order to surrender from his superior, but when the German emissary came to take charge of the French troops, he refused to receive him. He was still quibbling about leaving the fortifications. Reminding the military authorities that his sector had not been defeated, he requested that his troops be transported to the free zone.

As time elapsed, the Germans demanded an immediate surrender, threatening the French High Command with retaliation; if the situation was not resolved in a couple of days, they said, they would break the armistice and send panzer divisions to occupy the Mediterranean Coast. The French Government, now in Vichy in the free zone, could not take that risk and General Weygand, Commander-in-Chief, signed an order of immediate surrender. It arrived in Haguenau over a week after the signing of the armistice. Running out of options, the troops surrendered on 1 July. The Germans denied the request to send the men to the free zone, and the French troops were incarcerated in a temporary camp around Haguenau.[13]

It would have been relatively easy for the officers to leave and go home during the weeks of late June and early July, but they felt at heart that it would be just a matter of days before they would be demobilized. So, why leave? There were also practical considerations: threats of court-martial for leaving without being demobilized and fear of possible retaliation for their comrades and families. Over half of France was occupied; they could not go through the demarcation line to enter the free zone without a pass. Even if they reached the free zone they would not have the proper identification papers, let alone for some, be with their family.

There was one more consideration. My father fought in the Haguenau sector and was taken prisoner on 1 July. With all the contacts he had in Alsace, he could have left the camp while in Haguenau. From a traditional military family, he had shunned the family's demand to follow in his forefathers' footsteps. Instead, he pursued a literary career and was an officer in the reserve. As a reservist, he kept a strong attachment to the duty to serve his country and like many of his comrades believed in upholding the honor of the military. That honor, my father reminded me after the war, meant that an officer could not leave the encampment and his troops.

He abided by what military honor required, but he expected honorable treatment in return. I still remember his intense protestation in one of his rare comments about the war that he should never have been taken prisoner, since he was forced to surrender about nine days after the armistice had been signed. Yet, years later, he never doubted his decision not to have taken the opportunity to leave when it would have been possible.

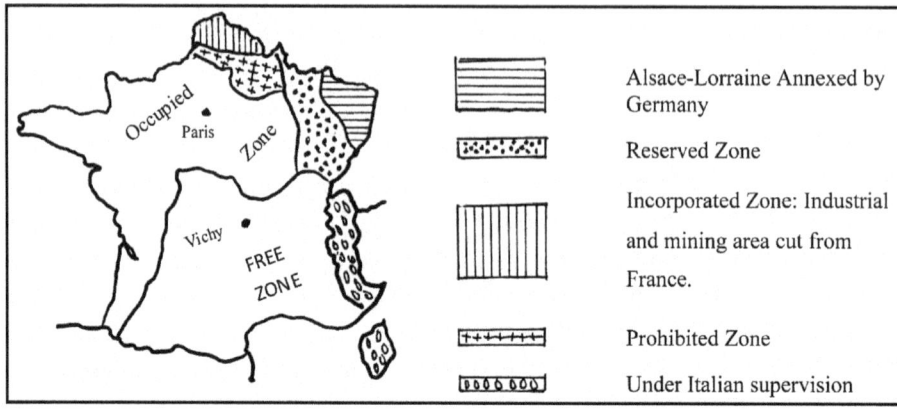

France was divided into an Occupied Zone and a Free Zone after July–August 1940. The Occupied Zone was divided into separate pieces: Alsace-Lorraine was annexed outright to be integrated into Germany. The Incorporated Zone was placed under the jurisdiction of German Administration in Belgium. War refugees were not allowed to return to the Reserve Zone, intended for German settlers. The demarcation line between the Occupied and Free Zones was like a border, crossed only with special permits. The Germans occupied all of France in November 1942 (Jacqueline Vautrain Collins).

On 25 June Marshal Pétain spoke to the nation to announce the conditions of the armistice to the French people. In general terms he declared, "The conditions are severe: a large part of our territory will be temporarily occupied, our army and navy will have to be demobilized.... (Yet) the French government remains free to administer all of France and its colonies, and you will soon get back to your homes. At least our honor has been safeguarded."[14] The day after the speech, the writer André Gide, who had earlier praised Pétain, now asked, "Was Pétain really speaking of his own free will? Is it possible? How can he speak of France as intact after handing over more than half of the country to the enemy? Is it not enough for France to be defeated? Must she also be dishonored?"[15] The men on their way to captivity were likely to be asking the same question, as they waited in vain for their return home. Instead, they would make one more stop in Oflag XIII at Nuremberg before going to Oflag XVIIA at Edelbach.

3

Betrayal and Humiliation
22 June–3 July 1940

The unit of the writers of the diary was stationed on the western slope of the Vosges.

22 June 1940—The cannons are silent and so is the rattle of machine-gun fire. A few thumping explosions rumble and echo in the deep valleys of the Vosges; our munitions are exploding. A light mist rises from the earth. Here and there, the golden dots of a few small lights disclose the presence of isolated farms. Night falls. It's all over.

23 June—Cramped from sleeping three men in a cot for two, we are up by 6:00 a.m. Rain pours through the leaves. It is eerily quiet. Not one German in sight, and yet we know that they are right there on the periphery sixteen hundred feet away. They neither prevailed nor captured any of our fortresses or blockhouses, but they surround us and are now waiting for us. We are trapped. Strange liberty!

By noon we go out to explore the field of debris. In front of us, the ground is littered with grim piles of helmets, mess kits, hoods, tents spilling out a flood of linens, letters, and muddy books. On a box, a lonely banjo reminds us of more joyful days. The slope is a gigantic and pathetic flea market, a grotesque wastefulness that attests to our defeat. In the distance below, broken-down trucks block the road. The entire area blotched with large pieces of decomposing meat covered with flies reeks the stench of a slaughterhouse.

8 p.m.—Dinnertime. After setting up a sheet of tarpaulin supported by four stakes, we cook in full wind. On the menu, *singe* [monkey, nickname given by the World War I soldiers to boiled beef, which was distributed in cans with the labels of Madagascar hence the name monkey] cooked in Chambéry, the last remnant of an ancient splendor. It is still raining.

Forced surrender tomorrow at 1:00 p.m.

24 June—One by one the cars reach the first German post. *Waffen*! [Weapons] Consumed with rage we surrender our weapons. The search is perfunctory. A *Feldwebel* [military police] raids playing cards, binoculars, and cameras. *Weiter!* [Go on]. The door slams shut; we are now prisoners.

25 June—Sélestat—We spent the night in the barracks of the army base, sleeping on a concrete floor that had been covered with a layer of straw. It was impossible to sleep. In our state of nervous agitation how could we ever relax? Only a few days ago, these walls sheltered Frenchmen, and today these same walls serve as our jail. Everything looks hostile and bleak. A bitter truth torments us.

Outside, a crowd of women and young people presses anxiously behind the fence, looking for some news of the fate of loved ones. They are ruthlessly pushed back by the sentries. Nevertheless, defying orders we succeed in establishing contact. Our hearts go out to the Alsatian population.

We crossed the Vosges yesterday at the Col de Saales [mountain pass]. Harassed by German motorcyclists, who shoved us like cattle, we were going through towns and villages at top speed without stopping except at the intersections, where a few bareheaded Nazis in brown shirts with a swastika armband wave their arms.

We passed many army units walking east, flanked by green uniforms.

In a state of shock these men were silent and dazed, crushed by the double burden of the sun and their backpacks. Their look conveyed a misery and distress we will never forget. Four miles from Sélestat, a German first lieutenant, a big bully with a round face, blemished by acne, thin lips, and steely eyes, stopped our car and ordered us out. *Raus!* In an instant our luggage flew into the ditch. The ruffian grabbed the steering wheel and started the motor, taking all the provisions and blankets with him. Guilefully, a young German second lieutenant walked up: "It is wartime. But to end soon, eighty thousand parachutes on London. In three weeks you go back home." After being picked up by a small truck, we catch a glimpse of D. and N. walking along the road, and soon their two silhouettes disappear on the horizon. Without doubt they were victims of the same treatment. Despite our shouts we could not stop. We are dumped in front of the army base in Sélestat.

26 June—We have been living on our meager reserve of food since last night, unable to come close to the single field kitchen in the middle of the courtyard. Thanks to the Alsatian civilians, however, we have been able to get some bread, and unbeknownst to the sentries these people are taking it upon themselves to mail cards and letters to families and friends.

A few incidents: when General E. refuses to salute a first lieutenant, he is threatened with prison; he does not give in. A German soldier swipes the cigarette lighter of a colonel right from under his nose. Auspicious omen!!

The road was familiar to most of these officers. Their first stop after being taken prisoners, Sélestat[1] in mid–Alsace, had a well-established military base, which the Germans immediately used as the gathering place for POWs from all the neighboring fortifications of the Maginot Line. To be thrown helter-skelter into that base, overcrowded and with hardly any food, a place where they likely had been stationed while commanding their own unit during the previous months and was now serving as a prison, was doubly traumatic for some of these officers. The incidents, as noted in the diary, reflected the mounting anger and powerlessness of their situation.

The Cadet, whose unit had waited for the signing of the armistice in a clearing, was now in Sélestat. Expressing the general sentiment reflected in the diary, he wrote: "On the walls of the halls and rooms of the main building the troops had painted frescoes proclaiming the major victories of the French Army in 1914–18, Verdun, l'Argonne, and l'Yser. It was a very strange situation."[2] *The diarists wrote,* "A bitter truth torments us." *They were prisoners in rooms which glorified the achievements of their fathers.*

27 June—We left Sélestat this morning at 6 a.m. on an empty stomach, marching in columns of five amidst a sea of bayonets. The field kitchen is staying behind in the army base. Lacking advance notice we hurried to sort out what to put in our backpacks, a random exercise: one or two shirts, a few pairs of socks, toiletry, and provisions, reaching what seems a senseless choice.

9 a.m.—A small unit pulls up and stops: suddenly, D. and N. appear and rush into our arms. Outburst of frenzied joy! They have spent three days in a marshy meadow about two miles from us, sleeping on a water-saturated ground parched by the sun. Constantly drawn machine-guns, bursting with sudden fire, were controlling a mass of fifteen thousand men and officers, parked there helter-skelter with only a few pieces of bread and muddy water for food. Some men died.

5:30 p.m.—We arrive in Erstein in the late afternoon and are locked up in the sports arena behind a high circular fence. The Germans have placed a machine gun on the balcony of an attractive villa overlooking the stadium. The sky is overcast, and it is starting to rain. We have traveled fifteen miles at an exhausting pace, dazed by the yelling of sentinels who were goaded on by a fierce and scowling small noncommissioned officer. Our feet are bloody, and we are exhausted. Our luggage that was stowed at random, badly balanced and tied with tangled strings and ropes, broke loose at the first bump requiring constant repair. We are told that trucks will pick up our many comrades who fell by the way side in the ditches.

We would have reached the nadir of distress, were it not for the aid and support we received from the Alsatians, who are massed along our route. In the medieval hall at X. the town people give us bowls of soup they had prepared. Famished, we devour it. All along the route, women and young girls offer us a glass of wine, milk, or brandy, and give us some bread, pieces of cakes, and fruit. Their shout, ceaselessly repeated, sustains us: "Have courage! See you soon! You will come back! Vive la France!" Our frustrated guards chase these poor people, destroy their presents, and knock down their buckets and bottles. One soldier grabs a jug and hits a woman on the head.

28 June—6 a.m.—We spent the night in a large warehouse of the corps of engineers overflowing with surplus material, sleeping on stacked sacks of concrete.

8 a.m.—Leave for Strasbourg, crossing Erstein for the second time. Persistent, the town people wave to us for the last time. Again, they display a poignant and painful support with the cries: "You will come back! Courage! It's not over!"

11 a.m.—We are pushed back to the side of the road with full-throated yells. *Recht halten*! [Keep to the right]. A swarm of German military police in greenish raincoats passes us at top speed, followed by an over-sized car bristling with machine guns. Coming behind are cars full of officers. In one of them a man is standing, his arms outstretched. It's Hitler. [It was Hitler, who was reviewing his troops in Alsace at that time.] At his side sits a fat potbellied pig. Could it be Goering?

3:30 p.m.—The column stretches out and becomes a disorderly horde. Our guards have lost control. Could we escape? Where would we go? The Germans are everywhere. And we are footsore and bone-weary. We know that the armistice has been signed. What's next?

Before entering Strasbourg the column regroups to enter the city, where a crowd welcomes us, shouting a cry that erupts from every mouth. Vive la France! Singing, stiff, and heads held high, we make our way in a slow march, the most we can do to keep our decorum and pride. On the side, a group of German officers observes in silence, unable to prevent the outpouring of sentiment.

The officers marched north on the Alsatian main road from Sélestat to Strasbourg. Alsace pulled on many emotional strings for these men, particularly under their present conditions; poignant feelings shared by the Alsatians all along the road. For centuries, Alsace had been a disputed territory between France and Germany. The home of well-established German princes, it became part of France in the seventeenth century and was fully integrated into France after the French

3. Betrayal and Humiliation

Revolution. After her defeat in the Franco-Prussian war, France was forced in 1871 to cede Alsace and Lorraine back to the Germans, who tried to integrate these two provinces into Germany. But obstinate, the population resisted the Germans, and in return the French gave them a preferred place, when they became part of France again after World War I. The bond remained very strong.

These officers felt called to defend Alsace, so it would never again become part of Germany. Instead, the Alsatians were now taking care of them. It was a particularly tragic situation the officers responded to by showing as much decorum and pride as they could muster, as they entered Strasbourg. The Cadet expressed his own feeling more precisely. Toward the end of the day, when he caught sight of the spire of the cathedral, he wrote, "It was for me an emotional moment. I had been deeply marked in my childhood memories by all the blue-horizon mythology of the return of Alsace to the fatherland, symbolized powerfully by the spire of the cathedral of Strasbourg."[3]

Strasbourg, a major city, could very well serve as a demobilization center, but as the gateway to Germany, it could also be their last stop in France. These thoughts were on the officers' minds: "We know that the armistice has been signed. What's next?" Yet, they had been treated "like a herd" and profoundly humiliated, hardly a good sign. In five days, they had traveled about fifty miles, a short physical distance, but eons in emotional and psychological time.

30 June—Sunday—We assemble in Kehl in front of the train station, located in the center of an immense square. Huge red banners with the Nazi emblem, fluttering in the gentle wind under a blue sky, hang all along the street in front of the houses. The town people stare at us with solemn curiosity. The men wear tricorne hats with cords draped around the crown of the hat, decorated with feathers or fur. The women wear shimmering colors. Posted close to us, proud as peacocks, stand already indoctrinated and disciplined units of youths in khaki uniforms, who belong to the Organization Todt [a construction outfit founded during the Third Reich working for the military to build the fortifications on Germany's western frontiers].

We had left the barracks of Stirn at 8 a.m. Strasbourg, a silent deserted city, is still sleeping. We cross the Marne to the Rhine canal and then the Rhine River on a narrow footbridge, built between the abutments of the destroyed bridge. A flock of storks flies swiftly west. Toward the west is France; the separation is now complete. To captivity is added exile.

The day these officers crossed over the Rhine and set foot on German territory, 30 June, was a very dark day. The diary writers expressed it poignantly with the mythical symbol of Alsace; a flock of storks flying west becoming the messengers of all their fervent hope for a return to their country. A captain wrote in his memoirs, "The transfer to Germany meant an uprooting from our national soil, worries of being far away, no end in sight, being brutally seized by captivity, all feelings that were very deep."[4] As they entered Kehl, they also had to endure its church bells, vigorously ringing to celebrate the German victory.

1 July—2 p.m.—Mainz. Marching through town, we pass by sets of rustic tables and verdant green chairs. Producing the unexpected atmosphere of a suburban open-air café, a loud speaker, fastened to a chestnut tree, screeches nonstop a fife and drums music, alternating with schmaltzy Viennese melodies. Is this a garden, a public square, or a park? They serve lemonade. Our destination is the polar opposite: barbed wire and the old citadel with a massive tympanum, adorned with an undecipherable shield over the entrance. Mainz, a major revolving junction and the world's crossroad where all races mix, is from where hundreds of thousands of men leave for the Reich's [Germany's] heartland. We rub elbows with admirals and generals.

Some German noncommissioned officers, who speak our language, spread the news, obvious propaganda: "Imminent attack of Great Britain, Jersey occupied." We lose ourselves in speculations about our future destination. Will it be Poland or perhaps Austria? Does it matter after all? We receive our first hearty meal, served in a large earthenware bowl by Senegalese orderlies. It is a heavy slop of potatoes. With it we get a dense gray bread and synthetic honey. A few, famished, soon throw up this indigestible mass.

We are assigned three men per two straw mattresses: another night without any sleep. The heat is stifling, and the continual moan of piled up bodies is discomforting. In addition, British planes attacked the town during the night and were met with a furious response of antiaircraft fire that shook the windows and produced bursts of lightning, followed by silence.

After getting up, we look for traces of damages from the bombs and are deeply disappointed. The city is still intact with its numerous pointed slate roofs, its spires, its steeples, and its domes. The lush foliage that forms a luxuriant belt all around the city still displays all its shades of green, and in the distance the Rhine River, a wide gray ribbon, still glistens nonchalantly in the sun.

7 p.m.—We leave the citadel, marching between two rows of curious folks, who are quietly standing along the sidewalks staring at us, indifferent and silent. Do they fully realize the meaning of this colossal roll of the dice, which has handed them yesterday's masters? Does some foreboding not overshadow their joy? As we arrive at the small train station of Mainz-Süd, a train is getting up steam. It is ours. In a sharp contrast, some good bourgeois stroll peacefully in the public garden whose weeping willows and well-groomed lawns rise in tiers above the bank.

3. Betrayal and Humiliation

Mainz is situated at the edge of a disputed land north of Alsace and east of Luxembourg, an area on the left bank of the Rhine River, a natural buffer for France that would provide a secure barrier along the Rhine. After World War I, the French asked the international community to keep it indefinitely a demobilized zone. France lost that support[5] and despite engaging the population in French culture, the area reverted fully to Germany in the rising German nationalistic wave of the 1930s. The diary's musings, "Do they fully realize the meaning of this colossal roll of the dice, which has handed them yesterday's masters?" likely reflected the wish that the people of the region had remained attached to France.

The Citadel in Mainz stood on a hill at the edge of the city with a sweeping view of the town. An easy building to guard, the officer POWs could move freely once inside. From the top floor they had a bird's-eye view of the entire town's roofs and of the cathedral spire, undoubtedly the place they went to, to look at the hoped-for-damages of the British bombing during the night.

Mainz, the last stopover before being sent to separate oflags, was designated for officers only. They came from all parts of the front: France's interior, the battlefields of the north and the bunkers of the Maginot Line. They belonged to all the different services of the army: artillery, infantry, armored divisions, motorized infantry, and cavalry. They represented the entire military hierarchy from second lieutenants to generals. In addition, a lieutenant recalled the almost comical sight of policemen, custom officers, mailmen, and sheriffs among the crowd, "offering a curious and even amusing spectacle despite the circumstances."[6] The German Command had instructed its troops to pick up anyone wearing a uniform; a number of men, who did not belong to the military, were taken prisoner and presumably were sent home later.

For the first time these men had a chance to get a comprehensive overview of the battles beyond their own districts, an opportunity they eagerly responded to. "Conversations were buzzing from morning to evening. So many topics! So many reflections! So many testimonials! So many unbelievable stories," wrote a lieutenant.[7] These were stories of courage and endurance, panic and fear under German bombardment, success followed by retreat for lack of support, grief and loss, resignation and determination. The German historian Karl-Heinz Frieser, after reviewing the German officers' reports of the 1940 combat noted the French soldiers' fighting spirit. He wrote: "The collapse of the French Army cannot be blamed on the soldiers, but rather on its command. Whenever these men were correctly employed, they displayed astonishing examples of bravery."[8]

Churchill, recalling the resistance around Dunkirk, recognized these men in his memoirs:

They (the French) fought gallantly for many days to cover the evacuation of their British and French comrades. They were to spend the next years in captivity. Let us remember that but for the endurance of the Dunkirk rearguard, the re-creation of an army in Britain for home defense and final victory would have been gravely prejudiced.[9]

By the afternoon of 1 July, a few thousands of these men left Mainz for their final destination, Oflag XVIIA at Edelbach, a village in the hills of the northeastern corner of Austria, close to the Czechoslovakian border, where they would stay for five years.

2 July—In the train: Night falls. Light sleep, populated by confused recollections and vague images linking us to a past so near and yet so distant. We would almost attain a contented state, if only our stiff bodies were able to relax. With our legs bent under the seat our upright torso, propped up tightly one against the other, is almost rigid. We are subjected to a constant sway made worse by the sudden jolts of the brakes and the passages of switches; every wide curve throws us on our neighbors like disjointed puppets, and every dead stop tears us out of our torpor. We have been traveling for the last

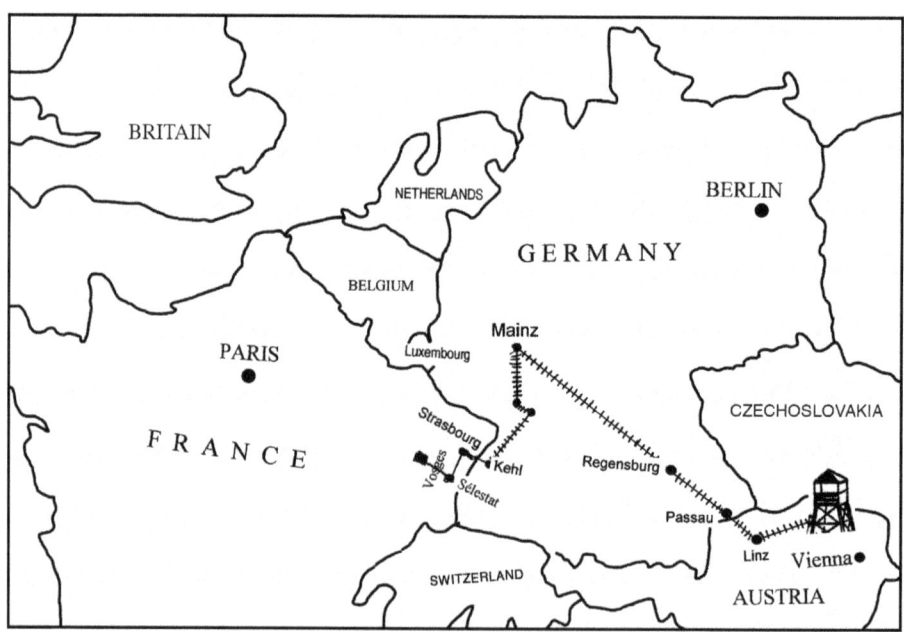

The journey to Oflag XVIIA of the first 3,000 to 4,000 POW officers. Some officers marched from the Vosges Mountains to Kehl, Germany, then went by train to Mainz, the triage center. Joined by others, they went by train from Mainz to Austria (Jacqueline Vautrain Collins).

3. Betrayal and Humiliation

twenty-four hours becoming more and more indifferent to the passing scenery. Tobacco smoke escapes in capricious spirals from this narrow overheated cage. Repetitive impressions follow one after the other; passing by villages, our eyes catch in a fleeting moment, a few colorful houses adorned with the ubiquitous Swastika banners. Then, countless flags appear all along the tracks; we are crossing a small town, where a red and black flag hangs from every house. Through the open windows, we catch glimpses of free people, smiling and happy to be alive and well-kept fields, where silhouettes stoop toward the ground. Kids give us the finger. When the train stops, we fill our bottles with fresh water. At a large train station, we pass a train full of German troops, which had stopped in the passageway. On its side, inscribed in chalk, the graffiti reads, "*Nach London*!" [To London]

At the outskirts of Regensburg the scenery is stunning. The tracks pass high over a spectacular deep precipice filled at the bottom with a slow moving river full of silt: The Danube. Stopover in Passau [German-Austrian border], then in Linz [Austria]. Second night.

3 July—We stop in the morning for an extended time at a small train station, which looks like a Swiss chalet. The train empties out. Without any food for the last thirty hours we invade the lunchroom. The sentinels are tired and indifferent. A slice of bread with jam costs 20 frs, cigarettes cost 10 frs. The stock is quickly exhausted. With nothing else left, hunger torments us. A few civilians, dressed in local attire, stand around. The men wear a brown vest with facings and frogs, short pants with suspenders, shoes with buckles, light gray stockings, tricorne hats, and always that ridiculous small blazer made of rough fur. The women wear short skirts with suspenders, garish blouses, and pointed headscarves tightly hugging their heads.

A second engine is coupled to our train. *Ansteigen*! [All aboard] Our guards rush around. The train starts very slowly, climbing a steep ramp and puffing, until it reaches an immense amphitheater of meadows ringed by high rocky plateaus. Here and there, white and red villages dot the landscape. Their onion dome steeples give the impression of the orient. We pass by small stands of meager trees and wooded rest stops that remind us of Black Forest toys. The train stops at a small station.

After a long stall on the platform at noon, when the sun is at its zenith, an impetuous *Rittmeister* [cavalry captain] launches into a long speech. A tall man with a bulging chest and wide shoulders, he fits tightly in his tunic. His flat cap tips toward one ear. His prominent chin rests on a thick padding of flesh that spills over his collar. His features are regular, but heavy. He looks like a mask of the gluttonous Roman Emperor Vitellius, obsequious and dull.

The train station of Göpfritz in April 2010. The village does not seem to have changed much since July 1940, when the officer POWs arrived (photograph by Patricia Jacqueline Hunt).

His rainbow-looking mouth and very thin lips, sagging at the corners, gives a scheming and cruel expression to an otherwise convivial looking face; all in all, a gentleman whose manners resemble those of a huckster. Someone whispers, "He looks like Mr. Loyal!" Heard among other things: "Gentlemen, please be disciplined! You will not carry your piece of luggage. The camp is just four short miles away. Soon after arrival, the gentlemen will be able to sleep. The gentlemen will find a good bed and will eat good soup." Punctuating each phrase, his chest dives forward. Genial! Much too genial!

Someone whispers, "He looks like Mr. Loyal!" Such a simple remark, yet out of context. Was the German captain named on the spot because of his attitude? I soon learned that so-named Mr. Loyal was Captain Trichtel, the Executive Officer of the camp. Living in France for a few years before the war as a representative of a large German soap company, he knew French well. After marrying a French woman, he became an employee of a French bank. When war seemed likely between France and Germany, Trichtel, a loyal Nazi, returned to Germany to serve in the army. But still, why was he called Mr. Loyal throughout the diary? Reading a transcript given by an officer at a conference after the war, solved the

3. Betrayal and Humiliation

riddle. *In one of life's unusual twists, one of the officers, prisoner on the station platform, happened to be the son of the bank director, where Tritchel had worked.*[10] *Recognizing him, he called him by the name Mr. Loyal, given to him by the bank employees, when he loyally returned to Germany.*

3 July (continued)—Thirsty, worn out by exhaustion, and lack of sleep, we are on the move again on an empty stomach. We go through the hamlet of Göpfritz, not more than a single never-ending street. At the crossroad, the road sign says, Vienna [Austria], 80 miles. That makes us dream of escaping. It is too late. We soon leave the main road and turn onto a small rural road lined with sycamores. A rustic fellow, standing on his doorstep, clenches his fists and shouts insults. We are approaching an army camp on our right, which soon disappears behind the rolling hill. On our left, woods of firs and pines border the road.

Then suddenly, on the other side of the slope, the roofs and chimneys of a block of barracks come into view. It is the camp. From here, about fifteen hundred feet away, the web of barbed wire connecting the high watchtowers gives the camp the shape of an oversized rectangle. An alley in the center divides the camp in half. Toward the south, scattered houses form a hamlet around a small church.

At 2:40 p.m. we cross the first gate, at 2:45 p.m. a second. They are shut behind us.

The Cadet said it best, "The camp looked as sinister as all the POW camps in the world. It was a big flat surface, encircled by a double curtain of barbed wire with about fourteen feet in-between. Between the two rows of barbed wire, one had taken the precaution of placing rolls of spikes. Every three hundred twenty feet stood a watchtower occupied by a sentinel armed with an automatic weapon. In the middle, two long rows of low lying barracks faced a central alley."[11]

About half a mile from the camp stood a seventeenth-century church with a prominent steeple surrounded by a cluster of houses, the village of Edelbach. Before 1938 this large plateau of cultivated fields and grazing farm animals offered a peaceful scene. Things changed with Hitler's invasion [Anschluss] of Austria. For his own purpose, Hitler had transformed this area into a military maneuver ground, expelling seven thousand people from forty-two villages. The camp was built as part of the training ground. The village still stood, but was an empty shell. The camp occupied previously cultivated fields.

The first group of prisoners had arrived in Oflag XVIIA, at Edelbach, one of seventeen permanent Oflags housing altogether thirty-six thousand French officers. There were also sixty-five stalags, housing about one and a half million French noncommissioned officers and enlisted soldiers.

4

Defiance

4–20 July 1940

As soon as the first officer POWs crossed the threshold of the camp in the afternoon of 3 July, the guards subjected them to a preliminary search before letting them into their assigned barracks. The cadet described that experience: "Our column headed toward a barracks, and one by one the Germans let each man enter. Noncommissioned officers and soldiers in green uniforms under the watchful eyes of a young officer executed our first search. Some resisted openly; a lieutenant quietly destroyed all the items that could be taken away from him. He took his watch and stamped on it with his heel, and his pen got the same treatment." The cadet continued, "Without realizing it, I had entered a merciless and ruthless world like everything that deals with war. When it was my turn, the Germans immediately took my spurs. The spurs were of very poor quality in nickel, but I was very fond of them. They represented for me a symbol of a somewhat romantic vision of military life, a world that I dimly felt disappearing. As I protested, the officer responded with a glacial look, "You do not need spurs, mister. There are no horses here." I had not yet understood that I had no rights anymore, and that in fact I did not exist anymore."[1]

4 July—Wake up call! A rough hand pushes the wooden shutters in their tracks. A few blurry shapes form crude shadows in the light. Our hearts pound very fast with an agonizing pain. We are prisoners! Eight hours of brutish exhaustion on a narrow straw mattress had deadened our grief, but it is coming back now and settles in. A true cancer! We will have to live with it until the end, and we do not even know what kind of end. Despair is a worn-out word, but are there any other words that can express at once, anguish, deprivation, incarceration, defeat, powerless rage, uncertainty, and misery? One hundred ten men in this half barracks are emerging from the drowsiness of a slug. Some pound the wooden floor with their boots. Others cuss each other out around a bucket filled with blackish water, and still others try, unsuccessfully, to go back to sleep. All our misery winds up here in this atmosphere of a rabbit shed built on a human scale. It is dirty and it stinks. Ah! Some standards these Germans have! Three-tier bunks are our beds with the frames attached to four posts. We use the third frame on top as the luggage dump. By way of a mattress we have a sack of wet straw. If that were not enough, there are neither closets nor tables. Not one chair. None! Ah! Remember the words of the *Rittmeister*: "A good bed, good soup is waiting for you!" The soup! It consists of lukewarm water with a few pieces of lettuce and potatoes with their skins served in a quaint serving dish, a bucket and neither bowls, nor cups. Did they say they were expecting us? D. eats from a Band-Aid container he had picked up on the way. Another fabricates a ladle with a can attached to a stick. It is cold and we have just one blanket. Rain pelts the windows. We don't have any coats. Yesterday afternoon we froze to the bone in the rain while waiting to be assigned to a barracks. Then, it was a mad rush to leap on the meager straw mattress and call a corner one's own. We jumped into it like a dog into his doghouse.

5 July—Have just completed a grand tour of the camp with R. We walked along the barbed wire fence in order to come back to our starting point. It was a confusing undertaking, as the camp is a kind of puzzle, divided into squares of four groups of barracks opening to a field, each enclosed by barbed wire. Gates connect the squares one with the other. We counted twenty-eight low-lying barracks surrounded by fields, vestiges of meadows left to their natural state. A few blades of grass here and there form patches of green. Our dreary domain, called the *Hauptlager* [main camp], is separated from the *Vorlager* [the German side of the camp] by a double gate. The *Vorlager* houses the administration and all the services. The eye embraces an unspectacular earth with bare meadows and arid hilltops, dominated by a dark sea of pines. Nevertheless in the southwest, a green ravine reminds us a little of the grace and delicate pattern of a French landscape. We gaze on it for a long time, united by the same thought, but as our stare on the iron spikes grows more precise, our contemplation becomes unbearable as soon as we discover the horizon through the grid of the barbed wire.

The German administrative area, separated by barbed wire from the rest of the camp, included the infirmary, one building for showers for the entire camp, sleeping quarters for the German guards, and a few other buildings. Immediately outside the enclosure was the Kommandantur *(headquarters) and the sentries' posts. The twenty-eight barracks of the main camp were divided into seven squares of four barracks with each a field and one building in the back for a latrine. The entrance to one half of the barracks faced the central alley and the entrance to the other half faced the field. In an eighth square, about three-quarters of the way from the front, were three brick buildings: a kitchen for the entire camp, a building housing a variety of rooms, and the jail of the camp.*

Recriminations against the Rittmeister, *Mr. Loyal, started from the very beginning. He had willfully misled the men at the train station by reciting the Geneva Convention regulations, but not the actual conditions of the camp. The articles of the Convention, which cover how prisoners of war are to be treated, specify buildings with sufficient hygiene, a minimum cubic airspace, bedding similar to those used by the detaining power's own soldiers in base camp, and similar quality and quantity of food as depot troops.*[2] *What they found was far from what they expected.*

6 July—The barracks looks, and feels like an anthill. All our wretchedness is penned up in here. It is about fifty meters long, and ten meters wide [about 5,400 square feet]. In the center there are three small rooms: a lavatory, a kitchen, and a utility room. On either side of these three rooms are two rooms, housing about 110 men, each. The inner walls are double, insulated with broken glass. At each end, there is a small vestibule, which opens to the outside. The kitchen is a cramped space equipped with an old-fashioned small stove. The utility room, slightly larger, looks more like a junk room than a utility room and is used to wipe the dishes clean. With all the grime and filth it looks like a dirty stable. The lavatory, more spacious, is in constant use. From five in the morning to ten at night the faucets are open, letting the water stream on the nude torsos before it disappears in the white ceramic basin. Some take pleasure in acrobatic baths, reaching with their hands the body parts inaccessible to the water in this primitive setting.

7 July—Sunday—It should be a day more joyous than all the others, but today it is cruel, obsessed by the memories of Sundays in freedom at home. In the morning, we attend an open-air mass. At noon, we partake of a meager soup of potatoes complete with their skins, bread, and margarine, followed by a catnap that brings back memories as bitter as ever. Four fanatics play bridge.... Others pound on nails.

The officer POWs in the camp included men from all corners of France: Paris, large and small towns, from provinces in the north, south, east, and west. They were active duty officers and reservists of all ranks belonging to all services from first lieutenants to colonels, and navy captains. The reservists represented an educated class from all walks of life and professions.

Each officer POW, however, knowing but a few men in this crowd, felt isolated. In their distress, they did not even find the spiritual uplifting that religion and celebrating Mass would provide later. Instead, on that first Sunday the rituals became bitter reminders of their faraway family, home, and the freedom they had lost.

The conditions of the camp were the ultimate indignities—220 men in a 5,400-square-foot-space with only three-tier bunk beds for furniture. The lighting was very dim. The lavatory consisted of pipes running just below the ceiling, pierced at interval with a few holes to let the water through. The water flowed into a waist-high receptacle resembling a trough for cows. There were no showers.

8 July—The administrative machine has been set in motion. At 3 o'clock we are led to the *Vorlager* to establish our personal files and fingerprints and conduct a random capricious search. The presence of officers renders this procedure even more vicious. No luck. One of the officers prowls in our corner, mindlessly parading the body frame of a sleek animal with low forehead and square jawbone. It is evident that his intelligence does not extend beyond this dirty work, which appears to give him great satisfaction. One by one, our sacks are turned inside out and every item is subjected to a picky scrutiny; fountain pens, tweezers, and a slide-rule are deemed dangerous and disappear into a large envelope. R., who is wearing boxer shorts, is ordered to take them off. Right away a guard pushes into his rectum. The soles of our shoes are examined with suspicion. Watches and pens are snatched. Raincoats, air mattresses, cameras, belts, everything goes. They say they will give them back later.... We receive a metal tag on which is engraved a series of numerals. We have become numbers.

9 July—Food is still meager. We receive one loaf of bread for five men, about eleven ounces a day, a soup made from a base of potato skins, in which there are no sparkling greasy circles, a starchy brew, and a few tough meat scraps, amounting at the most to one mouthful per person. The officer of the day [a daily rotating assignment in each barrack], derriere high and his head buried in the bucket, tries furiously to stab each piece with a three-prong fork. In the evening no soup, but instead, one slice of sausage and a spoonful of marmalade or synthetic honey. Our bodies are beginning to float in our jackets, our stomachs are receding, and our wedding bands are not staying on our fingers. The chubby B., who weighed two hundred thirty pounds, has already lost forty-four.

10 July—We have still not received anything, neither tables nor benches, or dishes. According to Mr. Loyal the *Kommandantur* gushes with promises, advice, and hollow sympathy. To remedy this lack, we take things into our own hands and loot a civilian construction company, which is building a block of barracks in the camp. On its site, we find nails, paper, pieces of wood, and scraps of iron, which we raid at random. Stones will be used as hammers, and knives that have escaped the search will become saws. The inside shutters become tables, and little by little coarse benches appear, as well as shelves attached to the walls with bolts. Shoes, bags, and clothes will hang from the ceiling. Strings, weighed down by multicolor pieces of cloth, are stretched from one bed frame to the other, making a picturesque jumble that looks like the Alleys of Marseille or the Trans-Tiberian.

11 July—The shock of defeat, a truly disintegrating force, is destroying the unifying principles, which are the bedrock of the human personality. An English writer comes to mind. "A certain framework, as well as an orthodox principle of continuity, becomes dominant in any given period." Come the shipwreck which destroys both the framework and the principle and the human personality disintegrates. Only basic vital needs survive. This leads to a moral breakdown, which could be seen in the painful daze of servitude. To escape this enslavement, we rush headlong into all kinds of feverish activities, expressed mostly in intellectual games. The majority talks about France, attempting to connect the future to the past as a way of finding a reason to live and hope. Some tell stories; true verbal orgies. Others, the impressionable ones, listen. Many hang on to their professional memories. As a result of the general understanding of the need to act, everybody starts writing, thinking, and speaking. Foreign language courses and talks are improvised in the barracks, in the kitchens of the barracks, and anywhere a few men can gather. Is the foremost thought motivating this whole awakening, a way to escape the wretched conditions of the slave, and regain the dignity of free men? In the absence of paper to write on, pieces from bags of cement are torn off sideways.

In just over two weeks these officers had met a fate which overnight removed them from commanding armies to being destitute and humiliated as prisoners living in primitive barracks. They had been sucked into a swift and disastrous defeat not of their own doing that forced many to surrender against their better judgment. These men felt their honor trod upon and felt betrayed by their high-ranking leaders and politicians.

They had reached the bottom of the abyss, feeling in my father's words that "an unexpected brutal, relentless, and inhuman fate" had come upon them. François Mitterand, a sergeant in 1940, taken prisoner, was typical of many soldiers. He wrote of these days, "I was a defeated soldier in a dishonored army, and I felt bitter towards those who had made that possible, the politicians of the Third Republic"[3] *[French government since 1871].*

4. Defiance

The diary's acerbic tone reflected the men's reaction, as they met face to face with the harsh reality of their situation at their arrival: dismal physical conditions and nonexistent food, numerous roll calls and searches. Worst of all they were not masters of their own lives anymore and did not know how long their captivity would last. They had become numbers.

Camp routine, roll calls, chores, and daily tasks occupied part of the day, sometimes most of the day, when the men were subjected to special roll calls. Nonetheless, they had a substantial amount of idle time. To escape the crowded barracks, they went to the fields, forming a big circle, walking along the inside perimeter of the barbed wire enclosure, "transforming the fields into a moving sea of khaki uniforms," a Red Cross official reported later. In these first days, they talked with anyone willing to listen, "true verbal orgies," notes the diary. This camp-wide mixing of all the men, however, put them in contact with one another, paving the way for the prompt organization of the community.

"We arrived in the camp under a gray foggy sky. Our hearts were just as joyless.... Yet, we began again to laugh and sing," recalled a lieutenant.[4] My father added, "We turned to the community for support, which provided each man an opportunity to give his best to entertain, document, and teach his comrades."[5] This spirit of cooperation would provide them with the means to live with dignity and honor. As we return to the diary they had reached a turning point.

12 July—In the barracks' entryway, a poster in three languages: no accosting of German women. Very funny! Little by little we transition from a gregarious status to a formal structure. Announcement of the establishment of a French hierarchy, which allows us to shift from a chaotic state to a more formal structure: at the top, our most senior officer of the highest rank assisted by a small general staff. He is the designated deputy. Under him will be the leaders of battalions—one battalion = four barracks—and under them, the leaders of the barracks. Every evening, reading of a communiqué consisting of a report, the notification of German orders, and briefing from our Commandant.

In Barracks 28, Lieutenant K. gives the first seminar: history of French literature. A multitude of listeners crowds the bunk beds in clusters, hanging like grapes on the grapevine and packing the floor between the bunks. For one hour, we forget this nauseating misery. An attempt to reach some intellectual endeavor is, however, difficult with an empty stomach.

13 July—Mr. Loyal has decided that we will be counted according to the rules. At 9 o'clock every barracks empties of its content. We all converge in the First Battalion's field. We line up at first in sets of three, being counted and recounted. First setback: there is a discrepancy between the total number of men and the number on the lists. Second attempt: we are counted in sets of five. Second setback: no doubt due to the shuttle game played by the insurrectionists. Astounding results and enjoyable interlude; frustrated non-commissioned officers run like dogs along the groups to extract the secret of the Number from this multitude. It is a fruitless endeavor. The figures still do not match. A bitter cold rain penetrates our clothes. Obdurate, Mr. Loyal decides not to leave the field, until he knows the Number. Then, begin a series of strange developments that defy any meaning. Every prisoner, carrying his tag, steps out of the line, walks toward the holder of the list, gives his number and then, joins the group already counted. The numerical call complicates the entire enterprise. This genial family party lasts until sunset. Chilled to the bone, we return to our dwelling. Has arithmetic become a speculative science?

14 July—Second Sunday in the camp: we attend mass in Barracks 13. A bright light falling on our shoulders from the bare window links us together in the same rush of fervor. A cross, made with two planks, rises in the back against the ochre stucco wall. Next to it stands a red white and blue flag, the colors of a piece of cloth that awaken in us a powerful throbbing and images of the absent homeland. In front of the altar stands the tall figure of Priest J. We kneel. There is a long silence, but in this particular moment it seems that the sounds become louder and are warped in a dreamland.

In the afternoon, an awful day peopled with too many memories.

15 July—An extraordinary rumor is running wild in the camp, news that is whispered from mouth to mouth and distorted as it is circulated. On second thought, it turns out to be absurd, but we believe it for a moment, particularly because it revolves around a pipe dream, being set free. It is difficult to trace it back to its source. Where did it come from? Nobody knows, except for the author, and no one tries to get to the bottom of it. From past experience, we have learned that it takes two hours for a rumor to come back to its point of origin, and by then it is unrecognizable. It is a canard. Some gullible individuals bathe with pleasure in this soothing formaldehyde, but in the end, they come out hurt. Such a one is P. He greets you with these words: "Do you know a gossip?" If you don't, he looks crest-fallen. If you do, he examines it, critiques it, discusses it, rejects its likelihood, but finally adopts it, and with great zeal circulates it in his circle. He takes a vainglorious delight to be a person-in-the-know, the best-informed person; he is a rumormonger! Rumor of the day: imminent signature in Versailles of a peace treaty between France and Germany. Ten armored divisions will march under the Arc de Triomphe. Another canard! By the way, what's happening to our liberation? It was supposed to start on 12 July. Another canard!

4. Defiance

16 July—In Barracks 28: a new lecture, given by Lieutenant B. on Shakespeare. High literary caliber!

17 July—All the furniture arrives. "They" deliver tables and stools. The heights of comfort! These are chunky and difficult to move but better than nothing. The other news of the day: barbers will be available. We are not allowed to grow a beard. There is no lack of humor. "Would Les Messieurs, who are not sure of their rank, come forward immediately," a guard announces. Is this to demote, or promote to a higher rank?

18 July—An agonizing hunger gnaws at us, quieted for a moment by swallowing a piece of black bread devoured in our ravenousness. But then our hunger is renewed even more ferociously. It haunts our dreams filled with feasts and hellish orgies. Every evening, D. and N. exchange gastronomic ideas from their bunks. One speaks of Chateaubriand servi bleu, with pommes soufflées, the other, of a lobster à l'américaine. Both agree that a dozen oysters with lemon juice are scrumptious. Threatening and abusive voices erupt from the adjoining bunks.

19 July—The entire camp swarms in front of Barracks 7 to read a public notice. It announces the schedule of seminars that will be given in Barracks 19, now empty.

The most diverse and unexpected topics: from Buddhism to the life of bees, and from Romanesque to Gothic art. Everyone tries to find a hobby. Certainly, all these are worthy endeavors that one may have dreamed of devoting one's idle hours in the past, but the demands of a normal life would have always ruled them out! In our present circumstances, everyone builds in his brain a course of studies worthy of Benedictine monks, studies that the first weariness will surely dim, until they are completely forgotten. Just like St. Paul on the road to Damascus, the halfhearted ones see their way illuminated now with a flash of divine revelation. So many fires of straw in a path, which demands the persevering soul of an apostle!

History is a popular attraction. This craze, no doubt, indicates the unconscious desire to resurrect old glorious times as harbingers of new ones. History, "the eternal renewal," is a science in which facts open a broad field of speculations. Will we experience new eras, and will these prestigious names of Iena and Austerlitz [Napoleon's victories] carry the seeds of future greatness in their power?

Within eight days after their arrival, they strikingly created order out of chaos. Turning to the familiar structure of a military hierarchy, they established their own French community with the most senior officer in the camp as their Commandant, who would also serve as their representative with the Germans (a difficult position to hold with dire consequences; usually being sent to a reprisal camp). The daily evening communiqué transmitted through the chain of command assured a flow of information from the top to every officer POW that became the crucial link during their entire captivity.

Establishing an internal command with their own leader altered the way the French felt about their situation. As the Representative to the German administration, the Commandant was able to advocate for the community, affording some modicum of protection for the officer POWs. It provided the means to reassert some control over their lives which restored a certain measure of self-respect and dignity in spite of their circumstantial powerlessness. New men coming into the camp over the following ten months integrated easily into the structure.

Understaffed to guard such a large number of prisoners, the Germans agreed to the French organization, since a self-disciplined community was to their advantage.[6] *The German administration consisted of a Major General, assisted by the Rittmeister, referred to as Mr. Loyal, who, speaking French, was the most visible person. A lieutenant was in charge of the sentries, and a few military police completed the contingent, totaling altogether about two to three hundred men.*[7] *An officer of the Gestapo monitored the running of the camp in the name of the Nazi party.*

Two barracks in the back section of the camp housed a detail of about three to four hundred French enlisted men POWs, who had come to the camp from a stalag, to do the manual labor and chores for the Germans. In addition to doing the work for the Germans, these POWs were assigned two to each barracks to help the officer POW of the day fetch the food vats from the main kitchen. According to the Geneva Convention, article 22, the duties of these POWs were: "(enlisted men) POWs of the same armed forces shall be detached for service to the officer POWs in sufficient numbers to ensure their wellbeing." The Germans in this instance were far from meeting these requirements, having assigned one orderly for one hundred ten officer POWs doing three chores a day.

These French soldiers, under normal circumstances in the army, would have been the orderlies attached to the French officers. Here in the camp, they were under the control of, and reported to the German staff, while performing some limited duty for the officer POWs. The officer POWs chose in this delicate situation to view the POWs as under more duress than they were, integrating them early on into the activities of the camp whenever possible. Later, they helped support these men's families, who had fewer resources than the officers' families in France. Over the years, the POWs became instrumental in providing crucial information to the officer POWs' clandestine activities; their daily work outside the camp, as the labor force for the Germans, gave them access to information not available to the officer POWs.

Not being required to work, the officer POWs were idle most of the day. Without access to supplies it could have been deadly (that requirement, however, was an essential prerogative, which the French officers affirmed with tenacity). Viktor Frankl, a Holocaust survivor, wrote, "There is nothing in the world that would so effectively help one to survive even the worst conditions, as the knowledge that there is a meaning to one's life."[8] These men understood that they needed to pursue worthwhile endeavors in order to survive. The idle time, instead of being a bane, became the crucible, in which they showed leadership, determination, and solidarity.

Concurrently with the establishment of the organizational structure, the first seminar, followed by another lecture three days later, culminated on 19 July with an entire schedule of seminars and lectures. In my father's words, "Freedom will certainly come some day; in the meantime we need to react. Our inner life must challenge daily this abominable and destitute material life. We must relentlessly establish the primacy of a spiritual life."[9] Many officer POWs came forward to share skills, which did not require material resources, utilizing the one resource they possessed, their combined abundant human knowledge and skills.

The implementation of the impressive list of seminars and lectures was, however, a daring adventure. First, they needed a space to meet; the French Commandant obtained the use of an empty barrack. There was neither podium, nor boards, or means of writing; no means of sitting down, unless each officer brought his own seat. There were no resource materials, except any book the men may have carried with them. All talks were given extemporaneously from memory. The scheduling was not as simple as one might think. Even though the prisoners were theoretically idle, except for meal times and regular twice a day roll calls, they were subjected to the whims of their jailers, who often lengthened roll calls for hours, or added unscheduled roll calls and searches. Posting a schedule of seminars and lectures was an act of faith and will.

Yet, after three weeks in the camp their communal life was taking shape, and intellectual and spiritual endeavors were paving the way for their emotional health. Already, on the second Sunday, their attitude was quite different from the prior week. They had obtained a barracks to serve as a chapel, which provided them with the more familiar environment of a cross and even displayed the French colors. With some measure of calm the men could take a few moments of reflection and find some respite.

As soldiers they had obeyed their commander-in-chief when he called for a cease-fire. As soon as they arrived on German soil, they realized that they had *become the pawns of political forces. Their options at that point were limited, but responding with a "fierce will to react," they created a meaningful environment that would defy their situation. Intimating a theme, which was widespread among the officer POWs, my father added in a moral, almost religious tone, "Our suffering could mark the beginning of a renewal of the spirit and the soul." The writer André Gide in France expressed the same attitude that "suffering purifies" when he asked, "Is it fanciful to hope that France will issue from this nightmare strengthened?"*[10] *Steadfastly and tenaciously, the men challenged their humiliation by their actions and achievements.*

20 July—Everything seems to get organized in this cursed city! New cogs, added to the old ones, engage each other and begin to turn. New habits take shape; everyone wants his own corner, his own path, and his own stool. The racks of the beds are full of familiar objects, pictures of our loved-ones, and a few knick-knacks. Does this mean that we are resigned to accept our fate, or is it a rational decision to make the best of the slightest possibilities? We are settling in captivity. What a paradox!

5

Settling In
21 July–15 November 1940

21 July—Third Sunday—We have not received any letters for six weeks. Our anxiety intensifies day by day. The extent of the catastrophe and our debilitating hunger have until now monopolized all our thoughts. Within the relative calm in which we live, the fate of our families is now coming back in legions and besieges us like a swarm of wasps. What has happened to France under the boots of the occupying forces? Where are our families? We know nothing about any of these things, if we exclude a few slanted articles in the *Trait-d'Union*, a German tabloid, written for the prisoners by the folks in Berlin. Also saw a particularly provocative picture on the front page of a batch of Viennese newspapers showing the Wehrmacht giving a concert on the Place de l'Opéra [in Paris]. Fortunately, there were few onlookers, but my God, what heartbreak!

22 July—We have just received fifteen marks as an installment of our pay.[1] In return, we are subjected to an obligatory sitting in a photo booth. In one of the barracks of the *Vorlager*, "the patients" with a slate, inscribed with a number and dangling from their neck, wait for the click of the shutter: two or three very original negatives. These gentlemen of the Gestapo are humorists without knowing it. A few K.G. [POWs] artfully distort their face; eyebrows plucked, head shaved, or face contorted.... No one shall ever ask, whether we have given up on life.

24 July—A small canteen[2] opened this morning. We are able to buy a bottle of beer and ten cigarettes. Big deal! There is no foodstuff. However, they are peddling Viennese junk: fetishes made of painted wood, tie clasps, and of all things, bath salts!

A few letters arrive via Switzerland for our Polish comrades, but still nothing from France.

Savor the first rutabaga soup.

26 July—Postal connections have resumed with France. Distribution of card-letters, quota of one for ten; they are drawn at random. The beneficiary passes on the news for nine comrades.

28 July—The lack of tobacco is severely felt. Pipes oozing a pungent smoke fill the barracks with a rancid air that makes you sick to your stomach. Clusters of herbs in small packages hanging from strings dry everywhere. Some prefer clover, others wild thyme, but everyone complains of sharp pains in the lower intestine.

29 July—Arrival of a few officers [POWs] picked up in France mostly in the West. In the bunch, a captain of frigate represents the navy. Mobbed, the newcomers give some fragmentary news. We are beginning to grasp the magnitude of the dislocation.

30 July—Barracks 19: This old son of a gun entertains us about the Mongols. A soldier of fortune-type, ex–Legionnaire, baked by every exotic sun and covered with medals, he walks around brashly dragging his wooden leg. Energetic, impudent, with the soul of a condottiere, and a specialist on noble weapons, he can chatter equally about the Macedonian phalanx and the wardroom of the Old Timers, or make a barbarian of the New Times appear behind the triumphant shadow of Genghis Khan. On the other hand, W., a biologist [Etienne Wolff, a renowned biologist after the war], fills the hall to capacity with a promising title: "The Twins and the Monsters." But it is a serious lecture, not a seminar. The sadism of the prurient busybodies clashes with the scientific stuffiness of the presentation. They will not come back.

1 August—In the field across from Edelbach, the Basques dance and sing the best melodies of their folklore. In the stillness of dusk, the sunset sky turns stale with shades of lilac, blue, and orange, blending little by little into the color of a dark amethyst. In the watchtower cages, the sentries' silhouettes stand out against the darkening sky.

3 August—Distribution of the first mail from France; the mail clerk is shoved, harassed, and pushed around. Half hidden, he breaks free and holds up a card, immediately wrested out of his hands by an eager hand. The human circle breaks off. Out of reach, the lucky one comes out of his dream, staring in the distance. The card has already been read. He will read it again and again.

4 August—It would be impossible to determine the anatomy of Herr General Kommandant, a domineering type. This man's external appearance looks like both a bulldog and a batrachian: a bulldog because of his powerful square jaws and set of teeth, and a batrachian because of his bulgy round

5. Settling In

eyes. We can, however, assume that the digestive track of this mammal supplants all the other organs, thanks to the overflowing cesspool. With short thighs, bowlegged, a purple-blue face, and pants flapping, he wobbles like a full flask. At a distance, a whole court of decorated men follows this little tyrant that has the soul of a *Feldwebel* [sergeant]. They stop as soon as he stops and start walking as soon as he walks. They sway their torsos, and click their heels as soon as he belches out an order with a hoarse voice affected by alcohol.

5 August—The roll calls always lack solemnity. The duty to stand at strict attention is never respected. The last rows are sparse at the expense of the front rows. Men swing from one foot to the other, and an intensive avalanche of stones falls on the unprotected heads. A continual eddy breaks up the line. The jackets and overcoats are sometimes decorated in the back with bizarre symbols, such as a fishbone made of paper. Without the owners' knowledge, the police caps are adorned with multicolored plumes. Sometimes, after the command, "Disband!" two comrades, tied together by strings, push and pull willy-nilly, and accompanied by howling jeers, our new Siamese brothers walk a few feet. These irreverent games are indisputable proof of a resilient will not to abdicate in front of our guardian angels.

8 August—The veterans of the First World War said: the Boches, the Fritz, and the Fridolins. For us it is the Chleuhs [a term for the Berbers in southern Morocco].

10 August—In the last few days, beside the *Trait-d'Union* we have received a new newspaper, the *Volkischer Beobachter*, [V.B.] which proclaims the official ideology of the *Partei* [Nazi Party]. Those who know German well attract a number of listeners, as they translate the bombastic prose of the victors. Usual slogans: war against democracies, claim of a vital living space and annihilation of the Judeo-Masonic plutocracies, and thunderous threats against anything that would prevent the free expansion of Greater Germany. Through the warped prism of this Nazi newspaper, we learn of the accession to power of Marshal Pétain, and the existence of what the paper calls, the "dissident pseudo-government" in London under the authority of the "traitor" General de Gaulle. Today, huge headlines on the front page announce the air attack on London. A winged skeleton playing the violin hangs over Westminster Abbey and "tactfully" displays the pompous Teutonic phraseology.

An organized structure of the camp was little by little taking shape. The opening of a canteen was not greeted with great enthusiasm, seen as a reminder that their captivity would last for an indefinite time. In addition, the supplies were not very useful; bath salts were the height of irony, since there were neither baths nor showers. There was, however, one silver lining. Someone figured out that the beauty cream jars contained enough grease to become candles as long as they could find something to twist to make a wick.³ With the electricity often cut off unexpectedly, these containers became a prized possession.

For the lucky men, news from their families started trickling in after six weeks of being completely without any news, but many did not hear from their families until October or November. They also had been without news of the continuation of the war or the fate of France politically. To add insult to injury, when they finally got some information, it came from German newspapers and propaganda machine in Le Trait d'Union *(the Union Arrow)*. Distributed regularly to all the camps, this tabloid, written in French and glorifying Hitler and his army, was despised particularly because a few French prisoners wrote articles for it. The men quickly dubbed the paper Le Traître d'Union *(the Union Traitor)* and noted that it was useful as toilet paper.⁴

In the months ahead, the prisoners were allowed to subscribe to French newspapers, published in the occupied French zone, also under German control, but these papers at least gave some idea of daily life in France. They were quick to assert their skepticism about the veracity of one of the newspapers, Je suis partout *(I am everywhere)*, nicknaming it J'essuis partout *(I mop up everywhere)*. They also found some practical use for these papers, shaping them into little balls to be used in their makeshift stoves during the winter.

The regular German newspaper the Volkischer Beobachter, *V.B.*, informed them of two crucial events for the future of France: the accession to power of Marshal Pétain,⁵ and the news of General de Gaulle having formed a government in London. The Nazi newspaper called it a "dissident pseudo-government" in London under the authority of the "traitor" General de Gaulle, a view shared by the Vichy government and Marshal Pétain.

They also wrote about General de Gaulle's memorable Appel *of 18 June*,⁶ and mocked his declaration that "France had only lost a battle, but had not lost the war," a catch phrase actually not part of the Appel, but printed on posters in July–August in England. Many officer POWs were likely not to know much about de Gaulle's Appel, as it was broadcast at the time they were taken prisoners. It was heard by very few people and was printed the next day only in the few French newspapers, which were still free of the German occupation. In addition, Charles de Gaulle, a colonel at the beginning of the war, was not well known by the troops.⁷

In the context of the circumstances in France in mid–June 1940, de Gaulle's call expressed a radical tension between the duty of the soldier and the sentiments of the patriot. He wrote in his memoirs, "As these irrevocable words (of the

5. Settling In

Appel*) flew out upon their way, I felt within myself a life coming to an end, the life I had lived within the framework of a solid France and an indivisible army."*[8] *As soldiers, the officer POWs had followed Marshal Pétain, but the patriot in them yearned for de Gaulle's call to resistance.*

12 August—Mediums, theosophists, and dowsers enhance the life of the oflag! One immediately gains great fame; an old colonel of the ordnance corps finds more pride in his art than in his stripes. The den of this modern Calchas is in Barracks 8, where he pronounces his oracles. Bent over his Tarot cards, he searches in the oscillations of the pendulum for the precise point where your wife, your brother, or your sister are now living. R. consults him and learns that his wife fled to the Orne region. Privately, those with independent minds snicker, and the pendulum swings furiously.

13 August—Rumor: armistice Anglo-German. C. takes us with unbridled lyricism to the Perigord. [Region in the southeast of France and so is Quercy.] We become acquainted with François Ménard, an illustrious man of Quercy. The patés de foie gras and truffles, found in abundance in this rich soil, overshadow all other elements. At a time when we cannot even find a stack of bread slices or smell the aroma of roast beef, lascivious looks lust after a lavish feast in silent anger. C. must have, in better times, lunched at Sousceyrac.

14 August—Chewing tobacco is now available in the canteen. N. stockpiles it. A skilled alchemist, he washes, grinds, pummels, salts, and dries this blackish carrot. Result: it is not fit to smoke.

Collecting cigarette butts, however, has generated the beginning of a black market, a prosperous traffic which enriches the trafficker; a fist full of cigarette butts goes for two marks. R. barters his cheese ration for four cigarettes. A tobacco pack is worth 25 marks.

15 August—Barracks 9 has become the camp's church, a modest wood sanctuary with makeshift altars, covered with white cloths. Leaning against the four rough inner walls these humble altars, consecrated each to a well-known saint, were built with rough planks. Somewhat simple-minded drawings decorate each altar. The main altar is a plain table standing on a stage. Today we celebrate the feast of the Assumption. The Cecilia Choir—about thirty members—conducted by the Midshipman L., bursts into the *Cantata à la Vierge* (for the Virgin) composed by Allain.

17 August—A streak of light flashes every so often. With both hands and a big circular motion, Captain A. strikes the ground with a long crooked steel rod, and his eyes follow a dot moving at a great speed into the sky. He then takes off with long strides to look for a goal he alone knows about.

A. plays golf. In his misfortune he had lost everything "except the club."

Oflag XVIIA in Austria 1940-1945

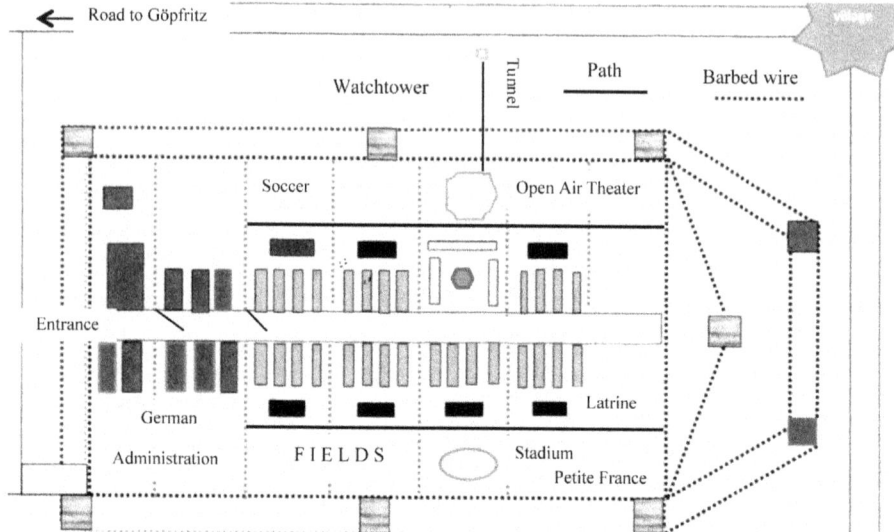

The layout of Oflag XVIIA. This drawing includes some of the improvements made by the officer POWs in 1941–42 as well as the escape tunnel of 1943 (Jacqueline Vautrain Collins).

In the distance, bodies leap around a ball, which looks like a basketball. Further away, some young men run in tight formation: soccer practice. Handball and volleyball players move around. Surrounding them, spectators stamp their feet, yell, wave, and applaud in the best tradition of sportsmanship.

20 August—Arrival of the month: two hundred officers [POWs] from Belfort, Neuf-Brisach, and Haguenau and five hundred from Nancy [all French cities]. Eagerly everyone looks for the face of a friend. The camp becomes a small town of more than five thousand inhabitants.

21 August—For a Frenchman, France is first and foremost, but the place of birth is also important. It attaches itself joyfully to the gentle shadow of a native steeple, and it shapes the true measure of the man. Every week, the *Bretons, Basques, Picards, Beaucerons,* and *Provençaux* [inhabitants of various provinces] get together. They exchange news and talk about everything that represents their regional soul. The accent of the province gives a warm-hearted richness to their chitchat.

23 August—Mentioning the menus in our letters is not allowed. Do not say, I am hungry or I am cold. Do not confess.... In all likelihood on behalf of free will?

5. Settling In

24 August—That we would be railroad workers! Ten employees of the S.N.C.F. [French Amtrak] are released from captivity. They are leaving today for the occupied zone. Our masters provide barracks 18 with a radio receiver. It is impossible to get close to it. At the center of a neutral zone, a Teuton messes around with the control knobs: exclusive Radio-Paris, French text, for popular use. Another source of more objective and truer information: the letters. Succinct analysis is read to comrades. They reveal deep political and social disarray, increasing scarcity of food, forced requisition, cruelty of dislocation and some shallow clarification on the armistice and accession to power of Maréchal Pétain.

26 August—Responding to a vibrant engagement in religion, Catholics are starting a cycle of courses for seminarians in the chapel, which includes dogmatic and moral theology, sacred texts, and canon law. Laymen are giving seminars of more general interest for everyone else. A small number of Protestants is engaged in biblical studies.

As the camp population shifted, some barracks became empty. Barracks 9, located toward the end of the camp between the POWs' barracks and the kitchen complex, became the church. By consecrating various altars to French saints, the men created a comfort zone reminding them of their hometown. Considered part of the national inheritance, saints occupied an important place in French culture, recognized in names of villages, towns, and regions.[9] *With each day of the calendar year dedicated to a saint, people celebrated the day of the saint bearing their first name.*

The priests, about eighty prisoners in the camp, chaplains in the military, had designated a head chaplain, organized parishes, and pursued their usual activities. A choir was the first attainable form of musical life, since it depended solely on the human voice. Without music scores, musical pieces were composed in the camp, or the choir director harmonized well-known folk songs and melodies. 15 August, the feast of the Assumption, an important date on the French Catholic calendar, celebrates the assumption of the Virgin Mary (from the Latin ad-sumere, to take away), not to be confused with the ascension (to ascend). The celebration signifies altogether, the death, glorious resurrection, entrance in heaven, and coronation of the Virgin Mary.

28 August—Whether or not a Frenchman ignores geography, as it has been said, he offsets it by loving community associations. He is always president, vice-president, treasurer or active member of something. "Distinguish Member," such were the characteristic newspaper reports in the past. We find here a considerable, impressive number of groups: alumni association of *Polytechnique, Centraux, Quartzarts, Cyrards, H.E.C.* [Institutions of higher learning]. Hunters have formed a circle of Saint-Hubert, an association of fishermen, a society of Fly Fishermen, and the mountaineers, an Alpine Club. The philatelists started their own group. In turn, the sociologists, rightly moved by this proliferation, gather to study this phenomenon.

... One more circle!

30 August—The Chleuhs announce that the prisoners whose occupation is needed for the resumption of the country's economy can be repatriated upon the request of the French government. Storm in our heads! Pie in the sky: who is not indispensable?

For the last two days the food has improved, now that the kitchens have been put under French management. Some barley or macaroni and a can of pork and beans occasionally replace the daily soup. Triumph of a giant pickle, preserved in salt, and swallowed voraciously as dessert. So sweet!

31 August—The lecture hall of Barracks 19 becomes the main office of *l'Université*. Leading it is an Academic Dean, L., tenured professor and a mathematician whose profile is well known here. A bit stooped, he walks with his eyes staring toward the ground, lost in some lofty speculations. The leather briefcase from which he never parts is such a rare object that one notices it immediately.

The courses are of two kinds: junior college and university courses, as well as classes predominantly tailored to benefit the average POWs. The former is designed for students wishing to finish their studies. Accredited professors—about thirty—will teach the subjects of the majors. At the end of the study, a series of tests will allow awarding certificates and diplomas, which will certainly be honored upon our return.

Concurrently with the official and academic instruction, an infinite number of practical courses are offered: shorthand, husbandry, modern languages, accounting, etc....

The lectures, however, retain an undeniable prestige, particularly those about history, literature, and music. Captain P., assisted by the violinist L., opens a series of talks in conjunction with recitals.

The founding day of the University, 31 August, was a milestone, which extended the academic influence on the community. One of the major achievements of Oflag XVIIA (some diplomas were recognized by French universities after the war), the camp university was led by a number of academicians and scientists who would become leaders in their fields after the war. The chosen Dean, Lieutenant Jean Leray, professor in the Department of Sciences at the University of Nancy before the war and an expert in hydrodynamics, had been awarded a prestigious mathematical prize. Fearful of being forced to work for the Nazis, if he were to reveal his field to the Germans, he taught instead algebraic topology and calculus during his captivity. Shortly after his return to France, he was appointed professor at the Collège de France *(founded in 1530, the Collège de France is a unique institution with fifty-two endowed professors representing science, art, history, and philosophy with the courses open to anyone), where he focused his work on non-linear partial-differential equations, stemming from mathematical physics.*[10]

At this early time, however, the Camp University was still without resources, books, or articles, except for what each officer POW may have carried with him. In addition to limited resources, there were very unique practical challenges: limited space, neither desks nor chairs. A picture, taken clandestinely and published after the war,[11] *shows the men waiting outside the barracks, each officer carrying his own wooden stool on his shoulder. Who would know that some of these drab-looking men had stood at podiums of town halls, in the halls of the Sorbonne, le Palais Bourbon, or commanded ships? But they were determined. A colonel wrote: "The mission of the university and of all the accomplishments of brotherly love, which were born and blossomed in our prisons, aimed to be superior to one's fate: as captives our bodies are shackled but our minds are free."*[12]

The Germans decided to assign some of the three hundred French POWs to cooking for the camp, a welcomed change for the officer POWs. It added another unintended benefit. It kept some of the POWs on the ground of the camp during the day, which gave the officer POWs an opportunity to talk and connect with their own troops.

1 September—Sunday—Good news. Two Polish officers [there was one barracks of Polish officer POWs] have been able to conceal themselves under the chassis of a big truck, which supplies the kitchens. This provides us with an entertainment similar to the one of 13 July. From 1 to 3 p.m. counting and recounting, numerical call, call by name, and finally, continual coming and going. We make a patsy of Mr. Loyal, who blows up. "Let's not create such headaches, I know that les Messieurs have left in the pickles drum. For the period of time les Messieurs have to stay, I am giving notice to les Messieurs: from today on, it will be hell!"

3 September—Slightly away from the rows of barracks, one barracks painted in a dark color stands perpendicular to the others. It's the "Brown House" [the common latrine, one per four barracks]. We also call it, *l'Académie*—irreverent connection—[name given to a Parisian literary group], because like the *Cenacle* it consists of exactly forty seats. Quaint details: the seats are separated sideways by simple room dividers, creating small open cubicles without doors. It is an odd style that will require getting used to.... Little by little, the shock of this situation disappears, however, and friendly conversations are struck between contiguous cubicles. Some ardent readers come to avidly finish a partly read chapter, less commotion here, while others come to discuss literature and philosophy, and still others come to address some fine points of a financial matter. All on the basis of the respectful and good humor that befits people of excellent company!

4 September—Rumor I.—Evacuation of the camp to make room for a Panzer division.

Rumor II.—The First World War Veterans will be liberated very soon.

It is a gorgeous day. The sky is lapis lazuli blue. It is strange how rumors need the sun to hatch out more profusely.

It is official: Scapini has been named plenipotentiary minister in charge of representing POWs. On what sides are the authorities?

5 September—M. is officer of the day. It is a cruel job. Subjected to murmuring and controversy, he wrangles furiously to divide the sausage. An engineer candidly offers him a caliper. He tries again. Loud boos. He falls back on the Roman scales, which a comrade, an evaluator of the Weights and Measure Administration, has built. Tempers simmer down. It starts again with the jam. With infinite care he scrapes the bucket with his hands. They are as red as beets. He would like to lick them, but does not dare. Finally, he has to scrape his fingers with a knife and portion out the excess of molasses plate by plate. What a job! Hunger, a continual tyrant, divides, hardens, and turns us into selfish people.

7 September—At last, the first packages. Censorship has taken effect, but fortunately the censors have not yet been trained. A package! Over there, no one understands what it all means for us. It has been prepared with love by cherished hands. It brings a fond radiance of our homeland. It revives our faraway home with all the daily gestures of the people of our flesh and our blood. It is, all in one, the country house and the city house. It is a piece of France.

10 September—Our two Poles are back. Ah! Who will express the sadness of failed breakouts! They are shoved into prison. Mr. Loyal gloats and cancels hell!

13 September—We now mix meat sacks and delicate batiste pillowcases. After the shelter for vagrants, the whiteness of the nursery! It is not yet a bed, but it looks a little more like it.

15 September—Captain R. dies without knowing the tragic end of his son, burnt in a tank. We had concealed the awful news from him until the very end.

5. Settling In

19 September—After the morning roll call: physical education classes with Ct. B., a trainer and follower of Isadora Duncan. We perform pleasurable combinations of crawling, squatting, rocking like a bear, human pyramids, and jumping rhythmically; this entire fauna huffs and puffs. During the breaks, the fine profile of Antinoüs and the pot-bellied Silène sit side by side.

"On what sides are the authorities," *the reaction of the officer POWs, very suspicious of the appointment of Georges Scapini as ambassador representing the POWs, was founded on his past actions. Georges Scapini, a lawyer and past deputy of the Paris Council, was the founder in 1935 of the French-German Committee, which had urged a rapprochement of the two nations. True to form, Scapini, in his new role of leading the Services for POWs, immediately established his headquarter in Berlin with an office in Paris,*[13] *hardly an auspicious beginning. His title also confirmed that the status of the POWs was permanent, one more proof of the lack of commitment of the Vichy government to their release, contradicting Marshal Pétain's claim that he wanted to obtain their liberation as quickly as possible.*

The description of the plight of the Officer of the Day in early September gives us a sense of the extent of their hunger. Weighing food was a great sport to make sure that everybody had the exact same amount. I still remember my father, in one of his few comments, explaining to me the elaborate ways they employed to divide rations to the last micro-ounce.

Conditions in the camp varied greatly over the five-year period. The historian S.P. MacKenzie wrote, "The rations given to the POWs were inadequate both in quantity and quality, when the enemy had to be relied on exclusively for support, as was the case for most prisoners in 1940–41 and again in 1944–45, and the ability of bodies to keep functioning came into serious question."[14] *In early September 1940 in Oflag XVIIA the food situation was dire. In 1941 the arrival of more regular packages improved the situation. The living conditions began deteriorating again toward the end of 1943, when the pressure of an expanding war on the German economy led to a reduction in the allocation of food as well as a lack of coal. By 1944, with the war raging in France, the men had been cut off from the packages as well, and there was nothing left around the camp to burn to heat the barracks.*

The writers of the diary expressed their distress only a few times. Like Pat Reid, recalling his experience in Colditz in The Great Escape, *they "avoided an incessant narrative during their captivity that could be read, as one great damn moan about the sufferings they went through. There is no need to repeat it at infinitum."*[15] *It cannot be forgotten, as a lieutenant in Nuremberg declared that "the glitzy surface (of activities) should not deceive those who know the human heart: captivity is a hard ordeal."*[16]

The day started around 6:30 to 7:00 a.m., depending on the season. After the wakeup call, the officer of the day walked over to the central kitchen to get the breakfast "juice," and helped by one POW soldier, hauled it back to the barracks on a hand-drawn cart. The Germans called this liquid "herbal tea." It was, in reality, a concoction of acorns, brewed in boiling water with the sap of maples and pines that are abundant in this area, hence the name, herbal tea. A short time later came the call for the morning roll call, either shouted in each barracks, or announced by a bugle. Roll calls lasted a minimum of three-quarters of an hour, with many lasting an extended time. Letters were distributed right after the roll call.

At 11:00 a.m. lunch, consisting of soup made with wheat flour, potatoes, dried beans, and rutabagas. The French dubbed it a casse-croute (snack). The same soup was served for the early evening dinner with one loaf of bread for five men. Once a week, they received a minuscule piece of beef, a slice of sausage, and a spoon full of beet jam (the so-called marmalade) or two-spoon full of synthetic honey. A roll call followed dinner. At sunset, came the call to get back in the barracks. At 10 p.m. the electricity inside the barracks was cut off. The outside floodlights were turned on.

The men were responsible for the housekeeping chores: all personal belongings and communal upkeep of the barracks. They washed their clothes in the barracks lavatory with whatever soap they may have received and hung them on clotheslines strung between the barracks. Historian S.P. MacKenzie reports, "With both soap and washing facilities in short supplies, a change into a clean outfit became a rare occurrence.... The most popular method is to let all one's clothes get dirty and wash a minimum number, when one wants to put on clean clothes."[17]

The proximity of the fields brought an abundance of mice and rats. They also endured the scourge of crowded quarters: lack of true hygiene with fleas, bedbugs, and lice. Lice were designated as the enemy number one of the prisoners. An officer wrote a detailed description of lice, their feeding on human blood and abundant reproduction, concluding: "Since lice find extremely favorable conditions in our communal life, we owe it to one another as comrades to eradicate this insidious army by keeping a scrupulous hygiene."[18] One clandestine picture shows men trying to get rid of these pests, catching them one by one, and one of the memoirs recalled some of the men sleeping on tables in summer to avoid the bunks' infestation.

Disinfecting took place when they took their showers. Each barracks took turn going once a month to a building in the Vorlager, consisting of a large room, where pipes and showerheads attached to the ceiling dispensed either freezing water, or occasional very hot water. Without partitions, the men, to their great distress, were crammed into that room regardless of age or rank. Once outside the room and without towels, they waited for their clothes and bedding, which had passed through the steam room to be disinfected. The clothes, all wrinkled and twisted, were thrown into a big pile, from which each prisoner retrieved his own.[19]

The Red Cross and families had done their best to send clothes—the men wore their own clothes and uniform—and with France equally without any resources, "the prisoners became more and more tramp-like in appearance."[20] "During the summer, shorts replaced pants," said one officer, and later, "When shorts became a luxury, the walkers went out in boxer shorts." For those concerned with sunburns, the fashion called for cardboard hats, mimicking the traditional straw hat. "From the outside, the camp must be looking like an asylum,"[21] declared a lieutenant.

These men abided as much as possible by a strict decorum, and were very determined to keep one presentable uniform for Sundays and special occasions. Some had carried an additional uniform. Others received one from home. For others, a lieutenant noted, "since there was next to nothing the families could buy in occupied France, some families raided their closets for old uniforms and sent moth-eaten uniforms, which had sometimes belonged to their fathers, or grandfathers."[22] By the end of 1942, the Vichy government sold new light fabric khaki pants and jackets to the officer POWs.

Footwear was a particular problem. The forced marches had destroyed socks, and shoes had lost their heels. They kept one pair each of socks and shoes to wear with the pieces of uniform reserved for Sundays. For everyday wear, one of the officer POWs created something like a sandal, a style that spread throughout the camp. He cut a small piece of wood from the bottom plank of his bunk and fashioned it in the shape of a sole. Gathering nails, in abundance on the construction sites, and using a stone as a hammer, he pounded the nails around the edges of the sole, weaving a string from nail to nail to form the top.[23] When the weather was warm, they went without socks and often "barefoot like on the beach."

22 September—"Art in prison," an exhibition in the canteen: Paintings, drawing, and chess pieces sculpted with a knife. Particularly striking is a series of poignant sketches in pencil, visions of nightmares and dreams by the Pole W., who shows an unquestionable mastery in an original and bold medium. The Chleuhs are flabbergasted.

25 September—With the arrival of food packages a new science emerges in the camp: the art of eating better. The stove roars in the kitchen of the barracks. There are two stations, each for fifty mess kits. Not to miss any food requires patience and endurance. One moment of absent-mindedness can cost you a larger portion. The large canned-food pots give off a marvelous smell full of kub and garlic.

The "Art in Prison" exhibit was the first attempt to engage the artistic talents of their community, improvising with the available resources.

By mid–September food improved slightly with the arrival of a few packages from home and the Red Cross. But packages were still few and far between. They pooled the food they had received by half barracks, cooking these extra meals in the barracks' small kitchen. Lacking cooking utensils, they improvised and fabricated their own big pots, welding together empty canned food containers. (These cans would prove to be one of the most used materials to fabricate all kinds of equipment throughout their captivity.) As they received more food, they divided into smaller kitchen groups, each cooking their own extra meals.

27 September—Significant incident: posters are displayed in the barracks, showing a French ensign sinking into the sea with these simple words, "Remember Oran." Almost all of them are torn down. A few posters keep only the ensign, cut out and glued to the wall. Punishment: Our top representative, Colonel V. and two captains are sent to a detention camp. Letters and packages will be held back for four days. "Very serious matter," mutters Mr. Loyal, "I am sending a report to Berlin."

These propaganda posters, displayed in France in July, showed the drowning of French ships sunk by the British Navy on 3 July. This was the great naval tragedy of Mers-El-Kebir, a port near the Algerian city of Oran. The swiftness of the officer POWs' response to the German posters was a measure of the stirring emotions these posters elicited in the men.[24]

It was a tragedy which the Germans exploited in France as well as in the POWs' camp, trying to stoke a latent antagonism between the French and the British. The officer POWs, however, did not take the bait and reacting aggressively to the propaganda, tore the posters. Posting the French ensign on the board was a warning to their German jailers not to meddle.

28 September—Crossing paths—Arrival of a contingent of enlisted men [POWs], followed by the departure of three hundred senior officers [POWs], they say, for a more comfortable stay in the countryside. In addition: arrival of one hundred fifty physicians and pharmacists. We are losing count of personnel.

30 September—Bare barrack: In the dim yellowish light of the light bulbs, Captain P. stands with his alto under his arm. In a familiar gesture, he takes off his glasses, and while his fingers play with the strings, he speaks with a somewhat weak voice. In a few insightful sentences, he evokes Mozart and introduces the musicians, who will play one movement of the quartet in E major. We already know the first violin. It is de La M.R., conspicuous for his emaciated face, fiery eyes, and high forehead under sparse hair. Second violin: L., and cellist: R.

Has music a soothing effect? Images emerging from a distant childhood come and go. One sound triggers a whole flood of emotions. They gush from a deep source, awakening a tenderness that we thought dead. Then, it is a total obliteration of time and space. Abruptly, one comes out of the dream. Heavy is the fall that leaves us hurt to be still in this awful cage of planks in which we are prisoner.

5 October—The V.B. [*Volkischer Beobachter*] announces a meeting between Hitler and Mussolini at the Brenner Pass. Galactic alignment? What are these two accomplices plotting?

8 October—The Germans have entered Romania.

15 October—The weather, very pleasant until now, has turned to overcast. The forecast predicts a cold night. From our bunks, piled up with our pea jackets and coats, we see the night officer navigate erratically through the obstacles of tables and stools. The poor fellow, holding his hurricane lamp, pushes the interior shutters one by one and opens the windows. A blast of fresh air enters and blows out the acrid smoke of the tobacco. [*The night officer was the officer of the day, whose duty changed at midnight. The regulations required that he aerate the barracks every two hours, keep an eye on the stove for fire prevention, and make sure water was dripping from the faucets so the pipes would not freeze in winter.*]

In the distance a circle of glowing points awakens the painful memory of a fashionable beach at night. They are the high lampposts, which encircle the camp with a yellowish halo. At intervals a glaring light, searching the web of barbed wire, shines for a moment and disappears. The watchtowers' searchlights crisscross their beams of light. The sound of boots, husky voices, clicking of weapons; a patrol is passing by. What precautionary luxury! Even zoo residents sleep without searchlights.

17 October—The gray texture of a low sky is ripping apart this morning, revealing a few pieces of blue beyond the clouds. Winter is almost here. We kindle the old-fashioned stoves, high rectangular structures covered with yellow ceramic. The cold-blooded gather around them, a circle which grows by the hour. Captain M. starts a passionate debate with Lieutenant L. about the causes of our defeat, which renews the old dispute between the career and reserve officers. Infantrymen and gunners take this opportunity to insist on the superiority of their weapons; the tank corpsmen meddle in. A discussion that started on a high plane quickly degenerates into bickering over trivia. An aggressive disposition throws two best friends one against the other and each sees only misunderstanding and bad faith in their adversary. Vanity leads to incoherence and while the arguments ad hominem distort the discussion, their positions are too clearly established to allow them to cut it off. B. comes in, hell-bent. Even though he has heard next to nothing of the rhetorical match, he knows the spoiling words, uses them, acting as an explosive. A spark flashes and the quarrel is revived in an even more intense way. Suddenly, a shout rings out: "Soup time!" The beginning tirade is interrupted. All at once, everyone is gone and no one remembers the quarrel. O Byzantium! O Corinth!

27 October—We learn of a series of stunning events, and a deep maelstrom shakes our little world; the 22nd Hitler met with Marshal Pétain. Yesterday, Italy declared war against Greece. The discussions have resumed with greater intensity around the stove. In the meantime, the first snowflakes are softly falling.

The meeting between Marshal Pétain and Hitler in Montoire, a town in France, was especially disturbing, provoking intense debates, "a deep maelstrom." Since they learned about it from a German newspaper, it is likely that they saw the (in)famous photograph of Pétain shaking hand with Hitler prominently displayed on the front page, a picture that would shock more deeply than written words. For the officer POWs, it would only lead to speculations, as they did not know that a few days after meeting with Hitler in Montoire, Marshal Pétain delivered a speech in which he declared, "up until now I have spoken to you as a father. I am now speaking to you as your leader,"[25] *adding, "collaboration between our two countries is being considered."*[26]

Many officer POWs hoped that Marshal Pétain was playing a double game. It was implausible for most of them at that time that he would collaborate of his own will; people felt that it was Pierre Laval's doings. (Laval was Petain's right hand man.) A discredited politician, Laval was often seen as Pétain's evil genius. "Pétain, the hero of Verdun," wrote Michael Christofferson, "was not tarnished with the brush of collaboration, but Pierre Laval became fixed in the public eye as a devious Germanophile, someone who could not be trusted to lead the nation. After the 13 December 1940 dismissal of Laval, Pétain's popularity soared, reaching in France its highest point in the winter months of 1940–41."[27] *Laval, however, would be back.*

As musical instruments started trickling in, the officers organized quartets. Music was very much appreciated, apparently by the German guards as well. The officer POW in charge, Captain P., Marc Pincherlé, was in civilian life the

5. Settling In 63

artistic director of the prestigious Societé Pleyel *in Paris. The violinist L. was also a professional musician. And later, after more instruments arrived an orchestra formed, becoming an important institution in the life of the camp.*

31 October—A deep, white silence has enveloped us; it has been snowing for four days.

We have just come back to our barracks. The roll call lasted over two hours. Our caps are white, and our faces are purple-blue. Mr. Loyal is showing an acute exasperation, which reaches to the last sentries via the hierarchical line of command. It's understandable, after all. During the night, seven officers [POWs] have dared get free of these gentlemen. Seven, not one less! Like the Sioux, these pathetic *Französen* [Frenchmen] crawled to the barbed wire fence, concealed under sacks of meat, which were indistinguishable from the snow because of their whiteness. Pliers finished the job.

We think about them in this Siberian cold. In retaliation, we will lose our allocation of wood and coal. There is no doubt Mr. Loyal is a mean chap.

11 November—This is a day of remembrance.[28] The Chleuhs do not agree, but it does not matter; we celebrate it our way. There are neither classes, nor lectures, nor theater. In the evening, in each barracks we observe one minute of silence standing at attention and bareheaded.

15 November—Tonight, reading of a brochure of the clauses of the armistice: tirades assailing the actions of the Pétain Administration. Thirty-two pages dealing with the relationship between France and the United States are missing, torn off by the censors. The discussions have resumed with greater intensity around the stove.

There were twenty-four articles for the armistice, two of which related specifically to the French Armed Forces. One comment was added to Article 4, which declared: "All serving in the army, navy, and air force, will lay down their arms and be demobilized and disarmed within a deadline to be determined" *(my emphasis). The deadline, in common practice, is the moment an armistice is signed. The addition of an indefinite deadline, together with Article 20, changed the conventional understanding. Article 20 declared: "The members of the French Armed Forces who are prisoners of war of the German Army will remain prisoners of war until the signing of a peace treaty." Both articles together allowed the Germans to take close to two million men prisoners of war and keep the majority in captivity for five years.*

For these men this was the last straw; any vestige of hope for a general repatriation evaporated. They had already felt betrayed and their honor trod upon by their own leaders with the sudden call for a cease-fire. Reading now the conditions of the armistice, they realized that the French leaders had caved in to

German demands, and they would remain prisoners for an indefinite time. It reminded them once more of the apathy of the politicians and the incompetence of the General Staff. It reinforced the rancor they had felt about the lack of appropriate equipment for the army, and the arrogance and dilettantism of some senior officers. "The French military defeat of 1940 indicts first and foremost the politicians and generals who did not plan nor lead," wrote Karl-Heinz Frieser.[29] The prisoners had become the victims of the defeatism of their leaders. The military and political leaders had laid the blame of the 1940 defeat on the officers and soldiers, creating a lasting perception that the debacle was their fault. In his last official report General Gamelin, after being sacked as commander-in-chief, wrote: "Too many soldiers failed to do their duty in battle."[30]

The officer POWs, who had been on the battlefield, felt that they had served their country well. They never questioned their patriotism or their troops' patriotism. In the words of a lieutenant, "There is no glory in defeat.... And for the soldiers is added the bitterness of defeat." He continued, "But the memory of my lost regiment and the attitude of the officers and infantrymen have always been for me a reason to be proud, and a ground for hope."[31]

Another lieutenant echoed the general sentiment: "We think of the suffering of the troops, POWs in forced labor in commandos (in stalags) for having loyally done their duty. We have come to hate the failures that created such catastrophic result. But rather than blaming the people responsible and wallowing in useless regrets, we dedicate ourselves to transforming our lives. Our best hope for the future lies in rebuilding a more moral free France."[32]

6

Eight Months in Nuremberg
September 1940–May 1941

This chapter is written by the translator and editor.
While the diarists and a large contingent of officer POWs arrived at their final destination in Edelbach and organized for the long run, the men in the four temporary camps in France were still in limbo, not knowing whether they would be sent to Germany or demobilized and sent home. Generally, they remained optimistic. The Major expressed a common opinion, when he observed, "When we were taken prisoner, we had already known armed conflict, anxiety, defeat, dire hunger, and exhaustion, but we had kept the hope of being liberated very soon."[1] Uncertainty about the future crept in, when he and his comrades were separated from their troops and moved to a chateau along the Loire Valley. All kinds of rumors abounded; the optimists felt that they were a special group who would be liberated, and the pessimists imagined suffering the worst conditions in Germany.

In Laval, crowded and with little food but minimal German presence inside the building, the men kept their regular schedule, organizing activities with whatever supplies they had on hand, giving lectures, and utilizing the skills within their community. Their Commandant briefed them daily.[2] One of the officers wrote about his time in Laval, "At first, we were like a herd, tired and humiliated. The zeal and talent of our leaders gave us hope and made us a community."[3]

Contact with some families resumed. Those living in Laval came to talk to their men through the fence of the front court, where the men were allowed to walk. Soon, they were able to visit inside the courtyard on Sundays. It was sometimes hard for those whose families lived far away, seeing the families hug and the men coming back to their quarters with packages.[4] They were allowed to send a letter, but communication in France was still fragmented.

A number of families had not been able to return home after the huge displacement of the civilians during the *Exode* (as many as eight million people headed south in front of the German advance in 1940). They were often stranded in the free zone, either without a pass to cross the demarcation line with the occupied zone or without public transportation in a disrupted system.

As time passed, a great uncertainty about the future took a heavy psychological toll.

In Neuf-Brisach, the men enjoyed a certain degree of autonomy within the walls of the town, regulated by the military hierarchy, which their own General had established. To alleviate some of the hunger, they created an exchange desk, which allowed the men who had been stationed in the neighboring area during the winter and spring of 1940 to order all kinds of foodstuffs, soap, and other necessities from the local merchants. Lacking supplies in the stores, some of the local families sent the men their personal things. Two neighboring bakeries worked around the clock under difficult circumstances. Soldiers who were cobblers in civilian life set up shop to repair their badly worn-out shoes, using resources given by local civilians. Red Cross volunteers served as intermediaries between the men, the merchants, and other civilians. The young woman, who had helped previously, spent her entire day, every day, delivering packages to the prisoners.

A lieutenant, brooding over their situation, wrote, "It has been said, one must live as if one were never to die." For us it is, "One must settle in captivity as if one were never to be freed."[5] These men, looking for constructive things to do, decided to repair what the bombings of the town had destroyed, when the Germans invaded Alsace. They recruited electricians, masons, carpenters, and contractors within their community and re-started the electric power plant and waterworks.

Those without specific duties engaged in recreational occupations. On the main square, many turned to regional games, which reminded them of home. There were daily Jeu de boules (bowling), prominent on the Mediterranean coast, or games of quoits, and soccer matches. Board games and card games were also popular. Others organized a library in the town hall. They formed a band and created theater productions. Fairly quickly, they were allowed to write letters to their families. On occasion, the officer POWs were allowed to walk outside the walls, accompanied by German guards.

In the Haguenau district, the men, who had refused to surrender until forced to do so with the intervention of their commander-in-chief, entered a temporary camp in the town of Haguenau in early July. My father described that camp as "fairly fit to live in and bearable. The relationships with the civilians

6. Eight Months in Nuremberg

were easier, and we still breathed the air of France, which allowed us to keep invisible and mystical ties with our families. Not to mention the fanciful hope, nurtured daily, of a coming liberation."[6]

After the war these men continued their battle to obtain an official recognition that they had not been beaten. In the 1980s, some fifty-five years later, a plaque was unveiled with the inscription, "In honor of the courageous men in the fortified sector of Haguenau, who were handed over to the enemy without having been beaten."[7]

The degree of autonomy granted the officer POWs in the temporary camps in France led them to believe that their captivity would be of short duration. But as soon as the Germans established enough camp-like enclosures to house them on German soil, they moved the prisoners of these four temporary camps to Oflag XIII near Nuremberg, dispelling once and for all the illusion of a quick liberation. My father wrote, "With the arrival of the enemy we had experienced in a few seconds the radical upheaval of a peaceful and independent life. Yet, it was only the first stage of suffering."[8] The first men to leave for Germany were in Neuf-Brisach.

Marcel Poisot, one of the last men to leave Neuf-Brisach, recorded the closing of the camp. He rejoiced to hear again the buzz of the insects and the songs of the birds in the silence of the empty town. Walking through the deserted streets under a light rain the night before his departure, in a reflective mood at dusk he wrote, "this gentle and fleeting hour, the hour of memories, regrets, and affection permeate my soul," and recalling a well-known poem by Paul Verlaine (1844–96), he recited *"Il pleure dans mon coeur comme il pleut dans la ville"* (The tears burst in my heart like the rain pouring down on the city). At the sound of the church bell he murmured, "Freedom, who knows when we shall find it again?"[9]

After he and his group put the house furnishings back the way they had found it, Poisot went through it one more time and took a picture of his little group. The next morning he walked over to the Town Square from which they were to leave, noting the ornate façades of the church and the houses. At the square, the General bid his last farewell (generals were generally incarcerated in the Citadel of Königstein). The last remaining four to five hundred men formed three columns and marched toward the eastern door. The Rhine River glistened in front of them. As they arrived at the train station, the first question in everyone's mind was as always, would they be in passenger or cattle cars? With relief they found passenger cars. The train moved away, soon approaching the Rhine. They were going to Germany. As they heard a loud noise and felt the jolt of the train getting onto the bridge, they threw a last glimpse toward Neuf-Brisach. A few seconds passed, yet just enough time wrote Poisot, "for a last glance at the Vosges behind us, where the sky of our country is turning light blue. Accelerated beatings of the heart; we have just left the French soil." On 13 August they were on their way to Nuremberg.

Upon arrival, the men were divided into small groups and sent into tents with straw on the ground. Their daily fare in the morning and evening was a watery soup with some bread and water. After a few days, they were subjected to the dreaded search, which confiscated most of what they possessed, followed by a process of identification: fingerprints, photographs, and a matriculation number. Their heads shaved, they went through the showers while their clothes were disinfected. They were then assigned to their barracks.[10]

Coming from Haguenau, my father arrived in Nuremberg on 24 August, repeating a similar procedure. Crossing the threshold of Nuremberg, he declared, "Now we are prisoners, a rude awakening. There is no need for dark prisons, thick walls, and deep ditches. It is just necessary to pass through the opening of a sole and almost intangible thread of barbed wire to know that there is no more hope. We have arrived in the last definitive prison out of which we will cross the lintel, only when freedom comes."[11] (Unknown to him, it was not yet the last prison. He would still cross the gate of one more camp.) Summing up the general feeling, he wrote later, "We all arrived at the

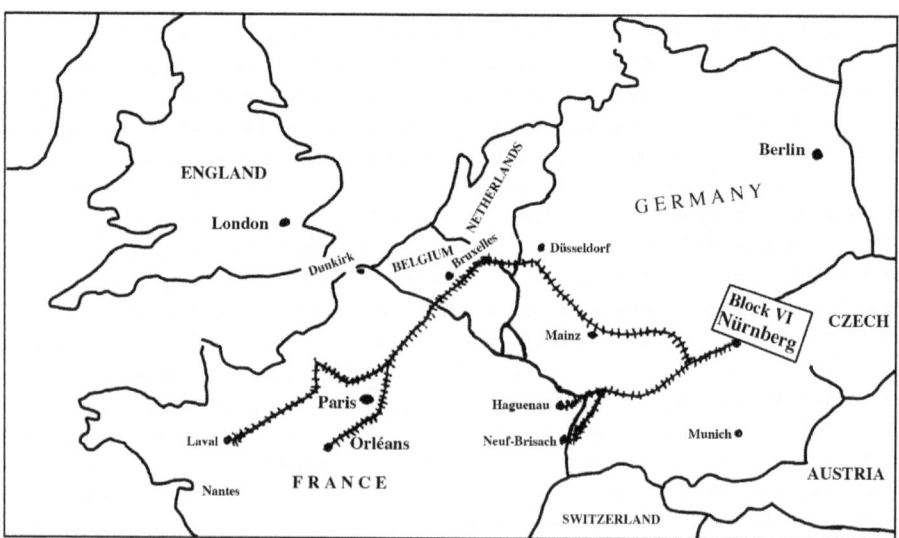

The train journey to Nuremberg. The four groups in temporary camps in France arrived in Nuremberg in August and September, 1940. The men will be transferred to Oflag XVIIA in May 1941 (Jacqueline Vautrain Collins).

camp after a great variety of adventures. Some of us had experienced all the gamut of emotions from courage to resentment, from the illusory hope of liberation to the harsh reality of marches. Others were picked up willy-nilly in some places deep in France, knowing only the torment of the sudden arrival of the enemy. We all experienced the radical upheaval of a peaceful life that had been its own master."[12]

Next, it was the turn of the men, who had been incarcerated in a chateau on the Loire with the unit of the Cavalry Major. They were picked up in passenger cars at a nearby train station by a train already full of officer POWs and traveled north without stopping until they arrived at a station near the Belgian frontier. They were ordered to step out of the train and once on the platform were told to leave their suitcases there. In a mad rush, they opened them to take out what they could, while the Red Cross "Ladies" promised to keep them in a secure location. After they got back to their seats, the train was securely locked. "No more doubt," wrote the Major, "we are going to Germany." They went through Belgium, Holland, and finally Germany. After five days and five nights without food, they reached their final destination. They entered the camp in Nuremberg on 11 September, passing through the same routine.[13]

The men in Laval were the last group to go. One morning they were summoned to meet with German officers and told they were to leave the next day. With heavy hearts they spent the day gathering what they could carry, destroying what they could not take and writing letters. The next day they assembled "looking like Bohemians with all kinds of carrying bags and sundry items hanging with twine from their clothes." The roll call lasted for hours. Some men, having chosen passive resistance or being unwilling to admit reality, had declared that they were sick and stayed in bed. Examined by German doctors, ninety percent of them were booted out and forced to join their comrades.[14]

Guarded by heavily armed sentries, the men marched toward the train station. It was a risky and emotional march. To get to the station, they had to go through the middle of town, passing through streets filled with a crowd, which included some of the prisoners' families. A few wives tried to break through to say good-bye to their husbands, and a little girl jumped into the arms of her father, only to be yanked away violently. At the train station, the guards, guns at the ready, kept the crowd at bay. There was a long wait before the train pulled up. Everyone's hearts sunk when they saw the cattle cars. They received some bread, and thirty to a wagon were locked in the dark for three days, stopping occasionally in the countryside so they could relieve themselves around the train tracks with German guards at the ready. Once in Germany the wagon doors remained unlocked and the train stopped at train stations to let the men relieve themselves in plain view of the population. They arrived in Nuremberg on 15 September. They too, went into tents for a few days before being assigned to their barracks.

September–December—The officer POWs in Nuremberg, like their comrades in Edelbach, were at first without news of their families. It was late October before my mother knew where my father was. A lieutenant wrote, "We tried to sort out the stories of comrades, who had witnessed bombardments and machine-gun fire in the provinces or towns, where our families lived. With such contradictory reports, our only hope was to receive letters. Until then, we knew only an anxiety that gripped our soul."[15]

As in Edelbach, they gathered by region. To that end, "they plastered the walls of one barracks with papers of every size and color inviting anyone of the region of...." to sign up to meet on a certain day at a designated place. They found comfort, reminiscing about a familiar landscape, people, entertainment, institutions, and businesses. The success of these first groupings led to groups forming around professions, alumni associations, and hobbies. These smaller groups became an essential element of the friendships, which over the years reinforced the solidarity of the community. It would pave the way later for their easy integration in similar groups in Edelbach.

A captain organized sessions of physical education, a task that proved to be challenging with men of all ages, from Cadets to World War I veterans, whose training and energy were quite far apart. "You could see old and young raise their arms to the "old Gott," or bow in lamentations. Others wriggled hopelessly." Nonetheless fifty men continued the classes through the cold and later on the snow.[16]

Hunters among the camp community recalled with nostalgia and good humor that their arrival in Nuremberg in September coincided with the opening of the hunting season. Tongue in cheek one officer POW declared: "What a shame! We have not thought of bringing our rifles. And come to think about it, we would be more like the rabbits, if we were to decide to leave our burrows for the neighboring woods."[17]

A number of the men in the camp, horse racing enthusiasts, got together to talk about a well-known horse of the time and discuss the standing of different racetracks. It led to the creation of an organization "which copied reality; *la Société des Courses de Nuremberg* (The Horserace Society of Nuremberg) with weekly horseracing, and a board game that mimicked a racetrack. A collection of wood etchings shows split drawings: on the lower right-hand corner, horse pieces on a game board and numbers arranged in the shape of a racetrack, and on the upper left-hand corner of the etching, the drawing of a jockey riding a horse. For example, if the horse piece is jumping over a hurdle on the board, the drawing shows a horse and jockey jumping over a hurdle, as it would look on a real racetrack, showing a stand in the background. There are a couple of dice on the side.

When the men were together, they maintained the atmosphere of a racetrack by speaking in a language that "was specific to horseracing enthusiasts and they auctioned horses between the games."[18] One officer POW wrote, "Sometimes, we closed our eyes, and immediately we were transported to Auteuil [racetrack near Paris]. Someone played a harmonica and the races began."

Harmonicas, the only instrument available at the time, were very popular. They would gather around the musicians and sing well-known melodies. One officer POW wrote, "Music is one of the most secure and pleasant means of escaping the difficulties of life. It is particularly true in a camp of prisoners, where the landscape remains constantly the same. No more barbed wire, no more barracks, when harmonious sounds are heard." Soon, a choirmaster in civilian life organized a choir, harmonizing regional songs. As in Edelbach they formed an orchestra, which grew to sixteen string instruments, one flute, two clarinets, three saxophones, three trumpets, and one trombone. A jazz band formed a little later.[19]

By the second Sunday of September, a few men took it upon themselves to entertain their comrades. They put together two tables in a corner of a barracks, called it a stage, and improvised a "timid" play. But nurtured by a sympathetic audience, the theater grew beyond all expectations. In a few months, new actors came forward, and writers created scripts, mostly comedies. They also produced a couple of classic plays, which some had brought with them. In four months, they produced a program of an average of fifteen shows per month. My father wrote, "The modest chrysalis opened up as a butterfly. The general theme, 'Far Away from the Camp' was an effort to take us over the barrier that encircled us, and to evoke our civilian life."[20]

In a dialogue from a satire called "Return" a bachelor officer is seen returning from captivity to his apartment building, where he first meets the concierge, a middle-age woman who leads him back to his apartment. "Please, step in front, Madame Carabol," says the officer. "Thank God, I still have an old reserve of gallantry that the searches have not taken away from me."[21]

Reading was a cherished pastime. Many had kept as many books as they could carry when they were taken prisoners. They began swapping books within their own barracks, extending the lending to their neighboring barracks. All this borrowing happened haphazardly with friends or just with someone they met. Without any control books were often lost or disappeared, diminishing the scant number of existing books. A few librarians by profession got together and asked each officer to give his books to be catalogued and used in a library system, which would benefit everyone. It sometimes took a bit of cajoling for men to give up their books, but by mid–September they were able to open a library with one hundred fifty volumes. By the end of September they had eight hundred books. Three weeks later, they had one thousand one hundred sixty. Those not donating a book could access the library by paying twenty pfennigs (cents).[22]

Very soon after arriving in Nuremberg, my father met Marcel Poisot, who in Neuf-Brisach, had written part-diary, part-reflections of his experience in that temporary camp. That draft immediately interested my father. Keen to document the conditions in the camps and show how the officer corps regrouped as prisoners, my father worked with Marcel Poisot to prepare the book for publication to be called *Prisonniers à Neuf-Brisach*. His intention was to publish it as soon as he returned to France, something he still thought would come quickly. He published two more books, which directly documents the officers' captivity, *Escale à Nurember* (Stopover in Nuremberg), and eventually the diary in this book, *6000 à l'Oflag 17A: ou cinq ans de captivité au fil des jour* (Six Thousand at Oflag 17A: or Five Years of Captivity as the Days Go By).

My father had now decided on his mission. As a publisher, he would establish a permanent record of how the officer POWs occupied their time in order to give meaning to their lives. He asked the various leaders of each of the activities to write about their achievements, highlighting the will, endurance, and dignity of the community. In introducing *Escale à Nuremberg*, published in 1945, my father wrote, "It is the common work of comrades, who wanted to show the unanimity of their moral endeavor and fierce will to react."[23]

A strong moral overtone recurs in many of the writings. The men commonly asked whether their swift defeat had been caused by a failure of their life style, but they were equally eager to spend their energy looking to the future. A Lieutenant wrote, "We all equally carry the weight of the failure of the past months. But, while our memory of the past is painful, and we are worried about the present, our best support lies in the hope of what the future can bring. We are all united in the conviction that we must make an immense effort with the goal of leading a more humane life built on a deeper morality."[24]

They saw their actions and achievements as living proof of their dignity and honor. By documenting the achievements of the camp's community, expressing their daily common striving and determination to sustain their self-respect as prisoners, my father hoped to help their families understand their concerted endurance during these five years of captivity.

1941

January–May—By the end of 1940 a number of officer POWs, who as civilians were teaching in the humanities, began planning a series of lectures, coupled with study circles. Speaking of their endeavor, an officer wrote, "Our mission is to transcend our fate. We are captives, because of the restriction inflicted on our body, but our spirit is free." Quoting the line from a poem, he added, "Your power stops at the threshold of my thoughts."[25] Capturing that consensus, my father wrote, "I think we are beyond our first encounter with suffering. Our freedom will certainly come someday, but in the meantime, we have to react.... Our daily inner life must challenge the conditions of our living situation. We must establish at all cost the primacy of the intellect by turning to the refuge of the mind, the memory, and the heart. There is no other way to endure."[26]

They began their lectures in January, as if it were the winter quarter of a university. The title of the series, "French Classic Literature from the Middle Ages to the Nineteenth Century,"[27] listed thirteen lectures, scheduled once a week. In addition, they met in the morning for more informal talks, which were called the *Cercle d'Études*.

Highlighting the major literary currents and authors over six hundred years of French literature was somewhat of a stretch. The officer POW in charge introduced the series with some words of caution. "There may be gaps and omissions that sometimes will produce a fragmented panorama of our classic literature, as we rely solely on the particular expertise of our comrades."[28] The context was similar to the one in Edelbach. Without documents at their fingertips, or the availability of texts in a library, they relied uniquely on the knowledge and memory of the lecturers.

In the introduction to the book written in Nuremberg, my father expressed similar words of caution. "In their fierce will to react, the writers may have represented the familiar atmosphere of a life, which was lived in a monotone and destitute environment, as an existence full of life, perhaps even attractive. Our intellectual endeavors were a deliberate attempt to transcend our sometimes abominable material life, to remind us of France and look forward to our return."[29]

What they could not provide in material resources, they made up in their spirit. The Navy Captain René Marie, who arrived in Nuremberg later in January, admitted being a "little skeptical" when he was invited to listen to the series. But later he wrote in the *Avant-propos* (in *Escale à Nuremberg*), "I beat my breast in the light of the power, clarity, and strength of the presentations. The written human language cannot adequately represent the intense fervor of our lecturers and our enthusiasm. It will be difficult for others to understand." (René Marie was very much loved by the officers as the leader of the whole block.)

Drawing on human resources, foreign languages were popular. A lieutenant recalled, "Every morning before roll call or evening before bedtime, we witnessed touching scenes of white hair comrades, assiduously reviewing German or Spanish vocabulary, words jotted down on a piece of paper. Their teachers, not always academics with diplomas, were comrades, who exiled and heartbroken like them, were compelled by an admirable spirit of solidarity to generously share their knowledge. A graduate from a prestigious foreign affairs institute found a new vocation teaching English and art, while an administrator taught the rudiments of Italian grammar. An engineer explained to a few comrades the working of the auto industry, or a functionary who had been stationed in the colonies evoked Syria or Morocco."[30]

A great number of groups became an essential part of the life in Nuremberg, as they were in Edelbach. Alumni, professional, and hobby groups provided special lectures and talks. The regional groups not only served as a connection among the prisoners but also often fostered solidarity between the prisoners' families. Some families, alerted in a letter by their husbands of a comrade's family nearby, helped other families in need.

Some groups looked to the future by developing their professions or talents. One of the most active was le *Cercle Pédagogique*, which included new young teachers and more seasoned educators, such as the national director of the French primary school system. In addition to creating many studies of general interest, experienced teachers coached younger ones.

Ping-Pong was very popular and a good example of how they developed their resources to create their environment. A lieutenant, missing his favorite sport, decided that he would form a club, but there was no place to play, nor did he have a net and paddles. He first arranged to obtain a vacant room in a barracks and then, asking around, found a comrade who had kept a net and four others who still had one paddle each, all items that had escaped the

6. Eight Months in Nuremberg

searches. With these on hand, they built a table with planks and presumably finding a few balls, they started a club, which grew to two hundred fifty adherents within days. Invigorated, they organized a tournament at Christmastime after which the German Kommandant decided to sell four sets to the prisoners and allowed them to set up a couple of makeshift tables. So many wanted to play that the club's rules were strict; each member was allowed to play one half-hour every two days. Another officer painted a large fresco on the back wall of the room, suggesting happier times. It represented a well-known Parisian luxury hotel and restaurant, submerged in greenery, "bringing us so close and yet so far from Paris,"[31] one officer observed.

As noted in the diary on 2 April, fathers of four children or more were repatriated from all the camps. In Nuremberg it meant that Marcel Poisot would be leaving. He and my father decided that, since the book was already prepared for publication, Poisot would take it with him and give it to my mother to be published. Some copies were published a year later in April 1942 and stashed away, but not before a few copies were given to members of the Académie Française, who awarded it a prize.[32]

In the first months of 1941 my father, impressed by the artists in the camp—some were alumni of the Beaux-Arts Institute—decided to utilize their talents to illustrate three books of French literature for a series he would call "Under the Sign of the Ram." He noted that "this Martian title seemed fitting for books conceived and illustrated in a POW camp."

For the first book of the series, he selected the *Petits Poèmes en Prose* by Beaudelaire. In the foreword a comrade wrote, "Jacques Vautrain chose this text for its writing in a minor tone, matching not only the art of the illustrator's charcoal drawings, but our sentiments of captives. He justified the choice of such works of literature to show our people back home the paradox of such a book being conceived, illustrated, and read while we were captives"[33] It was not a phony assertion. It was a text they had on hand and read that had been carried by one of the men and illustrated with the meager camp resources. To finance the future printing, my father, who thought they would be back in France soon, had gathered subscriptions.

In May 1941 they were transferred to Oflag XVIIA at Edelbach.

7

Creating a Town Behind Barbed Wire

16 November 1940–20 May 1941

16 November—The west room of Barracks 18 has become the theater, a real theater. Stools against stools, we take our seats very quietly in front of a green curtain, which shakes a little and will open later on a fictional story closer to real life than our own. The room does not matter anymore. What matters most is what is happening behind the curtain, as we hear the noise of hammers and some hushed voices. Impatient to hear the three knocks, the spectators stamp their feet and shout like in a real theater. Then, silence. The curtain opens to the scene of a Provençale kitchen, simple and sweet. The stage spotlights illuminate a backdrop full of wind and mistral [Southern wind]. Applause: also like in a theater. New scene: shimmering costumes in the style of the seventeenth century with a few slightly anachronistic banters. It's *Le médecin volant* [the Flying Doctor], a somewhat dumb slapstick comedy carried off with pizzazz. It does not matter; there are women and they are pretty. Lucille has a frail waist, and the maid, laughing eyes. Ah! The salutary illusion made of glue, paper, paint, and talent.

17 November—Life has solidified into a permanent routine, and it is during the dreary hours before the lights are turned off that the oppressive servitude of life in common weighs most heavily. The windows and shutters, closed as a precaution against the hypothetical danger of a blitz, turn the barracks into a sealed container full of smoke and acrid stench. Poorly lit by two rows of lamps, half the room is in the shadow made by the bunks, which stand in the way of the lights. Then this immense ship made of plank fills up with a deafening noise. A laugh bursts, a remark flies, bedlam increases, and always the unbearable pounding of boots on the floor, the scraping of steely

7. Creating a Town Behind Barbed Wire

soles belonging to the walking hysterics. The tables are mobbed to play games, read, and write, all in a miserly light.

23 November—About fifty British officers [POWs] are coming in Barracks 24. Speaking with them is not allowed. Those who know the language do not pay attention. Mr. Loyal grumbles, "There are two kinds of officers [POWs] in the camp, the British at war, the French almost at peace. There are talks in progress to liberate you. Please, follow the protocol and be disciplined! Do not do like us in 1918." What a good man, and how he takes good care of us!

About seven hundred midshipmen and physician aides leave us for Stalag XVIIA. A few officers [POWs] have arrived from Epinal [French city]. Human dough is continuously kneaded here. We look somewhat like a herd migrating from one pasture to the other. No ... rather, flies, which buzz to go from one cage to the other.

25 November—The primary unit in the barracks is a group of ten officers [POWs]. Each group has its leader. The group may be a cohesive number of comrades united by common dispositions, or a simple numerical formation of men joined together by chance, but not closely united by communal life. There are groups of ten, others of one, two, three, four.... Some barracks have addressed this fragmentation more tightly. Bunks attached in a rectangular space are walled off with partitions made of paper or cardboard, which makes the inside space look like a honeycomb, closed at times by a movable blanket. Nothing can prevent the filth and grime from penetrating it, but this partial isolation gives some measure of intimacy. It is a small island, a separation from the crowd with a little more silence. Honeycombs have their champions and detractors. The creation of honeycomb spaces produced a good deal of problems. It changed so many accepted habits that it required some very diplomatic handling to carry it through.

1 December—The chapel has acquired a harmonium, and the theater has a piano.

On 22 November in honor of its patron saint, the Cecilia Choir will perform a cantata composed by Midshipman L., accompanied by the harmonium and a quartet.

In the theater, we are treated to a recital of Schumann's first quintet, with Lieutenant F. at the piano, a duo with de la M.R. and a César Franck's sonata.

Housing one hundred to one hundred ten men, the room of the half-barracks, approximately twenty-four hundred square feet, served as sleeping, living, and eating area. The three-tier bunk beds were usually grouped in sets of four with the tables and stools occupying the empty spaces in between. In these crowded living conditions it was impossible for the men to have any private life, triggering its opposite, "men retreating completely unto themselves," wrote a lieutenant in his memoirs.[1] *As outsiders we have to imagine, always eating, day-in and day-out, with the same people, hearing every conversation, or even writing a letter to family with always other people around the table. Where would these men find a quiet place? They could go in the fields, but not during the winter.*

Another prisoner wrote that they felt separated not only from the world, but also lost the sense of time and of the seasons. On the other hand, he conceded that their adversity had strengthened relationships among fellow prisoners, discovering new human qualities in the forced close cohabitation of older and younger men. Noting their personal pain and bitterness he wrote, "Our comradeship is quite different, however, from the brotherhood of the battleground, where you feel joy in accomplishing a goal, or you are able to sacrifice for your comrades, and you can relax when you are relieved."[2]

A clandestine picture[3] *shows the walled-in units of bunks producing hallway-looking separation between the units, mimicking closely the space of a home, albeit in a makeshift way. Living with a fair amount of make-believe, the blanket, which closed the opening to their common cubbyholes, was often called the "door." The more realistic-minded called the entire contraption a box, honeycomb, or living in drawers.*

Winter settled in, bringing everything to a standstill. In this region of Austria, where winters are harsh in ways mostly unknown in France—the men called it the little Siberia—they hunkered down as best as they could.

3 December—Are we playing a Molière [playwright of the seventeenth century] comedy? The only talk around the camp is about sick people and illnesses. Illnesses spring out of the past, terrifying and with horrible consequences. Graciously with true sympathy, one listens to congenital infirmities, cancerous symptoms, enlargement of the liver, auricular and ventricular fibrillation, degenerating bladder, and other ailments, any one of them would without doubt end in death.

Reason: a short note in last night report, "Officers [POWs] who feel seriously ill shall present themselves to be examined, in order to be considered for repatriation." Thirty-eight men are declared ill.

11 December—Two successive departures: eighteen sick men repatriated. One hundred twenty-five Alsatians are sent back home. For two days, they jot down addresses. A crowd of friends escorts them to the gates. Contorted faces are glued to the barbed wire.

The departure of the Alsatians on 11 December created a great emotional upheaval. The Germans announced that "as a good-will gesture," they would free the Alsatians. It was attractive for them to go home, resume their lives, and take care of their families, but liberation came at a price and posed a moral dilemma. In return, the Germans demanded that these men, French officers, who had just fought in the French Army against Germany, sign a declaration that they would cooperate in Germany's prosperity and raise their children as Germans. There was little doubt that they would soon have to pledge full allegiance to Germany. As early as mid–July the Germans annexed Alsace and part of Lorraine, re-instituting the frontier of 1871 and setting up customs controls. Then, they imposed the German language on Alsace and expelled thousands of Alsatians and Lorrainers who did not conform.

Alsace had been a contested territory for many centuries. An Alsatian officer, a prisoner in Oflag XVIIA speaking to his comrades, noted: "Generally, Alsace remained firm and dignified in her support for the French. We all remember the moving and generous affection of Alsatians, lining the roads taken by the troops on their way to Germany. In fact, the German troops witnessed this outburst at the same time as they were subjected to an icy welcome. Even Hitler realized that, what he had done in the Sudeten Land, the Saar, and Austria, he could not dare do in Alsace, leading a German officer to declare: "While people hate us in Poland, Alsatians, here, scorn us."[4]

In another camp, a captain, father of many children, torn between belonging to the French nation and the great needs of his family, struggled with this dilemma. After his friends assured him that whatever he decided they would vouch for his service to the country, he replied that he would think about it overnight. One of his good friends recalled: "He came the next day, dressed in his full uniform and told us solemnly, "My friends, one million and a half soldiers died in 1914–1918, so that Alsace would become French again. Today, I cannot as a French captain disown them. I will stay with you to the end."[5] One hundred twenty-five Alsatian officer POWs left the camp. One hundred fifty refused to declare allegiance to Germany and remained prisoners for five years.

17 December—It is extremely cold. The thermometer is down to minus ten Fahrenheit, and the sky has turned cornflower blue. The harsh whiteness of the camp hurts the retina, and on the barracks' eaves the pattern of giant icicles forms a capricious fringe. Over the horizon the pine trees bend under the weight of the snow. It is worthy of an *Image d'Epinal* [similar to Currier & Ives scenes]. Here and there, snowdrifts glisten in the sun continually blown higher by the wind. It is impossible to go to the fields. Only small outings are possible on the plowed central alley. Hauled by ropes miniature sleds, carrying some bread and buckets, glide in front of the barracks. Strange looking men, wearing heavy mittens and wrapped in layers of multicolor woolens, walk about keeping their head snug in furry hats or ski masks, polar equipment that suggests weepy eyes and swollen noses.

Sensational news: Laval has been arrested. The ashes of the duc de Reichstadt [son of Napoléon and Marie Louise of Austria] have been brought back to Paris. The *Volkischer Beobachter* butters this up.

25 December—Christmas—It is futile to emphasize the agonizing character of the holiday season in prison. It is one of the paradoxes that fill the life of the captive. Is it possible to infuse a little merriment to days without joy? Or dress a wound with acid?

In the chapel: a crèche sculpted in wood, the collective work of officers [POWs] and enlisted men [POWs]. From 10 to 11 p.m. we sing French Christmas carols of the fifteenth and sixteenth centuries.

Midnight mass in the chapel, in the theater, and wherever there is room. At 1 o'clock, hot chocolate with a slice of gingerbread cake and a few dry cookies. Standing on a table, a small pine tree with its branches decorated with glass Christmas ornaments and junky garlands, which have been sent in care packages, the Christmas packages.

Tomorrow's lunch has been planned with care. The food for each course has been religiously set aside, removed from all temptations for the sake of this big day [using Christmas care packages]. There will be some foie gras, chicken, peas, and rice cake. Who dares pretend that we are not happy?

26 December—French prisoners are to be exchanged for the surrender of the fleet. Another version: No, not for the fleet, but for North Africa! This grotesque rumor makes us feel like vomiting.

German generosity! For Christmas, they have "surreptitiously" given us a bottle of beer and five cigarettes. Little gifts, as the saying goes, maintain friendship! After reflection, drank the beer, and smoked the cigarettes. That's at least something taken from the enemy.

However, our scale shows a great deficit!

31 December—The lights are turned off at 1:30 a.m., as it was for Christmas. Midnight: Explosion of joy! Is it real joy, though? At the most it is a nervous excitement and the need to get dizzy. A farandole [A linear dance of Provence and Languedoc, Southern France] spreads from group to group and from barracks to barracks. Happy New Year! Liberation! Handshakes and hugs!

At one o'clock—a few stubborn men are still awake and celebrate in their corners, and demonstrate a raucous joy that rings so false.

On this page our modest diary closes. No one could have anticipated that it would one day be filled with such bitterness.

The year 1940 has been a catastrophic year: phony war, retreat, defeat, and then, this cold jolt like a cleaver that is the prison.

How long will this sequestered life last to which has been added exile? This blacklisting, which isolates us from the world, this heartless deprivation of the universal rhythm, and the slow and undeserved torture of an honest man. One hundred eighty days have just slipped through our fingers like sand. One hundred eighty days spent running in circles, during which meaninglessness has wrestled with the dreadful emptiness of the hours. One hundred eighty days consumed in wild expectations, feverish dreams, and blind desperation. How long will this being stranded last and why is it that, every time we question, a single echo repeats this word: Wait!

Always wait! Wait for what? A letter, a package, showers, tomorrow, a betrayal, a faithful love, and above all a freedom that runs away like a shadow, a freedom, evasive and so dear! How many illusions, dead and left on the side of the road! The reality is; we are here tonight, and nothing can mask its implacable savagery.

Our home is decorated with a few sparkling baubles, but can one prevent captive birds from seeing the bars of the cage and the ominous body of the bird-catchers?

1941

1 January—It is snowing. Today day of congratulations and exchange of good wishes, as tradition and social customs cling to us in this bizarre environment. Lunch, fitting the occasion: no leftovers!

5 January—*Le Colis de France* [packages of France], an organized mutual aid, supported by in-kind donation within the camp, has given a Christmas package to every orderly [POW] in the camp and to the three hundred men of the adjacent stalag. This organization needs to grow.

At the beginning of the year, these men could look at some successes despite their dire conditions. In the first five months of captivity, they had established a functioning governance for their community, had formed family groups, popotes *(kitchen groups), and all sorts of other organizations. They provided opportunities for intellectual and spiritual development: giving lectures and seminars, which would later become the foundation for the classes of a university, establishing a small library and a "real" theater with an increasing number of troupes, forming an orchestra, and setting up a chapel. With the addition of physical education and the formation of sports teams, they had altogether laid the foundations of a community, which would mirror a small town.*

In a very basic way, however, it was not a usual town. Everyone was equally hungry, crowded in a space they were not free to leave, under the control of an enemy, and there were neither women nor children. At first, they had no resources or supplies except for what they could scrounge from within the camp enclosure, until little by little they received some basic items from packages. They relied on their memory and skills to entertain, educate, and make all kinds of objects from fabricating big pots made with empty tin cans to cook their food, to honoring their heritage by building scale models of Gothic cathedrals (later exhibit).

Indeed, building models of Gothic cathedrals was not an idle endeavor, nor were lectures on the history of French literature. As exiles in a foreign country, they intentionally created their community to feel like a corner of France. My father wrote: "The impression that a brutal fate, unexpected, implacable, and downright inhuman had come upon us, we all feel it with the same intensity.... We have turned to our natural community to provide the forces of our survival."[6]

Le Colis de France *was not a package coming from France, as one might imagine, but an in-camp gesture of fraternity. The POWs, working in the camp for the Germans, who under normal circumstances would have been the officers' orderlies, did not receive packages like the officer POWs. Early in September a captain, noticing that these men were in even worse conditions than the officer POWs, gathered a few items from his fellow prisoners who had received packages to give small packages to the worse-off POWs. Over the next few months, he expanded his work, charging one officer POW in each barrack with gathering whatever his comrades could spare. A core group put together packages to be distributed to every POW. From making forty-five packages in October, they produced another nine hundred by December.*[7]

11 January—The first three men freed on the merit of their files are arriving in France today. This event triggers off a wave of optimism. According to the letters received in the last few weeks, there is a file for every POW. What do we need in our dossier?

18 January—Who does not have his *Canard? Le Canard en KG*, a great source of information! Salesmen circulate among the groups, distributing the first issue of the camp newspaper. Has it been duplicated or typed? Not at all! It has been printed. Nothing less! A printing press, bought in Vienna and set up in the *Vorlager* [German Administrative Buildings], spits without stopping copies which emanate the good smell of oily ink. *Le Canard* has mobilized its own crowd of typesetters, editors, and reporters. Leading the team is P., his hair always in the wind, the nose of an eagle and snooping eyes, and a sarcastic smile on his lips. *Le Canard* proposes to reflect the life of the POWs, and aims at dispelling the blues. However, let us wish it a short life and prosperity of short duration.

The idea to acquire a printing press germinated a few months earlier and was one of the prisoners' first major ingenious stratagems. According to a rumor, they told the Germans that printing a newspaper would be an opportunity to publicize Marshal Pétain's leadership in France. A few officer POWs, who were in the printing business in civilian life, presented a request to the German administration to purchase the press and convinced the Germans to purchase it (it is likely that the prisoners paid for it). They also obtained French letters, which are different from the German script. Ultimately, they used the press to print forged identity papers necessary for the men who wanted to escape.

Félix Paillard, a French printer in civilian life, ran the press. At the beginning, a full size weekly six-page paper, le Canard en KG, changed a few weeks later to a fourteen-page-tabloid-size paper published twice a month, which rivaled any small town's newspaper.[8] The German censors read the proofs, and when approved stamped Geprüft *(approved)* on the copies before allowing it to go to press. Apparently, after some time passed, the printing team secured one or more of these stamps essential for authenticating identity papers.

The name of the paper, le Canard en KG *reflected the spirit and intentions of the men. Its name is a play on words;* "KG" *in German is short for* Krieg Gefangener, *meaning POW. The Germans had irked the French by painting these initials in large letters on the back of some of the men's vests. For the Germans, the name of the newspaper meant,* "The POW Duck." *However,* "en KG," *is pronounced* encagé *in French, meaning in a cage. In French, the full title meant* "The Duck in a Cage." *In addition,* le Canard enKaGé *was also a spoof of the well-known French satirical magazine* le Canard enchaîné *[The Duck*

The masthead of the camp newspaper, le Canard en ... KG from 18 November 1942 (Austrian National Library, Vienna).

in Chains], founded during World War I as a protest against the French government's censorship in wartime.⁹

In the first issue, the French Commander, who was held responsible by the Germans for the content of the paper, stated the purpose of the paper as one hundred percent French with the mission to affirm faith in the homeland and hope for the future. He added that le Canard would be "comforting and funny: funny because that is the way the French spirit fights gloom and feelings of depression." He enjoined every officer "never to forget that a country such as our homeland cannot and will not die."¹⁰

Le Canard contained varied articles from light humor to serious columns, from homilies to nostalgic stories and comic strips. Regular columns included: "In the Shadow of the Watchtower," describing places in the camp, and "Barbed Wire Spikes," a light-humor column about people, often pointing out the vagaries of the prisoners and sometimes of their jailers—one wonders sometimes how much the censors understood. The chaplain wrote a homily for the "Religion Chronicle" column and there were short announcements for the Protestants. A full page was devoted to crossword puzzles, chess games, and bridge with a regular comic strip, cartoons, and numerous jokes about different barracks. Theater plays and musical events occupied a prominent page or pages with pictures and detailed commentaries. The men wrote about French provinces, nostalgic reminiscence of their beauty, history, or birthplace of well-known people. There were serious articles analyzing a variety of subjects. Following the promotion of a story writing contest, le Canard published these stories, usually imagining a good life in a world outside the camp.

The southwestern corner of the camp, a hilly prairie, sloping gently down into a small valley and opening toward the west in the direction of France, had been christened Petite France. It routinely became a place where the men went to evoke their home. In the first issue of le Canard, a writer, honoring this collective yearning to feel close to France, wrote, "In these slow days of exile many officers (POWs) migrate toward the top of this hill at sunset, their hearts and thoughts turning to the gentle attraction of their faraway homeland. From our Petite France, we lovingly gaze at the slow descend of the sun, as it sinks over there, over there in the west, behind the horizon toward our loved ones. It is taking with it the invisible procession of five thousand loyal hearts, of which no barbed wire can prevent the flight."¹¹

The first issues of le Canard listed the university classes: three sessions of one hour each in the morning and four sessions in the afternoon. Still with only a few textbooks, the courses of study, except for the Baccalauréat (at the end of high school two exams a year apart for admission in a university), were fragmented on a great variety of subjects ranging from philosophy to biology, physics, geology, mathematics, history, and law. Instruction in German was given in each battalion—a set of four barracks—one hour a day, six days a week. Since there were many Alsatians in the community, there were plenty of instructors. The men felt the need to communicate in German and understand what their jailers said. Despite constant German surveillance, it seems that some of the surprising French achievements were made possible precisely, because they knew German and were free to speak among themselves without the Germans understanding what they were talking about. "One way to win over an enemy is to know his language," my father told me.

22 January—After ten vaudeville performances the "young 41" take over the stage of the theater with Jazz, energy and good spirits. The duo of Marc and Rémy sing works full of rhythm and humor composed by Marc, which everyone already hums. Several troupes are formed. They actively rehearse. In Barracks 13: musical revue à la Montmartre by G. and R.

25 January—Some games exude an aristocratic fragrance, others feel pedestrian. Their name alone is symbolic. What a gulf between the lofty game of bridge and the obscure "crapette." Here one plays the former and the latter without forgetting the popular belote of an origin which recalls a *"quarteron de dos verts."*

The schedule of classes of the Université de captivité Oflag XVIIA from *le Canard*, 18 January 1941 (Austrian National Library, Vienna).

Unquestionably, the game that requires the most concentration and strategy is bridge. Oh Albaran! Oh Culbertson! How many times have you been invoked!

The cold and impenetrable academic player brings an austere gravity to this game. He does not allow any lapses. The "bungler" hides his ignorance with overcalls and regularly misses one club. He will never learn, as one needs both genius and faith. Lower, all the way at the bottom of the ladder, is the modest crapette. It is a game for two players, and from time to time, one of the players shout "crapette." This shout has many meanings; it has become a curse word and a rallying cry. It may simultaneously mean doubt, joy, amazement, sarcasm, pain, or anger. It incorporates everything and explains everything, according to the learned interpretation of the psychic.

There are relatively few players of checkers and chess. A new game, Monopoly, where one sells and buys, is spreading like fire. The players seem to have a lot of fun, while those waiting for the table to be free sit impatiently, observing.

Obsessed players are few and far between and yet, there are a few. They move blind and deaf from table to bed and from bed to table, indifferent to anything that does not involve playing cards.

7 February—New transfusion of blood: One hundred officers [POWS] arrive from Spital after a painful trip in minus one-degree Fahrenheit. Their shoes were taken away to avoid any temptation, and guarded by big guards and police dogs, the entire inhuman equipment dear to the Chleuhs. These poor people are exhausted.

11 February—A constitutional decree declares Admiral Darlan the heir of Marshal Pétain. The British, forging ahead with their offensive, advance one hundred sixty miles beyond Benghazi.

13 February—Consistent with the law of polarities, friendships are forming between comrades of very different ages and the gap that often divides generations is bridged in the leveling of a common life.

The younger men are sometimes surprised by the youthful attitude of the older men, and the elder are astonished by the maturity of the young. Some men in their fifties even compete with youthful vigor, with those who are less than thirty years old. Boisterous and rambunctious, they reveal themselves tireless instigators of play, ringleaders, and glad rabble-rousers. They forget the age of their arteries, were it not for their arteries' dazzling reminders. One can see it after a bout of wrestling or a snowball fight, when, quite amazed not to be twenty anymore, they try to catch their panting breath and beg for mercy from their surprised adversaries.

14 February—Fifty-nine men, who are sick, return home.

Representatives of the Scapini mission are visiting the camp. They are received very coldly by reticent and suspicious prisoners, and inform us that there is no possibility of liberation. On the contrary, they exhort us to have courage. Easy to say!

The prisoners at that time learned about the outside world either from German newspapers or a few French papers controlled by the Germans. After the surrender of the Italian Army (from Libya), the British forged ahead. Their advance was of short duration, however. After Erwin Rommel arrived in Libya with the Afrika Korps, he captured Benghazi from the British. In the meantime, the Italians surrendered Koufra to the Free French troops, known for the oath of Koufra.[12]

17 February—The sports club has found a home in the west room of Barracks 17. With all the seriousness of a ritual, the physical education classes take place around a brand new ring attached to ropes, held by stout men wearing bulky pullovers. Captain M. leads it. A slight mist rises in the icy air of the room from all the exhalation of powerful breaths.

On the other side in the east room, the Ping-Pong fanatics carry on a frenzied game punctuated by the dry whacks of the balls. All of a sudden a vibrant song bursts out from the other side of the thin wall. The physical education lesson has ended.

20 February—Every week, *le Canard en KG* publishes the schedule of the classes and lectures, a program, which is becoming more and more crowded, and one must admire the hapless secretary of the University, who manages to implement it despite the stumbling blocks of the roll calls and meals. Observed for documentary purposes: *Guelfes* and *Gibelins*, Walking the paths of the Alps, Handwriting and character, Talleyrand, The beginning of Molière in Paris, Saddlehorse races, L' Affaire LaFarge.

Many conversations take place in study clubs: the Extraterrestrial Club, the Botany Club, and the Geology Club. A program in German, fashioned on the pattern of the Berlitz format, opens for beginners; due to the great interest, the classes will be given within each battalion.

The prisoner, who enjoys intellectual stimulation, can survey the cycle of human knowledge as he pleases without ever experiencing the kind of lassitude generated by boredom. He cannot, however, prevent the simultaneous listing of two classes, which interest him equally. He still has to choose one or the other, unless he positions himself, as N. does, in the center of the room, taking turns listening to two valued speakers. Buridan's ass would not have thought of that![13]

23 February—Today at 2:30 p.m.: symphonic orchestra conducted by D. with thirty performers. On the program: "Fra Diacolo," "Schubert's Military March," "the Blue Danube," some Tchaikovsky and ""Fantasie" from Carmen. Stooped, eyes glaring behind his glasses, head overburdened by the effort under a rare blond hair, D. waves his baton and looks like he is about to master a defiant beast. It is a big success with an excellent performance.

The orchestra started their first concert with a military march. The diary entry does not elaborate, but it is reminiscent of the first concert in another camp, where the military march became the occasion for the officer POWs' patriotic enthusiasm and an embarrassment for the Germans. An officer from that camp described the circumstances in his memoirs. The orchestra started the concert by playing "La Marche Lorraine,"[14] *a patriotic march (Proud children of Lorraine, from the mountains to the plains, we guard the access to the French soil), which invokes Joan of Arc, a French icon. Spontaneously, the men got up and stood at attention while singing their hearts out. As required the German senior officer was sitting in the front row. When he saw everyone standing at attention, he hesitated, not quite sure of what to do, and finally decided to stand up and salute. Naturally, all the other German officers followed suit to the great delight of the French, prompting the orchestra to play the stanzas over and over again. The officer concluded, "One has to live such moments to truly appreciate what a national hymn or the flag mean."*[15]

The 8 February issue of le Canard *honored the village of Edelbach by displaying on the front page a sketch of its church, which the men could see prominently from the camp, and a poem adapted to a French folk tune. Was it an expression of common sorrow with the Austrian villagers, who had been forced by Hitler to leave their land and become refugees? "I see a village on my horizon, / A gray hamlet with low lying houses.... Without smoke rising from its roofs / It seems to dream, frozen and deaf, / A deserted village."*

28 February—Too many letters! Too many packages! Write less! Eat less!" That is what the Chleuhs are saying, single-minded in their desire to reach their wicked goal, which will begin in March: two letters of twenty-seven lines, two cards of seven lines, two packages of eleven pounds per month. Thanks to the always-kind censors, the letters are kept for a long time after their arrival. One more turn of the screw.

3 March—The Swiss ski resort of Saint Moritz has come to the camp! There are three ice-skating rinks! Enthusiasts of this sport thrust themselves, glide, and whirl in gracious arabesques. There is only one thing missing: the skates!

15 March—A bookbinding shop is operating in the *Vorlager*, and in the

7. Creating a Town Behind Barbed Wire

Church of the village of Edelbach as seen from the camp. This church was an important landmark for the officer POWs. Drawn by an officer POW from *le Canard*, 8 February 1941 (Austrian National Library, Vienna).

same location are architects, painters, sculptors, and craftsmen. One goes from the art studio to the silversmith workshop. A tin can becomes a precious metal under B.'s skilled fingers.

21 March—A significant rumor spreads in the camp around the Barracks 13, 14, and 15 while armed troops keep the curious at bay. From time to time Mr. Loyal, showing signs of upheaval, appears at one door and then disappears like a jack in the box. Stone-faced and scowling W., the Gestapo Chief sticks out his primate snoot and sniffs like a bulldog, while workers in overalls pile a variety of materials in a cart. Painful history [Indicates that some prisoners were suspected of leaking the information, perhaps in exchange for a hoped-for repatriation]. A tunnel has been discovered. Thirty candidates for escape had worked on it since 15 October, taking turn in teams from six in the morning to ten at night. Enormous difficulties: lack of tools, rocky soil, water seepage, and insufficient aeration resolved by means of a giant blower. Lighting was provided, at first with oil lamps, then with electricity. Carts gliding on wooden tracks carried the soil away. A second tunnel starting from Barracks 15 to link up with Barracks 14 was also discovered. What a pity! The gallery measuring one hundred ninety five feet had already reached under the exterior barbed wire fence.

"If les Messieurs were to apply as much ingenuity to equip the camp," Mr. Loyal declares.... The rest is lost. We are subjected to the usual retaliation.

What seemed to have been fairly loose regulations of letters and packages was made more stringent and will apply for the rest of the men's captivity. Each letter and card had two detachable sections, one for the family member, and the other for the prisoner. Each letter consisted of a sheet of paper about five inches wide, glazed, which prevented the writers from using invisible ink between the lines. Censorship was now fully implemented. If anyone spilled over in the margin or added a line, the letter was thrown away. Everyone learned the art of writing very small.

The packages were also submitted to meticulous censorship. As soon as they arrived, they were put in a special room in the Vorlager under lock and key, guarded by a sentry and distributed at the whim of the German command. On the day of distribution, the French POWs, watched by German guards, loaded the packages into an old-fashioned horse-drawn wagon, which was then driven to a central barracks. The wagon stopped in front of an open window, and an officer POW under surveillance threw the packages to another officer POW inside, who under surveillance placed it on a table, where the guards opened it facing the recipient.

Everything was pulled apart to reveal the content: wrappings, boxes, cans, commercially sealed canned food. Their content was emptied into a mess kit and the cans were thrown away. Chocolate bars or cigarettes packs were torn apart to make sure there were no secret messages, and cardboard boxes were thrown away as well. Cigarettes were broken in two, soap sliced, cakes sometimes smashed. The books were taken to the censoring team. To mitigate this onslaught, the officer POWs sometimes used their knowledge of German to engage the guards in a conversation, diverting their attention during which they would spirit away a small jar or other small items suspected of containing a letter or a forbidden article.

There were other tricks. In one instance, after opening a package the guard zeroed in immediately on a can that seemed extra puffy. Somewhat suspicious, he pierced the top, releasing a nauseating gas, "Los! Los!" he shouted. (Get this thing out of the way, quick.) The prisoner was more than happy to comply, knowing that at the bottom of the can was a compass needed for an escape.[16]

Keen not to lose any supplies, the men persistently hunted through the garbage and refuse piles to retrieve what the Germans had discarded: cardboard, tin cans, and wrapping papers, which might also be an uncensored newspaper.

Overwhelmed by packages and names they could neither read nor pronounce, the Germans provided the officer POWs the opportunity to swindle packages, a lucky break the prisoners would strikingly exploit later on. The Kommandant asked the French Commandant to designate men who were post office employees *in civilian life or military mail officers to help sort out the packages. At first, the Commandant refused on the ground that officer POWs could not be asked to work directly for the enemy. On second thought, he realized that putting French officers in the room where the packages were stacked after arrival could be used to their advantage. Twenty men were selected to work in the mailroom under the surveillance of a guard.*

On 15 March the diary entry mentioned an art studio located in the Vorlager. *As a result of a special deal, an active group of about thirty architects (POWs) obtained the use of the building in the* Vorlager, *large enough to house their mock-up work on contemporary architecture. They later obtained recognition from the* École des Beaux-Arts *in Paris. Two architects, who had received* Le Prix de Rome *before the war, also worked with the University courses studying Roman and Gothic buildings.*[17] *Painters, sculptors, and craftsmen were allowed to use that space to set up shops for many artists in the camp.*

One officer created small boxes made of wood from the camp, with a cover inlaid with wood of different colors and shapes. My father somehow carried one home for me, inscribed on the side with Oflag XVII A 1942.

A bookbinding shop, an extension of the services provided by the library, was also housed in that building. The books suffered a harsh treatment, being shuffled all day long on tables, read in the rows during long roll calls, quickly put in a pocket, or folded inside out for convenience in small available spaces. They needed to be bound securely. Two professional bookbinders devoted their time to care for these books and began teaching others the art of bookbinding.[18]

25 March—"Conferencitis" is an illness whose level of virulence has never been measured, and yet it is a passion as consuming as love. It exists fortunately only as a sporadic condition. T. has caught it. From eight in the morning, stool on his shoulder and notebooks under his arm, he takes off for Barracks 19. He returns only at 11:30 a.m. to swallow his meager ration. From noon on he shows signs of nervousness and agitation; at 1:00 p.m. he can't stand it anymore and he is off again like a fast car on the race track of Barracks 19. At 4:45 p.m. he returns to the barracks in a whirlwind but does not stay and disappears again. He returns at 6:00 p.m. barely relaxed. He will soon miss an indispensable sleep that is as vital as lost time. To eat, what a mistake! A package, why bother! Let's talk instead of the viscosity of the culture of single cells.

28 March—Revolution in Yugoslavia: Protests against membership in the tripartite pact. In spite of executions and the muzzling of dissent, truth always manages to make its voice heard. It is found in the numerous letters, hidden in the packages; onion skin paper covered with tiny handwriting and

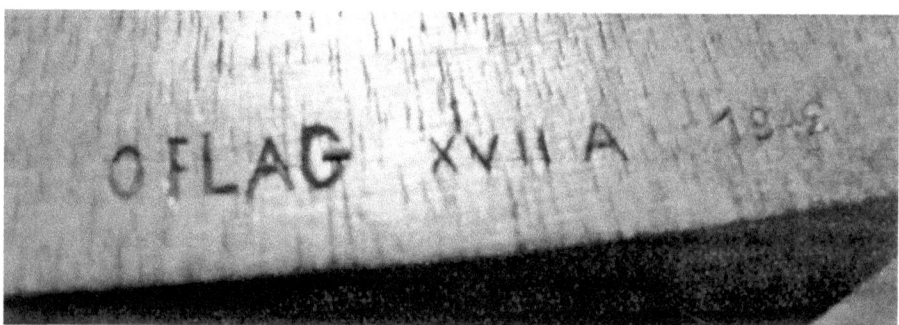

Top and Bottom: Using wood found in the camp, one of the officer POWs made small boxes with an inlaid cover of various shades and shapes, inscribed on the side with Oflag XVIIA 1942. The editor's father carried it back and gave it to her upon his return (photograph by Jacqueline Vautrain Collins).

hidden in a homemade cake, in a bag of candies, or inside empty nutshells. Compasses and pliers are concealed in canned foods and the double soles of wooden shoes, and well-chosen newspaper clippings used as wrapping paper, which one attempts to retrieve from under the nose of the censors. This is the way the French antidote neutralizes the German poison. News circulates under cover. It tells us that the entrapment of collaboration finds a growing resistance in France.

2 April—The first contingent of fathers of four children is repatriated. Our friend L. leaves us. Close comrade since 20 August 1939. What joy! What sadness! A long embrace!

7 April—The gniouf, a barbarian name of unknown origin, that's the pen. One never calls it prison. The gniouf and the kitchen are two of three masonry buildings, which stand out in this city made of wood. It is divided in narrow cells into which daylight enters through a casement window with bars. The gniouf has its regular occupants and even its devotees, the latter seeking it for its silence and during the winter for the quality of its heat. Smoking is not allowed, a prohibition not observed. One cannot receive any food except for the regular fare, but thanks to the complicity of the enlisted men [POWs], everything becomes possible and even easy. P. goes happily to the gniouf, taking with him a big volume under his arm. "Finally," he declares, "I will be able to read the Bible."

9 April—The Germans invade Greece and Yugoslavia; Salonika falls. When will they meet their Catalaunian Fields?

[The Battle of the Catalaunian Fields took place in 451 CE in the north east of France between the Romans and the Huns led by Attila. It was one of the major military operations of the Western Roman Empire, which resulted in the defeat of the Huns and prevented them from conquering Western Europe.]

12 April—The chapel finally has its bell tower. Four high posts, joined together by slanted braces, support a rustic small steeple made of logs. The sky sometimes laughs and sometimes looks sad through this rough construction. At the top, rising over the roof, a Gallic rooster and a Latin cross.

At 6:15 p.m.: christening of our bell, the Jeanne d'Arc, clothed with a tarnished silver gown by our skilled craftsmen. Its somewhat dull voice does not have the pure sound of bronze, yet, its timbre sounds like the far away tone of a bell in our homeland.

13 April—Today is Easter. We celebrate with a High Mass. A master altar sculpted in the dignified lines of the alder has replaced the original humble table, and the old Crucifix from the church in Edelbach[19] stands out in front of the altar screen. The orchestra and the choir sing the Missa festiva, composed by Midshipman L., achieving a magnificent liturgy. Faces have been carefully shaved, and our uniforms have been brushed and spruced up for the occasion. We wear our hats and gloves.

Flash back to Easters of time past.... Young girls in light colored dresses, childish voices, an old church, and a bakery full of gourmands!

The bell tower next to the barracks designated as the church. It was important for these men that the nondescript barracks, designated as a church, had a tower with a bell. The bell was bought and shipped from Vienna. From *le Canard*, 1 May 1941 (Austrian National Library, Vienna).

Last minutes news: fall of Belgrade.

The outside of the chapel was indistinguishable from the other barracks with just a number at the door, leading some of the men to propose building a tower next to the barracks. They obtained permission from the Kommandant (generally the officer POWs were allowed to improve the camp as long as they found the material and did the work) and ordered a bell from Vienna. The bell was made of an aluminum base alloy, sixteen inches tall and seventeen inches in diameter. On it they chiseled a border of small crosses, Joan of Arc's coat of arms, and the monogram XP for Christ. Around the bottom they inscribed, "Jeanne d'Arc Oflag XVIIA à Pâques 1941."

They performed a ceremony of the blessing of the bell. The chaplain said in parts, "a bell is a call from God to prayer.... It sounds through the clouds to provide a continual protection (from the enemy of our souls) and save our spirits and hearts." Then, he climbed the ladder to the top to bless the bell, which rang for the first time. In his remarks the Commandant recognized the chiselers and those who "patiently wove all the small pieces of strings into a rope. A bell gives us the illusion of France."[20]

Their first Easter in captivity was reflexive and morose. To cheer everyone up, le Canard *had requested submissions from anyone in the camp for its extended Easter issue, focused on "France, her greatness, her land, spirit, and the France of the future."* Nonetheless, at a time of joy and celebration, they profoundly felt their isolation and the weight of their exile, far away from their family, and most intensely the absence of their children from their lives. Writing about a new organization being formed by the Pétain government for children and youths in France, Les Companions de France, *an officer worried about their indoctrination, while he had no control over their lives. Feeling powerless, he remarked:* "We are so far and so ignorant of all the details of what this group's goals are; we unfortunately have only an abstract knowledge of what it does, and cannot assess what this new experience means for our children. Only our affection can replace our absence."[21]

20 April—"Messieurs, I am asking for some silence! We are practicing." On the stage, the actors in coats and wooden shoes are waiting. G., the director looks into the hall from behind his turtle shell glasses, which underscores his slightly bulging forehead with a black line. The courteous form of his request conveys a hint of some nervousness. No wonder! An army of stagehands is sawing, hammering, and grinding, led energetically by Captain F., the stage manager. The rehearsal continues with some difficulties in a relative calm. Script in hand G. repeats an intonation, or corrects a posture.

Captain G., cap over his ear, whose thin white goatee makes him look like a master mariner, casts an inquisitive look, while Rams, head decorator, armed with an over-sized brush, furiously paints a background canvas. In a few days, Beatrice, a play written in the camp by G. and R., will open under the footlights.

25 April—We are subjected to roll calls after endless roll calls. The reason: two officers [POWs] and one orderly have escaped, and Mr. Loyal is livid.

26 April—We suffer the usual retaliations, but they are more refined. Last night "they" cut the light, inciting a flood of vengeful speeches around the smoky and stinking oil lamps. We spent the day in a succession of roll calls and second sets of roll calls, standing in a bitter cold rain that casts a sense of gloom over the surroundings. A game of soccer scheduled for today is canceled, as Mr. Loyal has confiscated the ball.

27 April—The suppression of light persists today and excites a flare up of tempers. A growing anger coalesces into action; we must protest in a big way. This cannot last! Since "he" wants a fight, he will get one! At 1 p.m. the entire camp, en mass, descends on the first battalion and invades its field. The band plays some French marching songs, while Mr. Loyal, motionless, his forehead furrowed by anxiety, observes behind the barbed wire of the *Vorlager*.

We open the hostilities with a parody of a voluntary roll call, embellished by some clowning around, then, a soccer match engages two teams, confronting each other with wild energy around an imaginary ball. Booing gibes and catcalls prompts a Chleuh officer to rush up, dragging a bayonet behind his heels. He grabs a trophy, a panel on which is written "Big Match, *Morgenfrüh*" [tomorrow]! The Chleuhs are now riled up, forcing the crowd to flow back to the central alley, on which in a clever maneuver, Mr. Loyal at the head of a unit advances revolver at the ready. Shots are fired. No one runs away so to speak, but everyone "shows his back," and little by little the space empties. Fatefully, the barracks swallow this drifting population. It's all over. We are back-home and everything is grand, except for a few sore buttocks stabbed to the bare flesh.

All right! The drama turns to comedy. Mr. Loyal, worried about the report he no doubt has to send to Vienna, throws ashes on the fire. "…The electricity, just an error of the guard-house. We simply need to throw the breakers; here it comes." Tonight: light as usual encouraging bitchy commentaries. The faint-hearted protests against these stupid demonstrations, but the "Durs" [Tough Guys] bemoan the lost opportunity.

After the publication of the Easter issue, le Canard *changed format and became a bimonthly paper, replacing the weekly issues.* Le Canard *team explained: "For reason beyond our control,* le Canard *will be published twice a month, a newspaper of sixteen pages and smaller format."*[22] *We can only speculate what was "the reason beyond their control." Yet from now on, regular articles about the Pétain regime were published under the rubric "La vie en France" (Life in France), confirming the rumors that articles on Pétain had been one of the conditions for the German acceptance of publishing a newspaper.*

The column "Barbed Wire Spikes" disappeared. Its subtle humor may have been a little too pointed for the German censors, who were becoming wiser. The articles about the regions of France, their imagined lives in freedom, and the stories written in the camp remained. Under the rubric of "Nos Enquêtes" (Our Investigations), le Canard reported about the various "institutions" of the camp. Whole pages were devoted to the theater and music. The page on chess, bridge, other games, and cartoons was expanded. A regular column on staying physically fit was added.

The library (titled the National of the Camp, mimicking the National Library in Paris) was the focus of one of the first Enquêtes, conducted by an officer, who was a reporter in civilian life. Arriving early in the morning, he entered an already full lecture hall—over seven hundred men came every day—and immediately found the director. He noted how different it was from the interview he had conducted at the National Library in Paris. There, he had been escorted by ushers through stairs and hallways, and talked to a few secretaries, while waiting to meet the director. But the difference stopped there. Once inside, he was impressed to find the same ambiance in the hall: a study atmosphere and complete silence even more remarkable in the camp, an amazing contrast to the barracks. "It felt like an oasis, where it was possible to enter into some reflection."[23]

In the middle of 1941, there were a total of about ten thousand volumes, of which over three thousand belonged to the library and six thousand were available from individual officer POWs. The families and the Red Cross had sent many books, the German administration had bought German novels, the Society of Friends in Vienna (Quakers) had given French novels, and an office of the University of Paris had sent textbooks, basic study books, and references. More books were sent throughout the next two years. We do not know how many books they had in the end, as that section of the camp burned after the liberation of the camp.

A Center of Mutual Help for students in Paris sent course notes and manuals in all fields of study upon individual requests. The catalog included books from the Greeks and Romans to the contemporary period in science, art, the humanities, medicine, and law. The books were bound with a special cover.

4 May—Beatrice, Vaudeville à la Beaumarchais [well-known French playwright of the eighteenth century], a play written by G. and R., with music by F. is praised for a well-deserved success, notably, for the superb scenery and staging unequaled until now. Since January the theater groups have put on the performances of five plays written in the camp. Two more are being rehearsed with a new theater group: the Apprentices.

10 May—Mr. Loyal is all sweetness and light. Is it the proximity of fourteen beehives in the *Vorlager*, all buzzing with new swarms, which inspire him with the bucolic tenderness of Tityre and Mélibe? Does he hope to distill the honey of divine wisdom in order to feed his dangerous guests? A follower of Virgil, does he dream only of flowers and gardens? A greenhouse has already been built and parcels of land are distributed to groups in the camp proper. Seeds fly in the wind of the sowing season. Will Oflag XVIIA become an Eden? But why in the world, is Mr. Loyal so kind?

14 May—Sensational! Rudolf Hess has landed in Scotland. The V.B. [*Volkischer Beobachter*] implies he is demented. For us, he is a sage. Admiral Darlan visits Berlin. [*Hitler's right-hand man parachuted in Scotland with the intention of brokering some kind of peace between Germany and Great Britain. Imprisoned for the duration of the war, he was sentenced to life imprisonment in Nuremberg, and took his own life at the age of 93.*]

The May sun slowly dries the mud left over from the thaw and the unbridled imagination of the prisoners let giddy rumors blossom, rich in humor and fantasy.

15 May—Two buses have just arrived at the *Vorlager*, bringing thirty brutish looking guys in civilian clothes. They are the intelligence agents of the Gestapo dressed in light green and tea rose. Their heavy boot socks do not spoil the fashionable clothing of these shoddy narcissists. Let's not forget the funnel shaped headgear of these bullies with a tough looking visor.

Helped by a cadre of soldiers carrying bayonets, they surround Barracks 3 to conduct a search. Everyone's pockets are checked out thoroughly, the linings are ripped apart, and the wooden floor slats are pulled out. As naked as worms, our friends of Barracks 3 wait with stoicism for the end of this invasion. All of this for a meager booty: a few marks, one or two pliers, and two or three military maps. These scabby grasshoppers exit leaving devastated spaces behind them, worthy of marauders or burglars. When will we ever get even?

20 May—Departures and arrivals, arrivals and departures: the painful rhythm of displacements, which becomes noxious to write about. One hundred two men, who are sick and a burden on our non-existent medical care, leave, and we assimilate six hundred officers [POWs] transferred from a camp in Nuremberg.

Strange incident: a plane towing a tricolor cylinder flies over the camp. Intense emotions! Does this mean peace? Alas, it is only a signal for maneuvers.

It was the last stop for the men from Oflag XIII in Nuremberg, who would stay in Edelbach to the end of their captivity. Told of their departure just a couple of days before leaving Nuremberg, and not knowing where they were going, they faced the task of trying to take with them whatever they possessed. While they had arrived in Nuremberg with only what they could carry, their families had sent clothes and other items in the past few months. Their Commandant asked the Germans to allow one piece of heavy luggage to be taken by trucks. When that was granted, they scrambled to buy cardboard boxes at the canteen (PX) or fabricated boxes with the planks of their bunk beds, packing everything they could possibly take with them. My father packed up the already written essays, the completed illustrations for his book on Nuremberg, and the projected book on Beaudelaire.

Their train was composed of only cattle cars, each wagon taking forty officer POWs and securely locked. The trip took one day, following the same itinerary as the original group. It was very hot inside and they were continually thrown about, various items they had hung making an awful racket. When the train stopped and was unlocked they quickly relieved themselves before the train was locked again. Once at night, some shots were fired.

The arriving men had varied impressions about the new camp, perhaps depending on their state of mind. One, noting that the camp at Edelbach was "better equipped and more serene," welcomed the change. Another said, "Oflag XVIIA is considerably less comfortable than Nuremberg."[24] *In general, they had become part of a much larger crowd.*

The officer POWs in Edelbach warmly welcomed the Nuremberg group of six hundred men. Navy Captain René Marie, senior to Lieutenant Colonel Robert the commandant in Edelbach, became co-leader. In his short address in le Canard, *Marie wrote: "The officers of Nuremberg are very much touched by the welcome of their comrades, living in the miniature France that is Oflag XVIIA. This brotherly attitude bodes well for the recovery of our nation."*[25] *Since the lecture series in Nuremberg had been interrupted by the move, the officer POWs finished it in Edelbach, the Nuremberg professors enlarging greatly the faculty of the University of Oflag XVIIA.*

8

La Semaine de France (the French Week)
25 May–September 1941

25 May—Disgusting return of cold weather and snow! Will winter ever end? Yet, news that warms the heart: the Italians have surrendered in Ethiopia.

The weather is conducive to reading in the library, located in the east room of Barracks 9, equipped with rough long planks on sawhorses as tables. It is difficult to find a place. There are about three thousand books coming from diverse donations. As R. remarks, "One walks instinctively on one's toes." It is the house of silence.

29 May—A dreadful innovation: powerful loudspeakers flood the "central boulevard," with bellowing music. They function without stopping, amplifying from time to time the well-known voice of our "dear host," happy and proud to have the opportunity to play the broadcaster. "I would like to direct les Messieurs' attention to...."

4 June—The sun shines with a bright glare in a pure blue sky. Summer triumphs with abruptness in this land that ignores transitions. Already the sunbathers look for an ideal corner in the field, where sheltered from the wind, they can warm up their crumbling body. More daring the young take off their clothes and bask in full sun. The pale green of new needles outline the dark green branches of the pines, and one single blade of grass is good enough for life to burst out in spite of the oppression of our bodies and souls. One longs to shout, jump, and run! Impulse quickly suppressed, as the obsessive fear of a snare, always lurking day in and day out, is enough to destroy this purely animal joy. It is out of question to share in a universal life so unconcerned with our lot that it continues to create a reality we will never know beyond the barbed wire.

8. La Semaine de France (the French Week)

The dreadful innovation, the loud speakers, not only broadcast Mr. Loyal's voice, but even more distressing to the officer POWs it broadcast the voice of a Frenchman, known as the "traitor of Stuttgart." He had immigrated to Germany in the fall of 1939 from where he glorified the Nazi successes and cursed the French Republic, England, and the Jews. He was condemned to death after the war. The Germans used him for regular broadcast during which he told the French people that the POWs were housed in comfortable barracks with abundant food, lies that enraged them[1] and misled the French public about the conditions of the prisoners of war.

The group of officer POWs coming from Nuremberg found that a number of the men in Oflag XVIIA were Pétainists *(followers of Marshal Pétain), a designation that included subtle differences. A few were true believers of collaboration, ideologically in agreement with Marshal Pétain, and were devoted to him. Others ignored his declarations about collaborating, thinking he was playing a double game. Some simply followed him, because he was their nominal leader. And then, there were the opportunists, who hoped to be freed if they showed allegiance to Pétain. After arriving in the camp, many of the officer POWs from Nuremberg, seeing in General de Gaulle's resistance the way to sustain France's honor, bonded with the Gaullists already in the camp.[2]*

These different views came to a head when the Germans started a campaign to subject the officer POWs of Jewish decent to harsher treatment and planned to restrict the Jews to a separate barracks; it would be some sort of ghetto, which would subject the men to different rules, such as not being allowed to participate in the camp activities. There was, however, one problem. Jewish last names in French were often different from Jewish names in German. Who was Jewish? The Germans needed the cooperation of the French officers. In June they sent a notice to the French Commandant, Navy Captain René Marie, ordering him to establish a list of all the Jewish officer POWs "in order to isolate them." René Marie looked at it, and standing up very straight turned to the Oberleutenant (first lieutenant) who had brought the order and said: "Mister, I know only Frenchmen here, who have served under the same flag and the same uniform," and he refused to comply.[3] Discrimination was against the military code, which dictated that every man fighting in the army, navy, or air force was a French officer regardless of his origin.

Despite Marie's protest one hundred twenty-five officer POWs designated as Jewish were moved to Barracks 3. It was troubling for many non–Jewish officer POWs, and the list became the subject of heated and somber discussions within the camp, abuzz with accusations about who had provided the names to the Germans. There had already been some tension when a tunnel was discovered, fueling the suspicion that someone had told the Germans, as indicated by the careful diary entry of 21 March naming the discovery of a tunnel a "painful history."

The rumor spread that a group of officer POWs called Régénération was responsible for the leaks and the denunciation of the Jews. It was de facto confirmed a few days later, when two suspected leaders of the group were liberated as "deserving prisoners." But it was harder to know who the other members of the group were, as it was difficult to distinguish between hard core collaborators, opportunists, and others who may have made compromising remarks but would not harm their comrades. A general nervousness took hold of the camp.

There was, however, no doubt that there were stool pigeons in their midst, a situation that demanded action. Two officer POWs from Nuremberg formed a group of seven officers who made plans to find the detractors; at first, to watch them and warn others of their transgressions. Soon, they expanded their actions and recruited one trusted officer in each barracks in charge of watching those who were willing to collaborate—a betrayal of their duty as a French officer. The barracks leaders reported the transgressor to a designated person in the core group. He would often be barred to participate in some of the activities of the camp.[4] The group became known as La Maffia.

In the meantime, many officer POWs showed their support for their Jewish comrades. They visited Barracks 3 as soon as the Jewish officer POWs had moved. As a warning to the Germans that their action was unacceptable, some men slept in the barracks overnight. It had some effect; the original German plan to confine the Jews to the barracks and prevent them from participating in the camp activities was rescinded in the face of the demonstration of solidarity by their comrades, and the Jewish officer POWs were free to leave the barracks without restriction. Once separated, however, the Gestapo could harass Jews more easily, particularly when it came to conducting harsher searches.

7 June—An underground tunnel beginning in Barracks 23 has been discovered. *Trompe-la-Mort* [death-cheat], a Chleuh officer [heading a group of seven men, roaming around the camp to conduct haphazard searches] whose beardless face displays a morbid refinement and lymphatic nostalgia assists the search of the inspectors with smugness.

Rumor! One speaks of the departure of the World War I Veterans.

The British and the Free French Forces enter Syria.

11 June—Two comrades escape by blending in with a work party of enlisted men [POWS], who were leaving the camp. Will they succeed? In reality the unknown begins after passing through the barbed wire. An escape is an undertaking, in which the intangible plays such an important role that it requires a very detailed preparation aimed at staving off all hazards.

8. La Semaine de France (the French Week)

W., an expert, recaptured already twice, is a living example.

First, watch the choice of clothes. As much as possible you must eliminate ties and khaki shirts, wear a clean suit, and well-polished shoes. Above all, no military footwear!

Then, pay attention to the supplies. Beware of French cookies and of chocolate, which are rare in Germany, and do not eat them in the train. Do not show *Lager-marks* [The currency used to pay the prisoners their portion of their salaries], but Reich-marks, the legal currency of Germany. False papers have to show the seal of an indisputable official document. You need to know the exact schedule of buses and convoys, be in possession of maps and a good compass. Thoroughly know the entire escape plan. Walk at night and hide during the day. After taking all these precautions and with huge luck, there may be some chance of success.

At this point, of about twenty escapees it seems that only one has been able to reach Yugoslavia. The unlucky ones have been brought back to the camp without gentleness. As a way of consolation, they are rewarded with ten days in the gniouf in the *Vorlager*, after which they return to their barrack to dream of the next opportunity.

15 June—Slowly the Corpus Christi procession [Holy Eucharist], marches toward the altar, which has been set up in *Petite France*.

The diary announcement, the British and the Free French Forces enter Syria, was remarkable news. In a stroke of luck, the officer POWs had obtained a clandestine radio receiver from a lieutenant who arrived in the Oflag in the spring of 1941 and had managed to hide it from the Germans despite the numerous searches he went through. The radio was bulky and of poor quality, but they could now listen to clandestine broadcasts of the BBC and of a station in Switzerland, in spite of the very poor reception.[5]

The radio had to be very carefully hidden, and if found, there would be retaliation for the entire barracks. As it happened, the newcomer was in a barracks where some of his fellow prisoners violently refused to keep it. The radio was taken to the barracks next door, where other officer POWs took care of it.[6]

Most officer POWs were anxious to follow the progress of the war and discuss the French participation in the important combat raging in Africa, forerunners of the critical battles for France in 1944. An officer wrote: "We passionately follow the military development on all the fronts of the ground, sea, and air war."[7] After World War I, France had been awarded Syria and Lebanon, while the British took over Palestine and what became modern-day Iraq. In 1941 the Vichy government remained in control of Syria and Lebanon with French troops, who had kept allegiance to Marshal Pétain. The Germans, wanting a foothold in the Middle East, obtained permission from the Vichy government to use the airfields in Syria, prompting the British to invade Syria from their bases in Palestine.[8]

The knowledge that the British and the Free French Forces were fighting together on one side, and the Vichy government forces were on the other side, meant that some units of the French military were fighting against other units of the French military. It must have been disturbing for many officer POWs in the camp. General De Gaulle, speaking of the Free French troops, expressed this sentiment: "I realized that they were in exactly the same state of mind as I was. There was grief and disgust at having to fight Frenchmen, indignation with Vichy for leading astray the discipline of the troops, and conviction that it was necessary to march to make sure that the Levant (Lebanon and Syria) would not be acquired by the Germans."[9]

The fight in Syria impacted the camp directly. In mid-June, the Germans announced that eighteen prisoners would be repatriated immediately, a request of the Vichy government approved by Berlin. Once the prisoners learned that all eighteen were active duty officers who had served in the colonial armies, they realized they would be sent directly to fight in Syria without any choice but to fight on the Vichy side.

In addition to the liberation of the colonial officers who went to Syria, Admiral Darlan took the opportunity of his position as prime minister in the Vichy government to ask the Germans to liberate all the Navy officers. For Oflag XVIIA, it meant that René Marie, the outspoken and much-loved Commandant of the camp, would leave to rejoin the navy ships in Senegal under the control of the Vichy government. This order of repatriation put the Navy officers in a compromised situation, a fact that was not lost on Marie. To say his good-bye, René Marie called for a gathering in the theater hall. The room filled very quickly to capacity, forcing the opening of all the windows, so the ceremony could be heard from the outside. After the French fanfare, "Aux champs," (To the Fields), Colonel Robert began the ceremony, ending with these words, "Let us all shout, Vive la France," a shout everyone immediately roared.

Then, Marie came on stage and stated his unyielding position, blasting: "I have fought against the enemy, the enemy who is tyrannizing you, and whom I am leaving now to go serve in Africa! You can count on my patriotism: I shall not come to terms with him." Needless to say, if a German had come close to the theater, heard him, and understood French, his courageous attitude could have cost him his freedom.[10] He was one who, as de Gaulle said, "remained unscathed from the traps, which the armistice regime had laid for (his) honor."

An article in le Canard described the ceremony for Marie as touching, "a

8. La Semaine de France (the French Week)

testimony to the gratitude, trust, and friendship of the officers." It was noted that René Marie was the symbol of an immense hope for them. The article ended with a message from Marie, who said in parts: "Captivity enriches friendships, a precious gift we gain from the catastrophe.... It is not usual for the captain to leave before his crew; my most fervent wish is that you will follow quickly. Vive la France!"[11]

A dark silence gripped the camp after Marie's departure.

19 June—A plan for a public square following a French design has been sketched out for the center of the camp in the rectangle bordered by the kitchen, the canteen, and the central alley: flowerbeds, grassy borders, and a gazebo made of rough logs. The band inaugurates it, playing military marches and selections from operettas. There is always a need to recreate a familiar setting.

A persistent rumor rises again from the ashes: the liberation of the World War I Veterans.

22 June—A shrill voice, speaking at great speed, hurts our ears with its abusive diatribes. Tirades of extreme violence drowned out by hysterical acclamations; Hitler is speaking. Stunning turn of events! Germany has declared war with Russia.

29 June—For the last two hours the loud speakers have been screaming victory bulletins: two special communiqués intermingled with warring marches. The Germans have broken through the Russian front, encircling their army now in retreat. There are hundreds of thousands of prisoners.

3 July—This time the super rumor is not a rumor! The liberation of the World War I Veterans is officially confirmed, but the date has not been selected, which has the effect of moderating the enthusiasm. With the help of good weather a vague optimism rushes through Oflag XVIIA. After the Veterans it will be the turn of those who are over 35 years old, or perhaps the Oflag will be transferred to Innsbruck, why not? Good news naturally follows good news! Forced exile in a nicer region would not disappoint us.

11 July—The World War I Veterans are still here, but their thoughts are wandering somewhere else. We can feel that they are detached from the mental climate of our lives. Their departure is now a certainty and the buzz spreads of an upcoming liberation, one per month. An outrageous hope, but it electrifies even the most skeptics and acts as a new wine. Upon reflection, it seems that Mr. Loyal makes such public announcements from time to time to calm the heightened desire to escape. All his effort is aimed at making our stay enthralling. [Many escapes would reflect poorly on Mr. Loyal, who would then risk being sent to the Russian front.] A double row of flowers from the greenhouse embellishes now the central alley, and light green lawns have replaced the meager grass that was growing between the barracks. Elsewhere, there is a vegetable garden, and as an additional way of embellishment, the enlisted men [POWs] have built a stony pond where a few trout swim. A sundial, embedded in the lawn between Barracks 2 and 3, spreads out these words etched in the stone, "Tempus manat dum manemus" [Time passes, but we remain].

15 July—A contingent of the men of class 19 leaves today. The liberation is beginning!

Thirty officer POWs, architects in civilian life, proposed improving the look of the camp to the Kommandant, who agreed as long as the French paid for the material and did the work. The Germans were always glad to see the prisoners occupied, thinking they would be less likely to escape. The officer POWs planted small trees on either side of the central alley, the only paved surface of the camp, set flowerbeds around the trees, and built a path at each entrance of the barracks. About three-quarters of the way from the front of the camp, a U-shape area, formed by the kitchen buildings, the canteen, and the gniouf, broke the tediousness of the rows of barracks. To make it a space resembling a small French town square, they built the Gazebo, planted trees, and laid out flowerbeds. The barracks next to that area were already used as general buildings: the chapel, the library, and farther down the row, the university and the theater.

Keeping the morale of five thousand officer POWs was a continual challenge. In June le Canard en K G *publicized plans for a grand exhibition, "a festival to honor the richness and glory of France." It would represent all aspects of French life and utilize the far-ranging talents of the prisoners. Called* La Semaine de France *(the French Week), it was to take place in the fall. The theater troupes would present classic and contemporary plays to "show the evolution of our language and taste the French spirit." The orchestra and chamber ensembles would play pieces by French composers. Regional folkloric music and dances would also be well represented. Each region, including the French overseas empire, would have individual exhibits. Stands, representing family life, religion, and the education of children and youth, would emphasize French moral forces. Le Canard concluded: "This will help us break the monotony of our temporary stay."*[12] *For the next three months,* le Canard *recruited and organized this weeklong festival, celebrating the different aspects of French life and culture.*

17 July—Loiterers are not allowed in the field facing Barracks 17 west. A construction site has opened and a crew of workers with bare torsos, tanned by the sun, pounds with picks, digs with shovels, and pushes wheelbarrows. They are the sports enthusiasts building their stadium. Grandiose project!

8. La Semaine de France (the French Week) 107

An open space with a steep slope has to be flattened. The soil, torn off the side of the hill, is thrown downwards as if to balance the beam of a huge scale. Later on, tracks and fields will be built for a variety of sports. Skeptical onlookers watch this activity looking like an anthill. A stadium! What's the use? We will be far away before it is finished.

23 July—They are leaving! One thousand to twelve hundred officers, World War I Veterans, buckle their luggage once more and gather by battalions in barracks emptied for that purpose. As soon as there is an opportunity to accomplish the smallest task, a captive expends a feverish energy, and all over the camp groups of men carrying straw mattresses, crates, and bundles, rush from one barracks to the other.

Colonel R., our commandant, is transferred to a reprisal camp as retribution for the protest of 27 April. Mr. Loyal has a lasting grudge.

3 August—Four *Durs* [tough guys] tried to go AWOL by cutting the barbed wires of the *Vorlager*, but at night you can hear the smallest noise, and unfortunately they had not anticipated the long-range vibration of a wire being cut with pliers. Alerted, the sentry searched the field with his searchlight;

A - Sprints track
B - Distance track
C - Basketball Court
D – Volleyball Court
E - Weight throw
F - Javelin
G - High jump
H - Discus throw
I – Polevault
J - Long jump

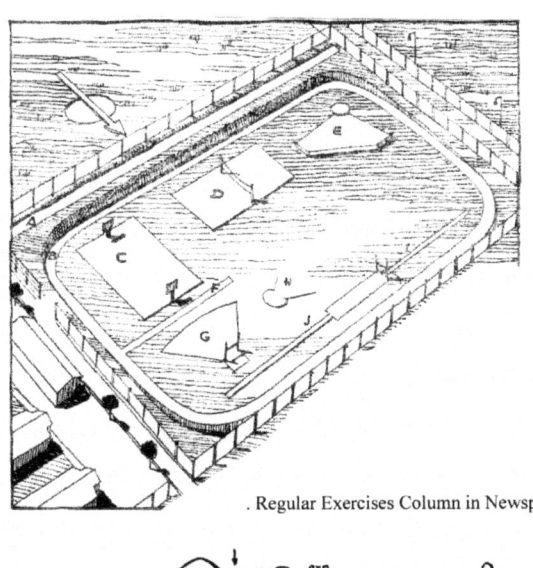

The Stadium, built by the officer POWs. Drawn by an officer POW. From *le Canard*, 1 October 1941 (Austrian National Library, Vienna).

nerve racking minutes. An hour later, a new unsuccessful attempt, and by that time the Chleuhs were stirred up. Our four guys must flee.

Sheepishly and full of rage, they returned to their bunks.

Le Cercle Sportif *had grown to an active group of eight hundred men. They had obtained an empty barracks, using half of it for Ping-Pong, the other half for boxing with some fitness equipment. The presence in the camp of three French boxing champions made boxing popular. They gave private lessons and helped build a ring that met official specifications. The utility room between the two halves of the barracks served as an office for the captain, who had organized the* Cercle *and directed its activities. In the exercise room, a couple of professional trainers taught physical education for teachers with the intention of awarding certificates.*[13] *The officer POWs' goal was always to make their time as prisoners worthwhile in anticipation of their return home.*

The men were also keenly aware that they needed to keep fit despite the lack of food. A regular column in le Canard *gave precise instructions for exercises, encouraging every officer to keep a regular schedule. They organized competitions, giving ornate cups at the end—usually made of paper—to mimic normal life as much as possible.*

As spring became summer, they began building a stadium, which opened in mid–August.

It was complete with tracks for short and long distances, areas for high, long, and vault jumps, basketball and volleyball courts, and disc weight-throw areas. One officer POW remarked that despite the description the stadium was still somewhat primitive.

The Durs *continually plotted to escape, despite the fact that escaping from a camp so deep in central Europe was a daunting enterprise. On the whole, very few made it back to France. But as soon as they were caught, they planned their next escape.*

7 August—Opening night at the theater, *After the Rain Good Weather*, a slapstick comedy, 1820s style: In the director's office used as a dressing room, Captain G., make-up stick in hand, brightens Angelique's freshly shaved cheeks with a scarlet red glow. In underwear, Lieutenant B. fastens two breasts of a young virgin's size on his hairy chest. Next to him, Dame Hortense cautiously combs "her" English curled wig made of hemp, while on the side Aunt Virginie, smoking "her" pipe nonchalantly, allows F. the dressmaker, to fit a huge dress, to cutting and slashing. Away from the uninitiated spectators, Buzard, financier without guts, hidden between a row of costumes and a pile of academic hats, tries out over half a dozen cynical grins in front of a cracked mirror.

8. La Semaine de France (the French Week)

"Hurry up in there, we start in two minutes!" yells the stage director, who runs backstage where the stagehands are finishing work on a secondary stage of painted wood and colored cardboard. Catastrophe, followed by a loud f...; the leg of a stool has just pierced the scenery that Rams repairs speedily by gluing a new paper. The public stamps their feet impatiently, while the two silent authors, green with stage fright, gaze over this prologue and bite their nails.

9 August—The Vets are leaving single file with a military band leading the way. They pass through the outer gate, the one that opens to freedom. Suitcases in hand or packs on their backs, they are trying to march in step in spite of their exhilaration and in spite of their load. As they march away, their eyes are constantly turned toward us who are left behind the barbed wire and must appear like insects. We wave handkerchiefs as good bye. At intervals, the somber blasts of the full sound of drums, bugles, and shouts come our way: "Goodbye ... Goodbye...." Climbing half way on the barbed wire, a big rogue tirelessly proclaims in a powerful voice: "So long old geezers ... so long old geezers...." Names are yelled until they reach their destination, and in return the faithful wind carries a shout or a goodbye. Little by little this swell subsides. Already, the column walks along the pine forest, which walls in the horizon.

Soon, we catch only a few weak vibrating sounds in occasional wind gusts. There is nothing left only an empty road. The desolate human herd resumes its dreary round in our field.

8 p.m. "They are down below! At the *Vorlager*!"—"That's not possible." Correct....

"There were no trains in Göpfritz." They have come back dragging their disappointment, their weariness, and their luggage. This luggage made and made over again with such love, in view of a departure that was pushed back ... and pushed back.

11 August—After two nights in the *Vorlager*, the World War I Veterans have permanently left at dawn, without drumbeat or bugle.

The repatriation of the World War I Veterans, in addition to liberating the men born before 1 January 1900, became an unexpected golden opportunity for the officer POWs who were left behind. Once back in France, the Vets made contact with the families of the prisoners, bringing them codes to be used in the letters, mostly to ask for forbidden items, and special signs to be placed on packages containing compromising articles. Codes were often simple grids such as the first letter of each line, or a small space between characters, which put together, allowed a knowledgeable reader to reconstitute an important phrase in the middle of an inconsequential one. *The signs on a package were to help take packages out before they came in front of the censors.*

The clandestine photographer, who had managed to keep a still camera from being confiscated during the numerous searches, had also dreamed of making a film with a friend who owned a camera. One of his comrades, a World War I Veteran, was charged with asking his friend's wife to give the camera to his wife, who would then send it to her husband. He did receive the camera and made a film, which was shown after the war.[14]

The repatriation of the World War I Veterans presented a particularly important opportunity for La Maffia group, as one of its members happened to be a World War I Vet. Taking with him the addresses of the families of La Maffia members, he instructed them on how to address the compromising packages. He then oversaw the shipment of special packages over the years. The packages were to be addressed to a Lieutenant Gedet (Gedet was the anagram of G.D., the initials of George Durant, who was the World War I Vet) with a matriculation number belonging to one of the prisoners who had died.[15] A member of La Maffia was one of the twenty officer POWs in the mailroom; he became the man in charge of diverting packages.

My father also took advantage of the return of the Vets, as it became clear to him that he would remain prisoner for some time. What he could not do personally he would do by proxy. Continuing the work he had started in Nuremberg, by July he had prepared for publication two more books in Edelbach: one, Alfred de Vigny's Poèmes de la mer *(Poems of the Sea)*, with charcoal illustrations, and the other, Voltaire's Zadig *with watercolor illustrations. In publishing these books his goal was to show that "despite their grief, ruins, and personal misery, the officer POWs had preserved their morale, energy, and will to live, in order to prepare a better future."*[16] He gave the proofs of the three books to a returning Veteran, who contacted my mother and with her help gave them to a printer in France. The books came out in 1942 with the drawing of a barbed wire as a logo on the cover. The first book was duly inscribed as having been prepared in Nuremberg and the last two in Edelbach.

18 August—The wheel turns. All minds are focused on a major artistic event, *La Semaine de France*. In the honeycombs and the empty barracks, individual craftsmen improvise. The Vienna Headquarter delivers rolls of paper, reams of cardboard, brushes, and tubes of paints [It is likely that they paid for it]. The robust ones lift the rolls on their shoulders and pile them in front of Barracks 21, the future exhibition hall.

In the meantime the Chleuhs advance in Russia, where they have just taken Smolensk.

8. La Semaine de France (the French Week)

24 August—Festival: The stadium is inaugurated under a bright sun with a brass band, coordinated movement, human pyramids, parallel bars, basketball, eighty meter races, relay races, and athletes with suntanned bodies. Twenty-five cubic meters of earth have been moved, representing eighteen thousand hours of work. The stadium is a welcomed creation with its white fences and high portico, but always that gnawing thought: we are settling in!

4 September—It is impossible to describe the exhibition in Barracks 21. It is the high point of *La Semaine de France,* the living synthesis of French art, craftsmanship and thought: picturesque mosaic, which portrays on a small scale the essence of each province, its sights, the variety of its products, and the originality of its costumes. It represents the miracle of the artwork of thousands of men, who, for weeks, have kept whole a strong faith. They have embodied all their memories, their skills, and their power in order to re-create the image of the absent fatherland. With the exception of photos, books, and objects of the homeland, received in the packages, everything has been created on site: decorations of the booths, murals, dioramas, watercolors, and models. Architects, artists, sculptors, engineers, professors, and craftsmen have worked side by side to make this a success.

Should we see in this cultural and artistic manifestation an act of defiance thrown to the enemy, the revenge against an unearned fate, and a victory over all the accumulated hurdles to act obstructing our path? Without doubt also, there is a desire to dazzle the Chleuhs, to show them that, in spite of the whip and the barbed wire, the Frenchman keeps a powerful potential in reserve.

From morning to evening a throng of officers swarms around the booths: one dreams in front of the miniature portal of a cathedral, another raves about a model farm, moved to tears by the contemplation of a simple peasant headdress.

The stated goal of La Semaine de France *was ambitious: "To express faith in the future of France by building on (our) past and tradition."*[17] *It became the largest exhibition of the five years, lasting twenty-one days. The exhibits consisted of a great variety of mediums: large panels, frescoes, mock-ups, scale models, and exposés. One officer had built a full-size loom on which he wove a tapestry. A collection of drawings by caricaturists spread over a large panel. There were photos, drawings, and sculptures. One half of the barracks was dedicated to stands, each with a specific focus: The Education stand depicted activities from pre-school to higher education, and another, titled Thought, exhibited a sample of a fake Carolingian manuscript and thirteenth century printing. The Architecture exhibit had mock-up models of many styles of cathedral vaults—The*

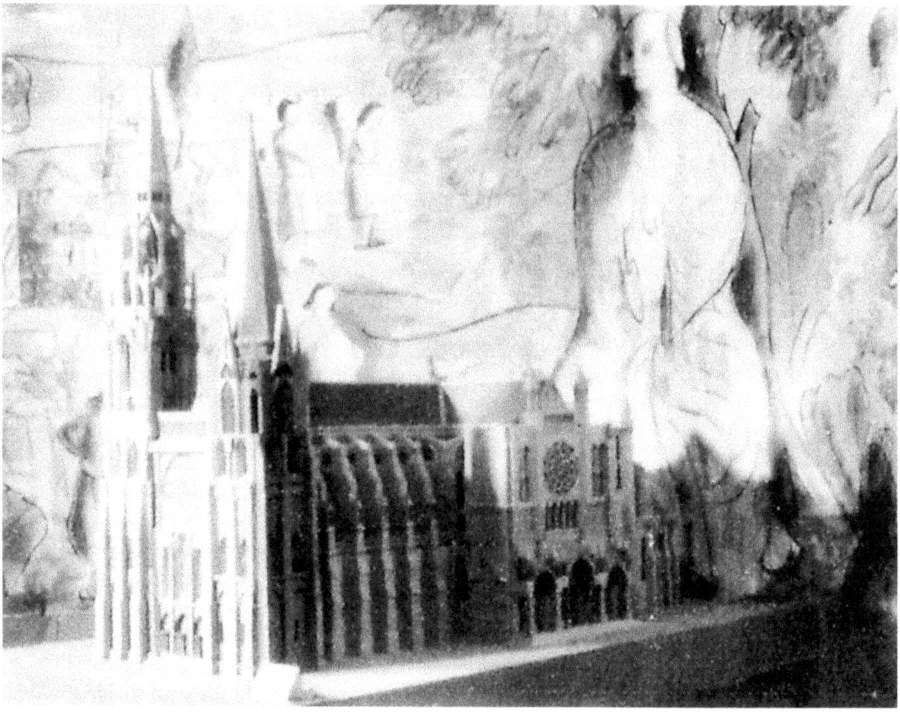

AFRIQVE NC
SENEGAL. NIGER. SOVDAN
DAHOMEY. MAVRITANIE
COTE D'IVOIR
TCHAD

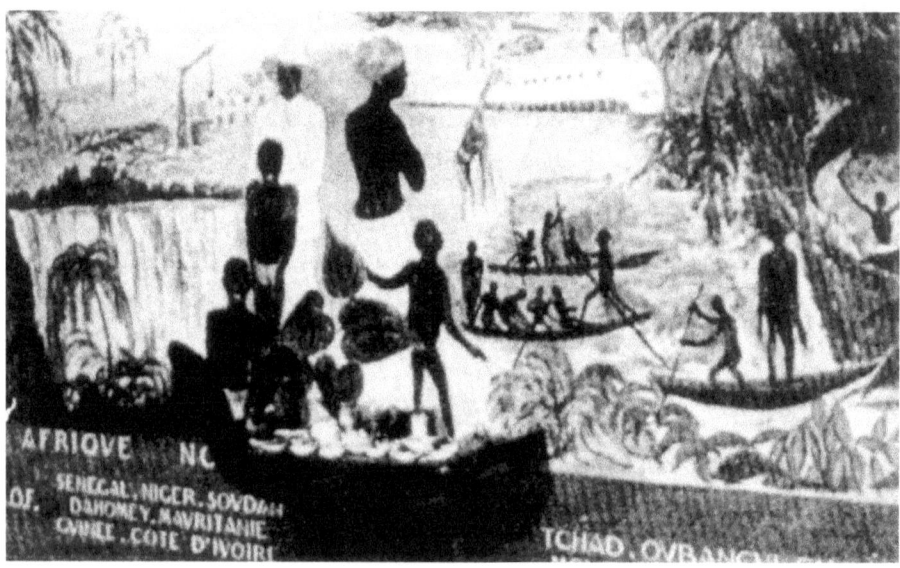

8. La Semaine de France (the French Week)

cathedrals of Notre Dame and of Chartres were meticulously reproduced—as well as provincial houses, and The Decorative Arts displayed a tapestry. The Agriculture display described the organization of a farm. The Industry corner, stunning with its red and black contrasts, depicted a mine, while the Colonies exhibit reproduced the atmosphere of faraway places: a Buddha sculpture made of clay, a pagoda, a minaret, rice plantations, deserts, and dense forests.

The other half of the barrack was dedicated to the provinces: le Canard

These four illustrations are part of the big exhibit called La Semaine de France. They are all done by the officer POWs. *Opposite top:* Model of the Cathedral of Chartres: A scale model of the cathedral made of cardboard from photographs with some fresco in the background. *Bottom:* Mural: A mural honoring the French colonies in Africa. *Right:* Buddha: A statue sculpted in clay. *Below:* Languedoc Dances: Men, some costumed as women, dancing the traditional dance of the region of Languedoc (all images from *le Canard*, special December 1941 issue, Austrian National Library, Vienna).

called it *"Le Tour de France in two hundred sixty two feet." Of particular significance was the Corsican corner. At a time when Italy was trying to claim Corsica for herself, the Corsicans had drawn a colorful fresco with the inscription saying in part:* "With all our soul, we pledge to live and die, Frenchmen." *The Southwest displayed a collection of dolls, wearing their rich-colored costumes, a scale model of a model farm, and of a port.*

The open-air theater, built for the occasion, used a gentle slope of a small hill for seating with a stage at the bottom. The men, wearing local provincial costumes—men and women apparels—presented provincial dances and music. There were theater productions, concerts, and lectures, and at the end, an elegant soirée, which was a gala for fundraising.

In the concluding lecture, "La France Eternelle," *the speaker declared,* "Our long captivity has not shaken our invincible faith in our destiny, and the inspiring splendor of our Semaine de France *has expressed the most eloquent testimony of the vitality of our country. In the crucible of suffering, the France of yesterday is the foundation of a new soul giving birth to the France of tomorrow.*"¹⁸

6 September—*Foire du Trône* or festival at *Neuneu* ? [Well-known yearly fair] The genial vulgar joy of a merrymaking populace spills over the enclosure of the fairground. Hoisted to the top of poles, banners vibrate in the wind, the rhythmic beat of the bands and the guttural voices of the hucksters all blend in a harsh cacophony: frenzied fair, where trainers and wizards move about, shooting games, archery, lotteries, the Edelbach-Barnum circus and its beautiful Fatima. Miraculous fishing.... Who has not won before will win now! At the Two Pigeons pastry shop, one finds doughnuts, toffee, and lollipops. Let's taste them in the bistro, enhanced by a thimbleful of white wine, the first glass in sixteen months! It feels good to spend our Lager-marks in the way we threw coins on the merry-go-round and the swings of the *Foire du Trône*, a long time ago.

8 September—Everything comes at the same time: opening of a movie theater in an unused barracks south of the camp. Pleasant surprise of a comfortable room brought to completion by Frenchmen.

15 September—*La Semaine de France* has come to an end, leaving us somewhat dazed by all the creative spirit it revealed. The matinees of folklore in the *Theatre de Verdure* [open-air theater] have allowed us in a few hours of accumulated evocation to revive our provincial soul expressed in its dances and songs. Glorious fresco!¹⁹

La Semaine de France has already collected 700,000 frs., which will be given to the National Art Institute. We would like to reach one million. A half barracks has been converted into an auditorium, thanks to the masterstrokes of

8. La Semaine de France (the French Week)

our decorators. The hall and bar are streaming with light. No bartenders but better, a barmaid! Or so it seems. Soirée in full-dress uniform. The Minuet of Couperin is presented in costume of the times. Also on the program: shadow theater, games, and entertainment.

During this entire week the theater performed special performances of *Le Cid* [Corneille} and *Barberine* [Alfred de Musset], the university presented literary matinées, and the symphony orchestra gave concerts. In the stadium, there were soccer matches, of pelote basque [traditional Basque sport], rugby exhibition, and for the finale a splendid athletics assembly.

One more entertainment outlet opened during La Semaine. *The POWs, who went regularly to Edelbach to perform sundry duties for the Germans, had noticed that the old movie theater in Edelbach was not being used, since Edelbach was empty of its inhabitants. Seeing an opportunity, the French Commandant proposed to the Germans to install the seats of the old theater into an empty barn in the back of the camp. The Kommandant, who was also very glad to have some entertainment, agreed to the proposal as long as the French did the work. The POWs were charged with getting the seats, which, even though old, were judged much more comfortable than the stools, the only seats available in the camp. The officer POWs installed them and painted the walls with paint provided by the Germans. The Germans obtained a good set of projectors and a screen. Sunday was reserved exclusively for the Germans, and the rest of the week was for the prisoners with a few German officers always in attendance. As part of the deal, current events, which promoted the war successes of the German Army, were shown before the films. The films were in German, with simultaneous translation by a French Alsatian officer. As a bonus the officer POWs used the sound equipment to play recorded music with discs they received from a variety of organizations.*[20]

29 September—Waking up in a dry nippy cold that already bites; L., bending down with his head under the bunk, pulls out a pullover from his suitcase. D. buttons his coat and grumbles: "Eh! Guys, we are still good for one winter." Winter! We had forgotten it. Silence weighs on the group. What a steep fall after the exciting days of festivals! With summer the last fires of *La Semaine de France* have been extinguished and "normal" life resumes, a hateful life from which nothing can be expected. A taste of ashes returns. It feels like we have searched to temporarily forget all our pain in the multiple games.

Some three hundred men found a positive way to channel their dejection. Immediately after La Semaine de France, *they organized a Santa Claus workshop, working on an endeavor close to their hearts: doing something for the children from whom they were separated and could not participate in their lives. They set a goal of creating fifteen hundred toys, finish them in a few weeks' time, and send them to the French government to be distributed to children of prisoners of war at Christmastime. After obtaining an empty barracks, they rigged up working surfaces and organized an assembly line to speed up the process.*

They used wood they could find in the camp: planks from boxes, wood from poplars, beech, and pine trees. One group planed and smoothed surfaces with made-up instruments, then another group cut and chiseled them into pieces of different shapes with pocket knives. Further down the line, a third group painted the pieces, passing them on to those who finally assembled the different shapes to make animals: jumping jacks, carts, pull toys, little wagons, and puzzles. A complete farm exhibited all the farm animals, including horses pulling carts. A hutch full of rabbits moved their legs to jump, run, crouch, and crawl. Donkeys and elephants moved their heads and tails when pulled. The puzzles represented different French landscapes, they copied from pictures sent from home. They finished quickly, packed the toys, and sent them early November.[21] *To each toy was affixed a sticker saying: "Offered by the Oflag XVIIA for your Christmas tree."*

But France was an occupied country, and the packages did not arrive until February. Nonetheless, it made somewhat of a sensation. The French exhibited the toys and decided to give them for Easter. A reporter describing the exhibit wrote: "Before Christmas, officers who are prisoners in Oflag XVIIA, using the

The men organized a Santa's Workshop, making toys to be sent to France and given to children of prisoners like themselves (*le Canard*, February 1942, Austrian National Library, Vienna).

8. La Semaine de France (the French Week)

means on hand, had the touching thought of creating toys for the little French children whose fathers are captives like them. One can imagine with how much affection they worked on these toys, intended to entertain the children of their brothers in exile, perhaps dreaming that these playthings would by chance find the heart of their own little ones. Fate is sometimes very kind."[22]

The reporter extensively described all the different toys and their background, particularly those representing specific French scenes. She ended:

"The crowning achievement is a board game called 'La Promenade Impériale,' a big board, which opens to show the five continents of the world against a marine blue background. The action is similar to the jeu d'oie[23] (game of the goose) and visits our French colonial empire. Each traveler has a ship, a locomotive, an airplane, and a car. The longest trip wins. The adventures are varied, evocative of the most beautiful colonies and their treasures, and cannot but awaken in our children the desire to go visit these faraway places.... One cannot think without emotion of the loving pride for our larger France, which must have guided this captive soldier to create a game that carries such a pure aura of patriotism. These toys made with love for their kids, faraway in their country, emanate the longing for their homeland and pride in our Empire."

9

Barbed Wire Blues
October 1941–May 1942

13 October—A seasonally premature cold brings snow. We have the good fortune of hearing the "soft" voice of Hitler, subjecting us to the usual saber rattling and the promises of unprecedented events before winter. The Chleuhs claim to have reached the suburbs of Moscow. We are getting less coal than last year. Odd!

17 October—Mr. Loyal experienced the most harrowing night of his career; fourteen men are missing at the morning roll call. The watchtowers have a fortunate defect, which the prisoner, astute observer, has not failed to notice. At night, the towers create a zone of darkness, which protects the prisoner from the light of the projectors. At about 7 p.m. a small resolute group, taking the opportunity of these shadows and of the throng of walkers, opened a gap between the feet of the watchtower which keeps watch over the central alley. They were followed immediately by a few amateurs of the out-of-doors, enticed by the lure of an extramural walk.

We are subjected to the usual reprisals.

30 October—With the heavy snowfall the stoves, surrounded by the same customers, are kindled and endless discussions resume touching on different themes, but led by the same participants. Dreadful feeling of déja vu and deadly repetition of what has already been said and heard: myth of liberation, false promises, and so much nonsense that we could join the old fogies.

At the end of 1940, a few months after being taken prisoner, the endless discussions centered on the defeat of the French Army. In 1941 the discussions were likely to reflect the various intense political factions which would overshadow the life of the camp for the coming months, but were never explicitly expressed in the diary. After the change of format, the regular articles in le Canard *detailed*

Marshal Pétain's changes in the governance of France. One by one, the articles described the basic tenets of each of the decrees promulgated by the Vichy government in the second half of 1940, representing Pétain's vision for the future French government, the so-called New Order, which would establish La Révolution Nationale *(the National Revolution)*. These were wide-ranging and breathtaking changes designed to restructure industry, commerce, agriculture, education, the family, and women's place in France.

A historian wrote, *"It is not easy to define* La Révolution Nationale. *Historians have spilled a lot of ink arguing whether it was fascist or authoritarian. It was neither, but some of both."*[1] *In* le Canard *one of the officer POWs expressed the general unease, simply noting that Marshal Pétain remained somewhat of an enigma, and in a noncommittal way concluded, "Let everyone respond as he thinks."*[2] *Over these articles, there often was a more partisan personal message praising Marshal Pétain and enjoining everyone to follow him as their revered leader.*

At about the same time, one officer noted that pamphlets of Pétain's speeches were distributed in the camp. One speech addressed the POWs: "Prisoners, my friends and children, I think about you with all my affection and congratulate you for your noble courage." Another was addressed to the families. "I think about them [POWs] because they suffer, they fought to the extreme limit of their strength, and it is because they stood their ground that they fell in enemy hands. Let their mothers, wives, and daughters know that I keep them in my thoughts, as they too are my children!"[3] *The men, however, knew that Pétain was doing nothing to liberate them, and censored French newspapers spread lies about the relative comfort of the prisoner of war camps.*

Titled "Principles and Tendencies of the Pétain Legislation," a series of articles assessed the intellectual basis of the proposed changes, and described their applications, establishing a complete change in governance. A new motto, "Work, Family, Fatherland," replaced the French Republic's "Liberty, Equality, Fraternity." "His politics included authoritarian and exclusionist principles that called for the elimination of democracy."[4] *More articles praising Marshal Pétain effusively followed soon after. The P.R. campaign was in full swing.*

The intellectual and moral revivalist tone pervading the justification for the New Order of the National Revolution found a receptive audience with a number of officer POWs, who had accepted their suffering as a way to transform their lives to be better persons in the future. Some, however, interpreted it in a very different way. An officer wrote: "Moral revival is a matter of personal human transformation. Changes in the institutions will not *produce a New France. Change will be realized by a new virtue in the hearts of French men and* women.... *Our goal should not be to repudiate our past, but to relate to our best traditions, and to follow in the footsteps of the best of our saints, heroes, and heroines."*[5]

The Germans added more pressure on the officer POWs, ordering to plaster color posters of a portrait of Marshal Pétain all over the camp, in the barracks and the public areas. Red Cross packages, which had previously been labeled, "Beef from the Red Cross," or "Tuna from the Red Cross," were now labeled, "Beef Pétain, Cigarettes Pétain, Preserves Pétain" prompting one of the men to quip, "Has the Marshall become a butcher, a grocer, and a Tobacco store owner!"[6]

The division of the early summer became more pronounced with the radicalization of Marshal Pétain's supporters, who joined together to form La Légion du Maréchal. An officer wrote, "Here suspicion and denouncing reign supreme. These rather disreputable officer POWs go much further than the obligatory collaboration with the Marshal and completely betray France in the hope of being liberated."[7] On the other side, La Maffia was more intent than ever on monitoring the members of La Légion and punishing the transgressors.[8] For the overwhelming majority in the middle, there were various shades of commitment, and uncertainty about Pétain, whom they still respected as an individual, while rejecting his politics.[9] One officer asked: "Could such a prestigious leader deceive the French?"[10]

On 2 November the officer POWs held special services and military honors in the cemetery in remembrance of their comrades who had died for their country. In the southeast corner of the camp, a small gate opened to the Edelbach cemetery, a section of which was reserved for the French who died in the camp; at the end of 1941, there were twenty officer POWs buried there. In the morning, the camp chaplain conducted three separate worship services inside the camp; one for each of the different branches of the military. In the afternoon, the French Commandant and a delegation of officer POWs were allowed in the cemetery with the German Kommandant. The camp orchestra played the Funeral March of Beethoven's Third Symphony, followed by the blessing of the tombs by the chaplain and a Polish priest. The short service ended "with a bugle playing taps, a call made more moving by the circumstances."[11] They marched past the camp Kommandant and the Commandant to the tune of Chopin's Funeral March.

15 November—Snow, snow, and more snow, a white cuddly toy softly pads the windowpanes, which become translucent. Moscow continues holding and the Chleuhs stall. The V.B. initiates a big campaign to gather furs, woolens, and coats to send to the Russian front. Was this old son-of-a-gun

9. Barbed Wire Blues

C.H. right? Beware of the unforgiving Russian winter! Here, there is nothing worth noting after the tremendous effort of *La Semaine de France*. Everything seems to solidify into a definitive shape. We take refuge more and more in the protective web of habits, and the physical slowdown, caused by winter, encourages the resumption of intellectual life. Reading is the universal pastime. The library, expanded by new collections [sent by the Red Cross], is now the proud owner of five to six thousand volumes. In addition, a number of barracks have their own library, and as a general rule, each prisoner owns personal study books and bookstores' latest bestsellers. After an extraordinary popularity, detective novels suffer an eclipse and the craze moves on to novels in English [*Gone with the Wind, Rebecca, Sparkenbroke*, and Pearl Buck]. French classics retain their devotees, but modern authors have their fanatics, in particular Proust and Giraudoux. Adventure novels, historical chronicles and travel stories are the books of choice. We need to wander intellectually in time and space.

20 November—The university is not the self-conscious debutante it was some time ago. Having acquired with age an official sanction, it is the hub, which attracts the cultural life. There is a very clear distinction between classes and conferences, between the student and the auditor. The numbers of study circles have greatly increased, including cosmography, botany, prehistory, and paleontology..., and poets. The Alma Mater of Oflag XVIIA is also the center of one of the most active groups: the pedagogic circle of elementary school teachers, six hundred members strong, full of energy and fire.

4 December—In the gray end-of-the-year, a cabaret opens its door, appropriately called *La Volière* [The Aviary]. It looks like a small elegant establishment of Montparnasse or Montmartre, [two Parisian artistic centers], adorned with the cozy charm of a pink and blue candy jar, the Cage, where a bird made of gold paper with a big beak sings itself hoarse. It is a darling of a cage, which allows us to transcend the symbolism of the sign.

De C. ... introduces the songwriters with a sharp voice and piercing eyes behind his glasses: G., nicknamed Tonton [Nickname for uncle], all meek belly D., coldly cantankerous, and P., a caustic spirit, a poet, and imitator is a perfect Victor Boucher. H., the very high-class director, circulates between the tables and shakes hands. The service is impeccable. The same cannot be said of the beverages: Lager Bier! [Lager in German means camp]. The audience is golden.

La Volière, utilizing the talents of the community, was conceived as an elegant cabaret to counteract the winter doldrums. The symbolism of an aviary was very explicit in le Canard*'s introduction of* La Volière. *The writer declared* *that one cannot—or should not—imprison birds in a cage "because they need to spread their wings." He continued, "They find freedom only when the door is open. And so are men made to be free. We turn without end inside our narrow prison. Our cage does not even have the smooth bars (of birds' cages) but our bars are like an iron cactus, products of war with thousands of menacing sharp points that tears our clothing and hands."* La Volière *was a smashing success, thanks to the décor, the live show, and the care taken in reproducing for the men, "the illusion of being free in an upscale cabaret in France."*[12]

7 December—Japan attacks the United States in Pearl Harbor, and Great Britain in Singapore and Hong Kong.

8 December—The United States enter the war. Strategists and tacticians face off around the stove in a huge oratory squabbling. Rise of a tremendous hope.

11 December—Germany and Italy declare war on the United States.

15 December—There are women in the camp! The news is dependable; the enlisted men [POWs], who work in the *Vorlager*, have seen them with their own eyes. Alas! They are only guards. Even worse, they are the harpies, who are charged with censoring our meager letters, taking the place of the Wehrmacht soldiers who have left to strengthen the Russian front. Poor Anastasie! How sweet and affectionate you seem next to these would be Valkyries.

The officer POWs were infuriated by the way these women censored their letters and those of their families. Not only did they block their families' information of life in France, but also blocked their expressions of affections and love. They also blocked out or returned the men's letters when they mentioned their hunger and cold, enforcing the prohibition against mentioning their poor living condition.

Naming the women censors Anastasies *was a purposeful choice. For almost 150 years the French had used the name* Anastasie *as a code word to mean censure, particularly, the control of information by the state. In 1874 the cartoonist André Gill drew a malicious-looking woman holding a pair of huge scissors, with an owl, a bird of prey of the night, on her shoulder, and the old fashioned hat of a concierge, often seen as an informant for the police. He gave her the name* Anastasie, *a popular name in the slapstick comedies of the time.* Madame Anastasie *became the archetypical incarnation of arbitrary removal of public liberties. Another satirist enlarged her family when the war ministry instituted a special information department; members of the cabinet acquired new names: her mother became Seraphine Inquisition, two cousins were named Vicomte Butor de St. Arbitraire and Agathe Stamp.*

Then, as soon as France was under siege in 1914, when the government censored all the newspapers, the satirical weekly Le Canard enchaîné *revived her Dame Anastasie. Finally,* Anastasie *was reborn once more under the Vichy Regime during World War II.*[13]

In its 4 December 1939 issue, Time Magazine, writing about the censure of French newspapers, described Anastasie *as a haggard, crotchety old maid with an immense pair of shears, "a characteristic creation of Gallic wit," they said. Time had its own interpretation of her origin, however. She was named, it claimed, after St. Anastasia, who had her tongue cut out for resisting the advances of Roman Emperor Valerian, who was in love with her. She shunned him and after many adventures, she took refuge in a convent, disguised as a eunuch. There is a* Sainte Anastasie, *but in the French Catholics' story, she is pursued by Emperor Justinian.*

Madame Anastasie. A cartoon which came to signify censorship of newspapers drawn by a satirist to lampoon the censorship imposed by the government after the Franco-German war of 1870-71. It was revived in different forms for every war thereafter (André Gill, 19 July 1874, L'Éclipse).

20 December—After a short closure, the theater announces the performance of *Volpone* [The Big Fox by Ben Johnson] in a hall updated to contemporary taste with appliqués of white ironworks made of cardboard and painted paper. The rows are built in tiers. The widened stage is fitted with the latest technical equipment. The performances gain in boldness and increasingly break away from amateurism. G., the stage manager, is well known for his cheeky humor, his powerful voice, and the thickness of his shell glasses.

December 31—The five hundred forty fifth notch is etched with the tip of a knife in the board of the bunk. That will be the last. What are the use of this childish counting and depressing expression of days empty of substance? Let the days accumulate side by side like a thread that lengthens and glides between the fingers.

1942

The men were on the threshold of a bleak and tumultuous year. The Germans were winning all the battles and had reduced the allocation of food and heating fuel at a time when the winter was particularly harsh. The mesh of barbed wire encircling the camp between the barracks and the fields was a constant reminder of their loss of freedom.

At the beginning of 1942, my father wrote what he could have titled "Barbed Wire Winter Lament." "We all know now that the landscape will not change. It is engraved in an indelible way on our eyes and mind. The monotone and docile rows of barracks will not change, for days, weeks, perhaps months. Also remaining the same are the sand and asphalt, walked over in an endless circle. Remaining the same and without end is the true orgy of the regular warp and woof of the vast fabric woven by the barbed wire, which places between us and freedom a transparent barrier, yet an absolutely insurmountable and relentless one, beyond which the eye can easily see, but cannot honestly eliminate."[14]

In its role of cheerleader, le Canard *posted in the first issue of 1942, "We wish you a happy year in 1942, the year of our liberation!" Yet, it added, "We never planned to post these wishes, having counted on* le Canard *being of short duration." And reinforcing their longing, there were two snails, at the bottom of the article: 1940 was written on one shell and 1941 on the other. Little did they know they would not be liberated until 1945.*

Inside that issue was a sixteen-page booklet describing the purpose and activities of the newly opened Centre Pétain. *The Vichy Government requested that this brochure be distributed in all the camps. As anything dealing with politics, the Center's opening is not mentioned in the diary. The booklet revealed that* le Canard's *articles, in the summer and fall, had been used for weekly discussions called* Cercles d'Etudes, *taking place once a week throughout the camp during the second half of 1941. It also detailed the Center's resources and activities, brazenly declaring that these* Cercles *were the center of activities in the camp, as proof of the "living incarnation of the camp's unity behind Marshal Pétain."*

The Centre Pétain, *occupying one half of a barracks, was stacked with numerous pamphlets and literature about the establishment of Pétain's new form of government for France and promoted Marshal Pétain's personality cult, extolling his unassuming attitude, honesty, hard work and tenacity, common sense, and frank language. It promoted such pamphlets as: "Think of the leader who loves you" (*Pensez au chef qui vous aime*).*[15] *One section of the center, advertised as a "comfortable reading room," served as a library for all journals, books, newspapers, and speeches about Marshal Pétain, while another section* was reserved for daily lectures and discussions, focused each week on one specific aspect of the National Revolution. These discussions were the core of the Center's existence, designed to provide the political education of the officer POWs, engaging them in discussions of the implementation of the New Order, the radical reforms of French institutions, political parties, and the economy.[16]

Part two of the booklet, called "The Doctrine of the Marshall, Gospel and Discipleship of the Legionnaire," spelled out the planned indoctrination of the men into La Légion du Maréchal. The disciplines of the legionnaire could be subsumed under one imperative: Obey the Marshal (Pétain) unconditionally, and become a propagandist for him. Pétain exhorted the officer POWs: "Follow me without reserve on the path of honor and national interest," adding "I hate the lies, which have hurt the country so much. I will never lie." Marshal Pétain was very up front about what he was doing. Indeed, he laid out an entire program, which openly implemented an autocratic state, and made no secrets of collaborating, but declared, "It is collaboration with honor and dignity."

Using his speeches, La Légion *laid out how his collaboration was commensurable with honor and dignity. Would the officer POWs who were struggling mightily to uphold their honor and live with dignity in a humiliating environment, agree that honor and dignity were compatible with collaborating with an enemy, who held them captive?*

When the Center opened, interest seemed to have been high. Vichy was considered the legal French government, to which the officer POWs were accountable. (The United States also made it clear that it considered Vichy the legal French government. Admiral Leahy remained U.S. ambassador to the Vichy government until April 1942.) In August 1941 Time Magazine wrote, "There was no question of U.S. recognition of Free France, since Free France is not a government."

For some of the men, the Center's activities could have sparked curiosity, or be a response to simple boredom or pressure from being prisoners. There also was what seemed to be a small group of "Ultra Petainists," who, for their own benefit, would report to the Germans their fellow prisoners who were against Pétain.

21 January—It has been bitter cold for days, zero degrees Fahrenheit on the thermometer of Barracks 7. We are reduced to an impoverished, withdrawn life. A winter day is identical to the preceding winter day with today's schedule looking like yesterdays. Our existence resembles one in the monastery, or is it the university, or the garrison, but even more so, without doubt, the prison.

5 February—The *theatre de verdure* [open-air theater] is the site for ski lessons. A few fanatics practice christianas. At the movies: two stupid and silly films. At the theater: *Volpone*, and *Un Tour au Paradis*. Concerns run high about a persistent epidemic of typhus in the nearby camps. On the road to Edelbach we saw yesterday two Russian prisoners who were carrying to the cemetery the body of one of their comrades, disjointed like a marionette.

9 February—Letters and packages are held back and the theater and movies are closed; two officers escaped by walking out with the "workers" [French conscripts] who work at the ski workshop in Edelbach. Immediate retaliation: first, the skis will be collected [they quickly disappear], as will also the Tyrolean backpacks [they also promptly disappear]. There will be no individual liberation granted for three months.

17 February—A big snowfall covers the ground. There is no water in the washbasins and because the supply of coal is depleted, the common spaces such as the theater and the university will not be heated anymore. That's the way it is, they say, in the schools and auditoriums in Vienna. Excellent! A laughable rumor runs through the camp: upcoming liberation of four classes.

One of the clandestine pictures shows graphically the extent of the harshness of the winter; feet of snow covering the ground, huge icicles hanging from the eaves of the barracks all the way to the ground, and barbed wire covered with ice, looking like the gigantic web of a fairy tale castle. On its front page, le Canard *printed the gracious picture of a snow statue, the nude torso of a woman a la Venus de Milo (second century Greek statue, named after a Greek island, recognized as representing Aphrodite), leaning against a big stone of ice. The caption: "The Frigid Woman."*

The skis were probably smuggled into the camp by the POWs.

27 February—Some good news circulates very discreetly among us: the Russians have kept up their offensive and recaptured Mojaisk. It must be true, judging from the black mood and malice of our jailers. Vicious searches and unpleasantness have resumed with full vigor. However, the distribution of packages under the dreamy supervision of the sentries we have christened *Cassecroute* [Quick-lunch], because of his bulimia, and another, *Coupe-Racine* [Root-Cutter], because of his Jackrabbit look, borders on a big joke. Specialists with "sticky fingers" steal everyday tens of packages, which contain precious riches in their inner depth: compasses, maps, civilian clothes, radios, photographic devices, pliers, false identity papers. P. … is the chief hunter with several hundreds of successful thefts. He has an office and operates for the benefit of others.

The big joke like most jokes carried a kernel of truth, if not the whole truth. Claiming that tens of packages were diverted every day was a gross exaggeration, but perhaps a way to hide a few facts. Remember, the diarist always had to consider being discovered. The statement "the distribution of packages under the dreamy supervision" of Cassecroute *and* Coupe-Racine *was likely a coded way to hide the identity of a couple of anti–Nazi Austrian guards in the mailroom who were willing to collaborate.* La Maffia's *mailman had very skillfully enticed them to look away as he set aside the packages addressed to Lieutenant Gedet with a false matriculation number while sorting out the packages in the storeroom. Before leaving the room, the* La Maffia *mailman would put a package under the big cape of the Alpine Troops and leave without being searched. The system had already introduced a couple more radios in the camp, informing the men of the Russian offensive and the German defeat in Mojaisk,"* the news circulating very discretely among us" (*news not likely printed in German newspapers*). "This courageous man, the specialist with 'sticky fingers,' fulfilled that function for four years, risking his life."[17]

When the packages were flagged, but not retrieved from the storeroom, the prisoners followed another system. After the packages were loaded onto the horse-drawn cart, and as it moved slowly on the gentle grade, a few men would gather around to accompany the cart. As usual, it stopped in front of the window of the barracks, where the packages were to be examined. As was customary, the designated prisoner, under surveillance, threw the packages through the window where another prisoner, also under surveillance, caught them and placed them on a table, where it would be opened and pulled apart. When the prisoner throwing the packages raised his arm, suddenly, a big loud noise filled the air. A prisoner, about thirty feet away and in the middle of a few curious bystanders, banged madly on a large pot. The guard, suspicious, would rush to the group. "Was ist das? Was ist das?" (*What is this?*) Even before he got there, the prisoner in the cart had handed over the package to a waiting comrade, who promptly put it under his invaluable cape, and walked away nonchalantly, the package securely under his arm. By the time the guard returned to his post, the first prisoner was efficiently throwing the remaining packages into the barracks.[18]

The men also found ingenious ways to hide items, particularly in homemade food. To obtain film for his camera, the photographer's wife hid them in sausages. The Germans, aware that something could be hidden in sausages, slashed them repeatedly with heavy knives. Her husband had noticed, however, that, being disciplined, they always probed the sausage in the center. Using an agreed-upon code in a letter, he informed his wife, who hid the films at both ends of the sausage.[19]

During some of the vicious searches, all the men in a barracks were sent outside while the Germans ransacked their belongings, leaving the inside as if a burglar had come in (as seen in one of the clandestine pictures). The bedding was thrown inside out and all the clothes piled in a big heap. Papers were scattered and torn, mess and toilet kits thrown in all directions, and pictures torn to shreds. From the outside, the men would see the Germans stepping on everything. Taking an inventory upon being allowed back in, they found that the chocolate bars, cigarettes, and biscuits sent by the American Red Cross, in scant supply in Germany, had disappeared.[20]

Since the barracks were searched at random, they had to hide anything that was compromising, or be ready to hide the items at a moment's notice. One prisoner, who was particularly anxious to save his knife, which he fondly described as including "blades, a screwdriver, files, a cork opener, little scissors, and a gimlet," recalled how he kept it to the end. When there was a search, he wore it attached to a string, lodged next to a place, he said, "where the searcher would not dare touch without shame."[21]

6 March—We witness a very tough morning for Mr. Loyal, which could have ended tragically.

Five officers, taking advantage of snowdrifts, which hid them from the sight of the watchtowers, crawled to the barbed wire that runs parallel to the cemetery and cut it. Two passed through, a third was between the two fences and two more were getting close when they were noticed. Without warning the sentry opened fire, wounding two of the men. Coming down the central alley behind the stretchers, Mr. Loyal was greeted with a unanimous cry of assassin. As the turmoil grew, the security guards rushed up on the double and cleared the ground, shoving men with bayonet blows on the way. There were multiple arrests, including captain H. ... our duty officer who tried to intervene. Our most seriously wounded comrade got a bullet in his chest, fortunately not a serious wound. But these shots had a repercussion, which Mr. Loyal had not anticipated. They killed the fiction of the magnanimous German, and signaled the end of a doublespeak. Is that what collaboration means?

9 March—Follow up on the last entry. In addition to the usual retaliation, the twenty officers, who were to be repatriated, will not be released because of the escapes. Furthermore, announcement that, since eight hundred officers [POWs] will be arriving soon from Oflag II B, barracks 1 [toys workshop] and Barracks 21, which shelters both the cabaret and the Pétain Center, will be closed. Everybody knows that there is no plan for the arrival of officers, but Mr. Loyal lacks the courage to tell the truth.

The shooting of the officers trying to escape was a turning point, and uncharacteristically the diarist wrote openly of the doublespeak of the meaning of collaboration, signaling a widespread understanding that Pétain's collaboration "with honor and dignity in the national interest" was coming to an end except for a few men. Ousted from Barracks 21, the Ultra Petainists, without their own place, continued to meet outdoors, or in other barracks. Le Canard, *which had regularly published the schedule of the study circles, stopped printing it after the March issue.*

The closure of Barracks 21 had a triple goal: in addition to disbanding the Centre Pétain, *it closed the cabaret,* La Volière. *The organizers of the cabaret required dress uniform or whatever best uniform the men owned, because they said,* "it was important to have a reason for a close shave, nails clipped, and polished shoes in order to find again our true individual personality." La Volière *was so successful in creating an atmosphere of a chic cabaret with well-dressed men that it gave the men the opportunity* "to act in full control of their dignity, fostering the complete illusion for a few hours that they were not prisoners anymore," *observed* le Canard. *The Germans saw it as potentially dangerous. As the men lamented its closure, they put the best spin they could, calling on the original symbolism that birds escape when the door of the cage is open and affirmed that there would be no need of a cabaret the next winter.*[22]

Finally, the main drive to vacate Barracks 21 had a darker purpose, not related to the arrival of officer POWs: the Germans built a wall between the two halves of the barracks, and moved the Jewish officer POWs to one side in an effort to isolate them even more; these men were reduced to one entrance of the barracks without access and contact with the men on the other side of the barracks. "One more humiliating action!" exclaimed one of the Jewish officer POWs, adding: "It has not, however, prevented a whole crowd of comrades to come and visit with us: it is a continual procession. It is so comforting!"[23]

13 March—The chapel is little by little getting a more permanent look. The secondary altars are now embellished with a uniform extreme simplicity, instead of exhibiting an individual appearance. The back of each altar is mounted with a light colored rectangular panel bordered by a brown frame. Set over against it stand a dark cross and each saint's image sculpted in terra cotta. The Stations of the Cross, sculpted in wood, are attached to the sides of the frames and to the chimneys, which are used as heavy pillars. The harmonium has been placed on a platform, and over it, between two French flags, are long panels, set side by side, with a list of our dead on the battlefield.

Our church has retained the humility of its ever-visible planks and kept intact the austere mysticism that emanates from its nakedness.

17 March—The *Kommandantur* has turned down the performance of the Polish ballet, rehearsing in the theater. Reason: "Poland does not exist anymore."

The weather is gorgeous. The sun is thawing the accumulated snow under a clear soft-blue sky. One catches a glimpse of pieces of earth between small islands of dirty snow. The birds are singing. Could spring possibly exist on this miserable earth?

19 March—Crash! An earth mound soaked by the thaw caves in, opening to daylight an underground tunnel close to completion. A group of young men, who dreamed of digging a tunnel, found an optimum location in the most off center barracks from the *Vorlager*. But since the work had to be done at night, whoever worked in the tunnel needed to disappear in order to escape from the roll calls and repeated roll calls. Two of them, who had hid in the camp during a previous escape and were assumed to be escapees, had been listed as missing, which allowed them to work undisturbed. The metro [Tunnel nicknamed after the Paris subway] grew its own good old way, soon passing the lines of the barbed wire. Alas! Everything collapsed in the mud. Our workers forced to give up climbed back to the celestial light and returned to their abode. The situation is now unsolvable; the roll call of their barracks shows two additional men, bedeviling our jailers at a loss how to register them.

24 March—It is cold and dry under a very pure sky. One would like to open wide all the windows and get rid of the lingering odor of grease and clouds of smoke that continually sweep into the barracks through the wide open kitchen door. There, our hapless teary eyed and coughing cooks, bending over a hellish stove, heroically prepare the dish of the day: roux of reheated potatoes, fried cod, beans maison. They are using a remarkable device: *le Cubilo* [they designed and built these small stoves in the camp with old canned food containers]. Made of two cylindrical tin plate tubes, this cleaver instrument is designed to consume the gas produced by the combustion of scraps of wood and paper balls. Designed to prevent smoke, it actually coughs up a heavy and noxious cloud of unbelievable durability.

26 March—Dudule enters: cheesy jaw, sculpted like a chestnut with very prominent cheeks, deep furrows, crooked mouth and sagging lips, stunted frame, a big flat cap and a shoe tread at forty-five degrees. A ruckus erupts. "No Hovations, messieurs, please"—It is Dudule, the number one clown of the *Kommandantur's* murder game as dangerous as his brothers in arms despite his simpleton look [immortalized in the comic strip called Dudule in *le Canard*].

27 March—Is this week's series of searches a fever born of the foretaste of spring? Among the impounded bounty are canned food, saddlebags, straps, color crayons, a bathrobe, and a pajama. Without doubt these are the prizes of war!

2 April—The month closes with a heavy snowfall and a sudden return of winter, but the theater reopens with *Barbara*, light-hearted play executed with dizzy energy by B., the star "vamp," and the passionate gallant C. in the picturesque role of a comical village mayor.

5 April—Easter Sunday: an extended roll call until 1:00 p.m. following an extravagant attempt to escape by Z., who slid into a sack and, with the complicity of the kitchen crew [enlisted men POWs] was lifted onto the flatbed of a supply truck ready to leave the camp. Suspicious, the sentry poked at the sacks. About to be discovered, our man leapt out and running down the central alley, rushed into the first accessible barracks, where he sat down at a table and was served the Pascal bean, which he quietly sampled, while his pursuer panicked in a useless search.

A most important factor in the men's survival was the food, sent by their families or the Red Cross, supplementing the meager German portions. It, however, presented another quandary. There was a great disparity between what families could send, as food was rationed in France. Families in the cities sent what they could, while the families from the countryside sent more substantial provisions. To remedy this inequality, the men pooled the food they received, and creating small popotes *(kitchen groups), cooked it in the small kitchen of the barracks. To accommodate the numerous groups, they fabricated the* cubilos, *ubiquitous stoves found in all the oflags. In addition under the rubric Le Chef,* le Canard *published a regular column of recipes and culinary advice. In one column, with some humor, Le Chef advised his neophytes of when to start the beans, so they would be cooked on time, while making sure the rice would not burn. In another, he gave the recipe for the "real Couscous Oflag." There were a number of colonial officers in the camp.*

On 1 April le Canard, *keeping up with an age-old custom, published a satirical tale making outrageous claims about some events in the camp, signed with the drawing of a fish* (Le poisson, d'avril / April's Fish = April's Fool Day). *Another camp marked the day with a cherished tradition: surreptitiously pinning the big cutout of a fish on the back of a person. The person they chose was a German officer, an arrogant warrant officer, who always insisted on being saluted whenever he passed by. Having succeeded in pinning the cutout without his knowledge, everyone who saw the fish saluted the German with gusto when he passed by, making him stand very tall. No one knows what happened when he entered the German mess hall.*[24]

The effort to root out the stool pigeons in the camp escalated. A notice was posted clandestinely announcing the names of a couple of offending officer POWs, warning of dire consequences. The poster was quickly taken down but a rumor circulated that these men had also been roughed up. The evening communiqué announced that they would be called before an "Honor Court" of ten senior officer POWs, who later decided to bar the offenders from all the camp activities and organizations of the camp.[25]

8 April—In a well-planned attempt at dusk, C. and B., two well-known recidivists, cut the wires of *Petite France*. So they would not be in the line of sight of the watchtowers, a team of bowlers played a raucous game next to the barbed wire, while, to cover the noise of the pliers, a few bold comrades repeatedly kicked the barbed wire network. A hop and a skip and they were outside. "Halt!" shouted the sentry. They ran. The sentry pulled the trigger. Everyone held his breath. They dropped down. Hop! They stood up again and not paying attention to the bullets ran at top speed, ghosts quickly absorbed by the haze.

10 April—Is it a revolt against the slow passage of days without joy and glory and against the useless succession of mornings and evenings? Attempts to escape, ever more daring and clever, have multiplied one after the other, giving our jailers a good reason to call escaping, the sport of the prisoner.

D. … tried using the packaging papers of the packets which are tied together every day in big bales and stacked up in the *Vorlager's* hangar, where they stay until trucks take them to be pulverized. Thanks to certain accomplices, D. was able to fashion a hole in a bale of the stockpile in which like Lavarede [The fearless young hero of L*es Voyages Excentriques* by Paul d'Ivoi, who intended to be compared to Jules Verne] he dreamed of slipping into and shut himself inside. At the appointed time he tried to enter the *Vorlager* in order to get into his moving hideout, only to be stopped before he could even reach it. Found carrying women's clothes, which he planned to wear after exiting his box, the *Abwehr* [counterintelligence unit], always full of humor, made him wear them, and with affability took a picture before sending him to the gniouf for ten days.

11 April—Five accomplices, including Lieutenant C., judging that a trip outside the camp had the potential of offering unsuspected opportunities for freedom, arranged for a way to be sent to a reprisal camp. To that end, they addressed an "anonymous" denunciation to the Gestapo, informing them that a group of thugs, enamored with a "belle," would gather that evening under the kitchen canopy. Faithful to the rendezvous, which they themselves had arranged, they saw their desire fulfilled, as they were surrounded by a patrol, revolver at the ready. A sixth fellow, who innocently chatted with them, was taken in the convoy, and a seventh who was loitering in the area was picked up in the same raid. But this seventh villain was one of those, who had climbed back into the camp in mid–March, [see above] and therefore should not be here, since he was thought to have escaped! This story, already very muddled, became beyond solving in the light of day. It also ended in the gniouf.

18 April—The Wehrmacht is catching up with events and issued a communiqué: "In the event of an escape, weapons will be used without warning against the Russians, and after three notifications, against everybody else." The French POWs, who refuse to work, will be interned in the reprisal camp of Rawa-Rouska [hard labor camp].

23 April—Rain is followed by sad dreary days. Everything is gray, gloomy, and dirty. At the theater, *Topaze*: it does not disappoint with D. who shines in the role of Topaze. An official French newspaper announced that, every year, three million hectoliters of wine in France is requisitioned for the prisoners of war. Where are they? We have not seen them. Our senior spokesman will protest.

26 April—No end to rain, falling day and night. Read sensational news in the V.B.; General Giraud has escaped, and a reward of one hundred thousand marks will be awarded to the person who captures him. A momentous joy spreads throughout the camp. How did he escape from a fortress high up on a mountaintop and a sheer drop? May he succeed!

After the doldrums of winter, spring set in motion numerous escapes or attempted escapes. Thirty-three men had escaped in eight attempts since February, triggering constant reprisals such as shutting down important activities, keeping letters and packages, as well as searches of barracks two or three times a week.

The escape of General Giraud was a most unexpected but significant event, not only uplifting for the officer POWs, but with enormous consequences for the following year of the war. Giraud, a five-star general taken prisoner in May 1940, was incarcerated with other generals in the mountaintop fortress of Koenigstein near Dresden. His two-room apartment was on the second floor of the fortress, built on top of a steep hill. The Germans had chosen that place because he had already escaped from prison in World War I. True to form he began planning his escape as soon as he arrived in the fortress.

When a terminally ill general was repatriated, Giraud gave him a code, so he could correspond with his wife to plan an escape. Back home his wife made contact with the SOE, the British Special Operations Forces, and with a nun from Lorraine, who ran an underground relay station. To become fluent in German, he convinced the Germans to let a professor come to teach him, under the guise that it would help in a future Franco-German collaboration. After about eighteen months, he and his wife had worked out every single detail of the plan.

On 17 April the sixty-three-years-old Giraud lowered himself one hundred fifty feet to the ground with a cord he had braided, changed clothes, shaved, and wearing a Tyrolean hat, walked to the nearby train station. A man (Roger), passing by him on the platform, said: "Morgen, Heinrich" to which Giraud responded: "Morgen." In the train, Roger left a suitcase in the toilet room packed with a civilian suit, an identity card, and a driver's license. Giraud had become Mr. Heinrich Greiner, an Alsatian industrial engineer. Roger and Giraud, each in their own compartment, began their travel by train toward France.

30 April—The Protestant Church is located in the former utility room of Barracks 9. "Where every two or three are gathered in my name, I am in their midst," these words of the Bible, inscribed in the wood, stand out against a wall covered with a light-colored paper. Over the Sacred Writing, are posted the profiles of Calvin and Luther and between them stand the Huguenot cross, sculpted in full. It all blends in a play of shadows and light. Another very humble cross, consisting of two logs, stands in stark relief so much so that it seems to spring out of the opposite wall. In one corner, stacked on a red cloth, are shelves with books, adorned with a few golden filaments on the back of the books. Next to the window, across from a row of benches to which are fastened narrow writing spaces, are a plain communion table and a stand with an open Bible, on which the slanted rays from the full light of the sky illuminate its exquisite waxed wood.

14 May—Spring seems to forego any signs of renewal, mirroring the reality of the days we are living through. There is not even one leaf on the trees and we catch sight of a sky without radiance in between the break of a persistent mist.

General Giraud must be free. If he had been captured, we would know it by now and the Gestapo is closing the library for inventory, they say. Is it a coincidence?

Military action has resumed on all the fronts after a quasi-standstill for many long weeks: landing of the British in Madagascar, fall of Corregidor [Philippines], and Russian offensive against Kharkiv.

The enactment of a regulation allowing French officers to work in Germany provokes violent reactions.

At the movies, an interesting film: Wally of the Vulture.

18 May—The theater is not closed, and yet, it is not open! All the costumes, the accessories, and the make-ups have been removed this morning under the direction of the clown Dudule. A large and somber crowd, chanting Chopin's Marche Funèbre, accompanies the cart, which carries the hot goods to the gates of the *Vorlager*.

An exhibition of crafts and industry designed and created by the POWs opens in Barracks 12: some beautiful handicraft, particularly in bookbinding and small machinery. A complete range of small-scale models of agricultural machinery in melted aluminum demonstrates marvels of patience and skill.

24 May—A soccer match pits the officer POWs against the POWs: blue jerseys against red jerseys. The referee is R. In a highly contested game, the officers lose.

General Giraud's escape was a great embarrassment for the Germans. In spite of an all-out hunt, Giraud reached Strasbourg without being detected. While there were people ready to help him, Alsace, annexed to Germany, was still dangerous territory. After hiding for a few days (some of the people who helped him were deported later, when the Germans learned of their activities), Giraud left for the unoccupied zone of France and presented himself to Marshal Pétain. Pierre Laval, apparently wanting to pacify the irate Germans, asked him to return to his POW camp in Germany. After pledging not to take arms against the Germans, he was allowed to go to his family estate in southern France, where he was under the surveillance of the Vichy government.

The American intelligence services immediately got in contact with him, asking him to take command of the French Colonial Army at the time of the planned Allied landing in North Africa. Giraud was a well-known general, senior to de Gaulle, and his escape had produced a sensation in France, catching everyone's fancy for its sheer adventure and success. He seemed to fit the top French role perfectly. Plans were made to arrange his clandestine travel to North Africa.[26]

The announcement on 14 May of a new regulation allowing French officer POWs to work in Germany was considered an insult to the great majority of prisoners. The Vichy Regime had waived the requirement (of not working for an enemy) at the instigation of the Germans. As an incentive, the prisoners were told that they would work in their professions and would be paid the same salary as their German counterparts, while still receiving their officers' pay. Application forms were printed on the camp printing press.[27]

It presented an opportunity for the prisoners to get out of the camp and not see the "cursed barbed wire" anymore. Many began dreaming of escaping once free in Germany. But it was an officer's prized privilege not to be required to work for the enemy. In full recognition of this privilege, the regulation had been very carefully worded as an open-ended opportunity, not a requirement. The men were given the possibility to volunteer, if they so desired, emphasizing that they were not transgressing the rules. This fine distinction did not sway most officer POWs, who still considered working for the enemy, whether willingly or not, an act of treason, particularly at a time when it would allow the Germans to free more men to go fight the war on the Russian front.

It was still attractive, and at first a number of men considered it, but after further considerations, only a few actually signed up. When a German official met with each of these men to discuss their appropriate place of employment in Germany, a crowd formed outside the barracks. As the men left the barracks, they were greeted with jeering, hissing and booing, and a rumor spread that one officer was even slapped on the face.

Doggedly soldiering on, many officer POWs and POWs stayed out of politics, organizing an industry and agricultural machinery exhibit. The men executed their work in great detail with materials from scratch. Clandestine pictures show a Belgian Brabant plow, made of tin cans, complete with a colter, a depth leveler, a share, a landslide and moldboard attached to the central beam. The hitch in front was made for horses with handles in the back for the farmer. There was another little gem: a miniature locomotive, which included all the pieces of a real locomotive, built with tin cans by a railway engineer.

Tongue in cheek, never at a loss for dry wit, le Canard *published an advertisement titled: "Holiday Resort.": "Fresh country air. Spend the summer in Edelbach, alt. 2035 feet, forest, meadows, sports, fishing, hunting, and horse races.* **Tolar Hotel.** *Complete comfort. Reasonable prices and lodging for families. Special prices for the military!"*[28]

26 May—The infirmary consists of two barracks located in the *Vorlager*. These barracks are similar to ours, divided in wards by corrugated partitions. There are no bunk beds but beds that, some time ago, had a box spring and a mattress. These have now become straw mattresses on a wooden plank. A quiet that is much striven for, however, reigns in this place. And then, does one ever know? Lists are drawn up in the infirmary, and from time to time, the gate opens for a handful of repatriations.

28 May—A sudden resurgence of late spring brings back the forgotten images of intense blue skies and the re-emergent green of pines. Once again a new life erupts around us. Its impudent outburst drives us one degree deeper into despair. At the same time, one more dying hope as the Russian offensive, stalled in front of Kharkiv, turns into a disaster. The V.B. reports it in bombastic banner-headlines.

31 May—The officers, who were ill or chosen for repatriation because of their dossiers and had left on 16 April, are now coming back to the camp after an extended stay in Krems. All repatriations are suspended. The record player which played a few programs of recorded music in the theater is taken away.

News of internal changes of great import: dissolution of the study groups of the *Centre Pétain* after a few months of eminence.

The total closure of the Pétain Center on 31 May foreshadowed the beginning of the end of the influence of the Vichy government's supporters and the waning of political dissention. Two of the leaders of the Center had quietly been taken out of the camp in early May, and a couple of weeks later, the head of the collaborators left the camp, it was said, to go to Berlin. His departure produced an obstreperous brawl. A lieutenant recalled in his memoirs: "Suddenly, yells were heard throughout the camp. 'M. is leaving!' A crowd rushed from the fields and the barracks towards the central alley, and surrounded by his friends, M. was on his way to the Vorlager. *As he passed by, everybody shouted insults and numerous catcalls: 'Shame! Traitor!' After crossing the gate of the* Vorlager, *he was said to be trembling."*[29]

Afterwards, the ruckus compelled the French Commander to go to each barracks to give a pep talk, admonishing the officer POWs to avoid political polemics, rumors, and hateful comments, so "they would not tear each other apart and tear the community down."[30] *On 31 May the Germans officially announced that, from now on, Pétain's speeches and messages would not be broadcast anymore, officially closing down all the activities of the Center.*

In the meantime, La Maffia's *resistance was increasing. The core group, mostly young officer POWs, recruited the support of older officer POWs, a group that became known as the Senate. They were charged with assuming the liaison with the French Commander, giving advice, and talking to all their comrades in an effort to rally the entire camp to their endeavor. The organization, which had started as a counterweight to collaborators and a defense against Marshal Pétain's propaganda, was becoming the larger enterprise of engaging all the officer POWs to unite regardless of their political preferences.*[31]

10

Reaching Mid-Point
June–December 1942

5 June—B. ... has just been recaptured in the pinewoods, which border the road to Göpfritz. He jumped too early out of the truck, in which he drove out of the camp. Noticed by the sentry in a watchtower, he was the object of a turbulent manhunt.

10 June—The stadium and the university are the only places kept open. The latter has been modified. Cardboard partitions divide the west room into three small rooms. The east room is reserved for the large lectures, which, lacking any other sources of entertainment, know a new boom.

12 June—Barbed wire on the left, barbed wire on the right, barbed wire in front, barbed wire behind, and barbed wire everywhere at all times. The only way to escape the obsession of this cursed grid; when the earth is warm lying down on one's back, and follow the moving changes of a cloud, the whirling of the larks, the migration of birds in full flight, or plunge into the infinity of the blue. For, they have not yet thought of putting a grid on the sky.

15 June—A wave of pessimism spreads over the camp; the British are defeated in Libya and retreat toward Egypt.

Unrest grows concerning work in Germany. In reality there are few volunteers. At the time of their departure they are subjected to hostile demonstrations, actually mistreatment, adding insult to injury to Mr. Loyal's exasperation.

The university had become such an important part of the camp that the Germans probably thought it would cause too much turmoil to close it and would add to the on-going resistance; trouble in a camp often meant a transfer of the German high ranking officers to the Russian front. The men were determined to make their study count, following as closely as possible the same curricula as they would pursue in France. The number of well-known academics in the camp ensured that the exams conformed to those given in France, and a number of diplomas were recognized after the war. The university was also a source of general education; about two-thirds of the men were auditors. Numerous seminars in many disciplines reached well beyond the formal learning of a university.

Officially, there were three major departments, sciences, humanities, and law, and in addition a strong section for elementary school teachers, which in France would have belonged to a different institution than a university. The sciences benefited from three well-known scientists: Jean Leray, the dean and a mathematician, Etienne Wolff, a biologist, and François Ellenberger, a geologist, who organized a lab in the lavatory with microscopes built in the camp. The humanities were headed by a number of the officer POWs who had come from Nuremberg.

25 June—A powerful storm transforms the ditches into torrents. We are getting deeper and deeper into a black hole. The Germans have crossed the borders of Egypt and are getting ready to push their superiority in Russia. The V.B. and Das Reich describe with smugness the great maneuver that should lead to victory; a gigantic vise closing on the Russian oilfields on one side, and the Black sea on the other.

On the other hand, *le Colis de France* carries on endlessly its good work. Through its good offices, the Oflag sponsors several stalags serving altogether seventy-six thousand men (sic). The contribution from our endeavors reaches 10,000 marks per month.

30 June—Several new tunnel openings have been discovered one after the other, originating from Barracks 26, the flowerbeds of the sixth battalion, the trash heap of the third battalion, and the stadium. Today, a team of investigators bursts into Barracks 15 and surprises S. in his bunk, a pick in his hand. Without saying a word the unfortunate S. is grabbed and dragged to the gniouf. On the way he passes by Mr. Loyal accompanied by pick carriers. He knows where they come from.

Barracks 15 is surrounded and a furious search begins.

Having torn apart the floor of the entryway, Mr. Loyal's team drills a hole in the soil and suddenly it is hollow. A tunnel opens to daylight. It is two hundred twenty six feet long connecting Barracks 15 to Barracks 14, and Barracks 14 to Barracks 13. The passageway is twenty inches wide, four feet eight inches high, located four feet seven inches below ground level. Parallel to the central alley, it is about ready to open to the outside. Its passing under three entryways of the barracks has made removing the excavated earth easy. The ventilation is obtained by means of a bellows that blows air through a pipe of jam buckets fitted one into the other. The tunnel is lit with electricity. The entrance hole is admirably concealed under false stilts similar to those that hold the floor of the barracks and have to be moved in order to open the trapdoor.

The thick brains of the detectives cannot conceive of this shrewdness. It is from the inside of the passageway that they fall upon the manhole; the trapdoor crashes dragging with it the stilts that protects its secret.

An oppressive nervousness follows this "peculiar discovery."

Le Colis de France, *which began as a simple act of brotherhood, grew to provide supplies on a regular basis for the POWs, who were under duress. Almost two years after it started,* Le Colis *had become an organization which sent thousands of packages to the neighboring stalags in addition to the POWs in the camp. The items, collected from what the more "affluent" officer POWs received in their packages, were stored in one of the rooms of the brick buildings, where they were sorted in different boxes to be later allotted equally to each package. The packaging material was obtained from the packages the men received from France.*

In a le Canard's *article publicizing* le Colis, *an officer POW proudly wrote: "The package is one hundred percent French," and added, "On each package one could write: 'Unknown comrade, we hope that this package brings you some physical and most of all moral comfort. May it show you that like us you are not forgotten, and tell you that all our families are also yours, since we are glad to share with you what they have sent to us. Remember it tomorrow, when home again you will have to participate in the common task of rebuilding a New France in which, amicably united, we will have to collaborate together.'"*[1]

In addition, when the officer POWs learned that some of the POWs' families in France were in dire need, they sent them some of the money raised from the entertainment and the exhibits in the camp. Building on this effort, the camp officially adopted two stalags a few months later, raising the officer POWs obligation to donate one-day's pay each month. The money was sent to France via bank drafts. "Give a little bit of your heart. It is above all affection that a person needs during sad times."[2]

The term "peculiar discovery" was the coded way to say that someone had denounced the existence of a tunnel. The men knew who the stool pigeons were, and the "oppressive nervousness" that followed meant that the six or seven men responsible for denouncing the tunnels were beaten up. Threats to hang them prompted the Germans to send them to other camps for their own safety. (These men did not represent a political ideology, as was the case for the collaborator on 31 May.) This time the French Commandant reminded everyone that communicating information to the enemy warranted court-martial after the war and that he would refer these officers to a military court after their liberation. A couple of weeks later, the Commandant himself was sent to a reprisal camp for having been overheard saying derogatory words about the Germans.³

3 July—A notice from the O.K.W. [Wehrmacht's High Command] finally admits: "some of the privileges given to the French officers were rescinded because of the escape of General Giraud." The speech is greeted with shouts of "Vive Giraud." Animated events in the sports barracks: boxing and wrestling demonstration for a small group and outside the ring.

14 July—A dreary summer with rain and wind produces muddy clay, which sticks to the soles and pulls out the wooden shoes from our feet. General roll call at 9:00 a.m.; two officers [POWs] have left through the gates with a detachment of POWs. It is said that one of them, keen on astrology, had discovered an accumulation of favorable conditions in his horoscope. Recaptured, these two men are ridiculed. There are always ill speaking tongues.

20 July—Mr. Loyal is looking for a fight; from now on dress code for every roll call dictated in advance, with or without a coat, no bare legs. You will be punished! You need some discipline!

Continuation of the black streak: the Germans have reached the Don and taken Sebastopol.

22 July—The line of walkers turns around in the field of the fourth battalion, and it suddenly freezes on the spot, anxiously looking toward the west. A few yards from the watchtower a man with an incredible resolve and speed climbs over the first eight foot barbed wire fence. He assails the second one a little slower, perhaps out of breath. He is now on the other side and runs. From the watchtower the sentries yell out the warning, but the man does not stop; one gunshot, followed by five more and he falls next to a haystack. The enthusiastic cheers cease, followed by a solemn silence. A little later, a stretcher brings back the body of Captain G.B., who died from a bullet in the nape for having loved freedom too much.

Since April as noted in the diary, numerous reprisals were an everyday occurrence after Giraud's escape. One particular, consequential privilege was taken away; the space in the Vorlager *where the architects and other craftsmen had been allowed to pursue their skills was closed for good.*⁴

By now the communication between La Maffia and their families was well established. At some time during 1942, diverted packages became so regular that the men called them "Diplomatic pouches worthy of the State Department." Packages included radios, sent either complete or with parts in different packages and assembled in the camp, letters, medicines, tubes for the radios, false papers, civilian clothes, and a number of French clandestine newspapers (L'Humanité—*in circulation today*—Combat, Libération, Témoignage Chrétien, and Franc-Tireur). *They even got a typewriter, a machine that could copy maps, and later handguns. It was dangerous business. While many of the participants remained unknown to the Germans, some men, including the two original masterminds of* La Maffia, *were sent to a reprisal camp toward the end of the war.*[5]

In addition, the wife of one of the members of La Maffia *put the group in regular contact with* La Défense de la France, *to which she belonged.* La Défense de la France *was a resistance group, founded as early as August 1940 by two students who had rallied faculty members of the Sorbonne (University of Paris, founded in the thirteenth century), prominent Catholics, and industrialists to publish an important clandestine newspaper of the same name (it became* France-Soir *after the war, still in circulation today). The group became a major support for the camp, keeping them abreast of the changing political situation and the inner workings of the resistance. In 1944, members of* La Défense *were also shipped to concentration camps.*

26 July—The Germans have taken Rostov.

Under a warm sun we watch a match of Pelote Basque on the *fronton* [The fronton is the name for a specific court for Pelote Basque, a popular game of Southwestern France] of the sixth battalion. The scores are sung. Between the games, the Pyrenean choir conducted by C. sings folksongs. Odd formality: in case of contention the umpires gather to solemnly deliberate in a low voice, beret in hand.

The exhibition game closes with a dance presentation: fandango and Yan petit under the direction of D.

18 August—Summer has arrived in full force: extreme heat that burns and penetrates. There is no shade anywhere except from the barracks. As a result of the dictate of this white-hot sky and the norms in vogue, there is only one uniform: the nude but in different degrees. The nude progresses from the half-naked, modest and decent, to the almost complete nude: a whole range of "negligées," from shorts to underpants. The actual age plays no role in this practice.

Aesthete or not, young or old, one lets oneself roast, laying quietly on a blanket or moving restlessly under the ultra-violet rays. Sunburns, be dammed! It is fashionable to exhibit a skin as golden as the crust of bread.

19 August—Exciting announcement bursting out like a bomb: the landing of the British in Normandy near Dieppe. The news kindles our hope, but not for long.

The landing in Dieppe, a French port on the Channel across from Great

10. Reaching Mid-Point　　　　143

Britain, called Operation Jubilee, was an Allied rehearsal to test the German defenses for a future full-scaled invasion of France. The Allied amphibious force, consisting mostly of Canadians, came ashore on the beaches of Dieppe, with the heavy support of the British RAF planes, sizing up the capabilities of the German Luftwaffe. Hearing the announcement first from the German broadcast, the news kindled new hope.

"But not for long." The men soon heard from the clandestine broadcasts that a flyer, thrown over the Dieppe region, explained: "This is only a special operation, not the invasion. Do not do anything that could provoke reprisals from the enemy. When the hour comes, we will tell you. We will then act together for a common victory and your freedom." The operation ended quickly, and the Germans announced that they had destroyed the force, taken most of the survivors and the equipment, proudly declaring that they had repelled the invasion with the complicity of the population.

The next day the Germans broadcast a special announcement in the camp, declaring that the officer POWs of Dieppe would be liberated as "recognition of their city's failure to support the Canadians."[6] A few officers from Dieppe left the camp in September. While Marshal Pétain may have been ready to cooperate with the Germans, claims of collaborating actions by the inhabitants were grossly exaggerated and discounted, as documented later.

22 August—Visit of doctors: the sick, three at a time, enter the consultation room. Some know what they want, and when the drugstore is not empty, receive a few white or pink pills they carry in the palm of their hands. Others do not yet know. After a brief examination they too receive a few pink or white pills they also carry in the palm of their hands. Impatient, the hopeful, unfortunate patients trample in the hallway, eager to obtain these miraculous panaceas, a triumph or a joke of the Chleuhs' medical care.

28 August—At the end of the month 653 officers [POWs] arrived from Hamburg. Among them was Colonel C. d'A. As usual they received a friendly welcome. They fit in as well as they can.

5 September—The horizon has become permanently bleak; the Germans have reached the Volga and have taken Novorossiysk. On the other hand, they have been stopped in front of El Alamein.

The oppressive heat is reduced in the afternoon by a violent storm, which interrupts the sports day. In this respect, it is worth noting that basketball has been the preferred sport this summer. Crowds have gathered in the stadium, where exhibition games have succeeded in re-creating the turbulent atmosphere of real sports arenas. Fans root for their teams: those from Barracks 23 with F., those from Barracks 26 with D., those from Barracks 25 and 28 with

Tse-Tse. The Barracks 26 team, the most popular, wins *le Canard en KG's* cup to everyone's surprise and the satisfaction of the largest number.

"They (the Germans) have been stopped in front of El Alamein" *(near Alexandria in Egypt) was major news. The men had followed closely the retreat of the British from Libya and Hitler's offensive. And now the British, Australians, and Free French Forces, led by Lieutenant-General Bernard Montgomery, stopped the Germans at El Alamein, winning decisively over the troops, led by Field Marshall Erwin Rommel. The battle lasted from 23 October to 5 November. Seeing the battle of El Alamein as the turning point in the war, Winston Churchill remarked: "Before Alamein we never had a victory, after Alamein we never had a defeat."*[7]

It was particularly important for the officer POWs, because the Free French Forces played an important part by holding for fifteen days the fort of Bir Hakeim south of Tobruck in Libya, a delay that was crucial for the British, allowing their forces time to receive new supplies and fall back to the defensive positions of El Alamein.[8]

Bir Hakeim was a simple crossroads in the middle of an arid desert, a naked and rocky place swept by sand winds, but in a strategic position.[9]

8 September—The camp grows with the arrival of 103 officers [POWs] coming from Choubine. Departure of the few repatriated Dieppois.

A passion was just born. Is it the fancy of a new youth, the realization of wandering dreams, or the simple love of do-it-yourselfers? On the pond of *Petite France* an Armada of tiny boats crosses from one side to the other. Yachts, sloops, thirty and forty-foot sailboats, and schooners pull broadside, on the way bumping a big dundee, a lougre [tall ship], or a Tartane [French Tartane, type of vessel developed in the eighteenth century on the Mediterranean Coast], while speedboats go round in circles, nose in the air, making deep wakes. At intervals the turret of a submarine emerges and dives in this miniature sea, a miserly pool without waves carrying children's toys.

18 September—Nautical exhibit in Barracks 17 west: of special interest is the stand for yachting, a complete mock-up in relief of Le Havre harbor, and an amazing collection of small-scale models, little masterpieces worthy of a museum. The orchestra provided the background music of a country club atmosphere.

The announcement is official. There will be a regatta soon.

3 October—Fog covers the camp like a veil every morning. It feels cold and already the trees along the road look like big bouquets of wilted foliage. Deadly, deadly is the heartless passage of the hours and the slow gliding of the days; an undifferentiated unfolding of grayness without end. From time to time a passing incident brings a bright spark to the night which engulfs us. But we are like stagnant waters, disturbed by the impact of a stone; turbulent for an instant, its ripples disappear one by one from the surface, which soon returns to its stillness.

5 October—We are in a stage of siege: departure of those who have signed up to work in Germany. The minuscule percentage of volunteers continues to arouse violent manifestations, despite their excused absence during roll calls. Mr. Loyal, in order to have the last word, has assembled a big war machine. A rowdy crowd forms at the conspicuous departure of four or five "crew cut heads," who are quite frightened. The soldiers in green, scattered in the crowd, intervene immediately making brutal arrests. Five protesters will be arraigned in front of the war council in Vienna. Motive: injury to the Wehrmacht.

16 October—Stunning news and general jubilation: Sir Loyal leaves us for the Russian front. The air becomes lighter.

26 October—No letup of an icy wind dragging ashen clouds that undulate near the ground like the smoke of factories, and as it unravels discloses between two spirals a few puny cabbages, the last vestiges of our gardens. Winter settles in for the third time in this grungy sky and earth. Slimy mud retains the water on the ground like shiny backwaters.

Closed horizons: every evening, we wait with anxiety for the news release about the Russian front, where a formidable fight for Stalingrad, the battle that will determine the fate of the war, is raging. It will be the Verdun of the Volga. It has become a contest of who will report the last lead wrestled, at the ultimate second from the owner of a radio. The emissary's words are weighted, commented upon, parsed, and his silences interpreted. After he has been wrung empty, pressured, and ground down, he is sent back to his corner like an old lemon peel. The supreme ingratitude: "we knew it already."

Mr. Loyal was a much despised man.

The nautical exhibit in September was a major event covered by le Canard *with a picture on its front page. Of note was the model of a three-mast schooner, a marvel of reproduction. One of the clandestine pictures shows the hull, made from a scrap of wood with a carefully shaped elegant bow. The three masts and the boom were tall and imposing. All the standard and running riggings were complete and the bulkhead and deck looked like fine wood. At the stern, a rudder looked so real it was an invitation to unfurl the sails and get under way.*

The departure in October of a few officer POWs going to work in Germany was the last rumbling of dissention in the camp. No one else signed up afterwards and all those who previously collaborated and snitched on their comrades had also left. From then on, the men could coalesce in tighter solidarity and engage in more subversive activities without worrying about being tripped. The diary entries reflect this freer attitude, acknowledging in an indirect way the presence of the clandestine radios on 26 October, as they followed hour by the hour the crucial battle for Stalingrad.

By the end of the year they were able to read uncensored newspapers, and possessing about twenty radios, they kept abreast of the news twenty-four hours a day. The most popular stations were the BBC, the Voice of America, the "French speak to the French" broadcast of the Free French and General de Gaulle from London. There were also the Free French major stations of Brazzaville and Beirut and after 1942, Algiers, Tunis, and Rabat as well.[10] A number of Foreign Service officer POWs, who were fluent in many foreign languages, also listened to the free radios of Eastern Europe in as many as seven languages. To remedy the fact that the Germans cut the electricity in the barracks at night, one of the men, an electrician, connected their grid to the electricity of the Vorlager.[11]

The news received clandestinely was a welcome counterpart to the German papers and broadcasts that trumpeted German successes. In addition, the Free French broadcasts were significant for the information about the increasing engagement in combat of the Free French Forces and for de Gaulle's speeches from which they had been completely cut off before. Early on they instituted a news service like the Associated Press, with professional journalists collecting the news twice a day. One officer from each barracks copied the report and read it every evening in the barracks as a communiqué. (A clandestine picture shows the men around a table copying the communiqué.) On occasion, there was a second communiqué during the day (a description of the news service will be noted in the diary in February 1943).

The news service required some other supporting groups; first and foremost to make sure that the Germans did not find an officer listening to a broadcast. Some men had lifted the wood of the barracks floorboard, which in some places was a few feet above the ground, a place large enough to fit in. (When I visited the site of the camp in 2010, one of the foundations of the barracks was still intact. It showed the entire rectangle with the base of the two chimneys, each heating a half-barracks. Because of the hilly nature of the ground, some parts of the foundation were about four feet high, making a large space under part of the floor.) At the hours of broadcast, a number of other prisoners were alerted and stood guard at the windows and door of the barracks on the lookout for approaching Germans. It took just seconds to get the place back to normal.[12]

1 November—The ceremonies in the chapel take on an extraordinary majesty, considering our situation, and display the entire liturgical splendor.

The Cecilia Choir has eighty-four members, joined recently by the twenty Gregorian choristers who came from Hamburg with Father C.

5 November—There is no end to the icy mist. The British attack in Egypt [El Alamein]. Beet leaf soup.

8 November—The "door" to our honeycomb suddenly opens. "The Americans have landed in Algiers!" "What?" Our group of ten, amazed, rushes into the hallway, where all the honeycombs propel their awestruck inhabitants. The news erupts and spreads like wild fire producing everywhere its incendiary effect. The Boulevard [central alley] is overrun by busybodies who bolt out of the barracks or dash back in. Messengers take off at a lively pace from door to door. Phenomenal humming that rises up and intensifies. "The Americans have landed in Algiers. The Americans...."

Light in the darkness.... Kick-in-the-pants that bring us back up from the deep. At least now, we hold the certainty that the beast, which has held us by a noose, will soon croak.

12 November—Events move quickly. We are briefed almost hourly. The Germans entered the free zone [of France] yesterday and the German radio broadcasts Hitler's letter to Marshal Pétain. All of France is occupied, breaking the armistice. Darlan dissents and Giraud is in North Africa. What will Vichy do? Most people think that Marshal Pétain will take refuge in North Africa, and one already envisions the Allies landing on the French coast. Miracle of the imagination!

"Light in the darkness" was Operation Torch, the landing of the Americans and the British in Algeria and Morocco; the long-awaited Allied offensive had taken place. There were many players, each reporting on their own terms. the Voice of America for the Americans, the BBC for the British, the official Vichy radio for Marshal Pétain, the official German radio, and the Free French broadcast for General de Gaulle. In the face of the complexity, the diary entry simply notes, "Events move quickly ... Darlan dissents and Giraud is in North Africa. What will Vichy do? Will Marshal Pétain take refuge in North Africa?" While they could not participate in person—the dreadful consequence of being prisoner—they passionately followed the complex unfolding drama, thanks to their news service. What was happening?[13]

"Most people think that Marshal Pétain will take refuge in North Africa" was the hope of the officer POWs, who still held out a belief in his integrity. It could be his chance to constitute a government out of reach of the Germans. In the end, with all the contradictory reports of the preceding four days, the men did not yet know what Pétain was doing. The only certainty was the complete occupation of France. They would sort out the political maneuvering in the next few weeks.

16 November—An awful murder: Captain R., who was walking in the field of the first battalion, is killed by a riffle-shot. Nothing can justify this unquestionable assassination. In various occasions gunshots from the watchtowers have been fired on one man without cause. The German General and his henchmen are booed. One would like to do more than that.

20 November—A cold dampness penetrates us to the bones. We are freezing in our dens. Neither wood, nor coal: the rations have been reduced to one fifth.

Against the vehement protests of our senior representative we are informed that from now on we will be treated as prisoners of war. What in the world have we been since June 1940? The food continues to be disgusting and insufficient. Latest novelties on the menu: inedible greenery called spinach, swimming in green water; and *Kriegsgefangenenmarmelade* [Prisoners of war preserves], these preserves originally came in boxes marked *Wehrmacht* [German Army preserves which were edible], corrosive mixture with a base of carrots or beets. Fortunately, we receive packages and three times a week potatoes in water.

Stimulant from three different kinds of good news: Stalingrad remains unconquerable and the Russians start a counter offensive, the British overpower the Afrika-Korps [German Army in Africa], and Algeria and Morocco are occupied. There still remains Tunisia. We would like it to go a little faster still!

There are no entries in the diary between 20 November and 31 December; five weeks that would shatter the men's last illusions. Marshal Pétain revealed his true intentions when not only did he not go to North Africa but also gave formal orders to fight the Allies. When Darlan, facing the reality on the ground, joined the Americans, Pétain declared that Darlan "had betrayed his mission." He published Giraud's letter, in which Giraud had assured him that he would not do anything contrary to the policies of the Vichy government. Finally, following a German request, he instructed the Resident-General (Governor) in Bizerte to allow the Germans to land in Tunisia.

Adding insult to injury, in the early hours of 27 November, the French admiral in Toulon, faced with the takeover of the fleet by the Germans, ordered the signal blinkers on the yardarms to flash the fatal message, "Scuttle, Scuttle, Scuttle! It was the greatest act of self-immolation in military history," wrote the historian Rick Atkinson. "What had been one of France's major hopes sank out of sight ... in the most pitiful and sterile suicide imaginable."[14]

Darlan was assassinated on Christmas Eve. "Not a tear was shed," noted a reporter.[15] *Giraud replaced him with the blessings of the Americans. General*

Giraud was well known by the officer POWs and his escape had enhanced his stature. In the void created by Marshal Pétain, a number of them turned to Giraud at this time.

31 December—The year 1942 closes its parenthesis with an absolute certainty: Germany will be defeated. The Allies are slowly climbing back up the slope. The Russians have advanced one hundred miles between the Don and the Donetz. The German parabolic curb has come to dead center and is tumbling down. There remains for us simply to wait.

Wait! Leitmotif of the prisoner, old tunes often whispered, but never with this joyous vivacity of today and this trust in the future. It seems that the heavy blanket of lead, which has crushed our shoulders, is weighing a little less. The air becomes breathable, and disregarding all caution a delirious euphoria drives us to plunder the supplies we had set aside as reserve.

Songs, laughs, shouts, and new spectacles, everywhere joy reveals itself: the veil has been torn.

The officer POWs had reached the mid-point of their captivity. They had been prisoners for thirty months. They never imagined they would be prisoners for another twenty-nine months.

11

The Great Adventure
January–14 October 1943

1943

Our jailers declare a truce for the holidays and the theater reopens. On stage alternating performances: *Knock and Marius* and *Faisons un Rêve* [Let's Dream]. All the stars are performing.

Knock with B.... The interpretation is intelligent and lively and despite Jouvet's shadow [French actor, producer, and director of la Comédie des Champs Élysées and l'Athénée in Paris] is not disappointing. G. ... has the heavy burden of being Raimus in Marius. He succeeds in this tour de force and shows the whole breadth of his real talent. He conveys a portrait of good nature, candor, and great tenderness.

Finally, G. plays les Sachas and R. the lovers. These uniquely Parisian three acts do not fail and pay off.

15 January—Foul weather. Mud, snow, thaw, and drizzle. With the exception of the central alley paved with stones, the rest is only a bog and a quagmire; the paths covered with logs, leading to the Brown Houses [latrines] and the planks which provided bridges over the ditches, have been hauled away to be used for fuel. Imitating the chrysalises, the groups shut themselves in their cubicles behind the protective cover of paper and cardboard. There are two solutions to fight the cold, either stay in bed or build a stove. That's how amazing heating appliances, made of clay and tinplate, were born. Rows of rickety and erratic pipes, made of cans, throw their foul matter through the windows. All this tinplate paraphernalia expels torrents of smoke and gives to the landscape the characteristic look of the slums. Gloomy, Mr. Loyal's successor does not object.

19 January—General Leclerc's Army [Leclerc was one of the first officers to join De Gaulle in England] catches up with the British Eighth Army after marching twelve hundred miles through the desert. The British enter Tripoli.

Our life remains in slow motion. The University is closed for lack of coal. There are no sources of entertainment except for a few books and card games. Some slackness in the discipline is creeping up and a growing number of pseudo-sick men miss the twice-daily roll calls. In each group the cook bustles about alone for the benefit of a half-asleep community, which hides under blankets.

26 January—Visit of Ambassador Scapini: There are no manifestations, only a void.

29 January—7:30 p.m.—In the chapel: Complin [the last of the canonical hours, Catholic liturgy]. The booming voices echo too loudly for this room without vaults. Their fullness powerfully conveys a burning plea almost too deep, muttering of prayers, and long silences. Is it the priestly frock that gives these men, kneeling side by side, the same loose and rough profile? The vision fades with the sudden flash of a gold stripe. Separation from the world and the looming of a fate too burdensome, including the austerity of the place, call for and justify this mystical fervor.

The news from the North African front was the only source of good news during these dismal days of winter. After the defeat of the Germans at El Alamein, the British marched west along the Libyan Coast toward Southern Tunisia, joined by a sizable number of French troops; the Free French Forces from Bir Hakeim and General Leclerc's forces, which came up from Chad through the Libyan Desert.

In the west, the French Colonial Army, whose troops had kept allegiance to the Vichy government, had now joined the American Army and the British First Army in Algeria, attacking the Germans in northern Tunisia. The colonies' mobilization plans, secretly prepared in the prior two years, had been activated. It gathered Africans and French Algerian settlers. It rekindled the pent-up desire of the men to join the fight by every possible means. They started talking about a mass escape, engaging the support of their entire community. The diary remains mum about it until close to the completion of the tunnel, when a few entries discreetly hint at some unusual activities.

Otherwise life in the camp continued at its own pace with the visit of Georges Scapini, the Vichy-designated advocate for the prisoners. A lieutenant described Scapini "of medium height and slender frame..., his face expressing a poignant sadness." Legally blind, he wore a black monocle on one eye while the other looked lifeless and walked with the help of his associates.[1] *Above all, for the officer POWs he represented the Vichy government collaboration. To show that he was not welcome,* they stayed in their barracks with the shutters closed, the void mentioned in the diary.

Ignoring him *"was as restrained an attitude as we could muster,"* reported the lieutenant. *There were rumors that some other camps had tried to prevent him from entering their camp, and when he visited the Koenigstein fortress, while General Giraud was still prisoner, it was said that Giraud had pinned a note to his door reading, "Do not enter, rabid dog."*[2]

3 February—Matter settled. The Germans quit the fight for Stalingrad.

8 February—The days are spent waiting for the news bulletins. It is common knowledge that the camp has at least twenty radios dispersed in the barracks and cleverly concealed. Secret well kept: only the insiders know each location. Each radio receiver has the mission of listening to one or more designated stations. The news, gathered and pooled together, abstracted and editorialized by a Committee led by moderator L., a diplomat, is dictated to about twenty recorders. The hand-written copies are read daily in the barracks.

Thanks to the astuteness of Lieutenant M., the "camp electrician," [French POW] a clandestine connection, hooked up to the *Vorlager*'s electricity, allows us to listen at all hours of the day and night despite the frequent losses of electricity. The repair service is headed by V., stocked with light bulbs and spare parts. The stocking of radios and other equipment, secured in large part by regular packages, requires an entire organization to divert the packages before they are opened by the censors.

Every morning the bulletins of the previous evening spread by the enlisted men's [POWs] work parties are passed along from Kommando to Kommando, [groups of enlisted men POWs] miles away, bringing them the comfort of the Allied news. They are published in English, Russian, Serbian, etc., for the use of our prisoner friends.

12 February—Eight days of stormy weather: An icy wind, its violence not slowed down by any obstacles, assaults the barracks and strains the weakest joints. We huddle close to the little stoves, which sputter smoke gushing back in small tornadoes. The roll calls take place inside the barracks. The men of the two rooms are piled up in one room from where they pour forth into the other, much like an upside-down hourglass. Those present are counted as they pass by the bottleneck of the lavatory.

15 February—The chapel offers the oasis of its silence and the refuge of its peace, a welcome change from the noise and throbbing of the barracks. There, we master our despair or doubt. There, we soothe our bitter bereavement, as families of exiles are not spared any more than other families. The exiles hear nothing of the drama. The illness has been concealed and they hear only of the death. The news, already old, is included in a few sentences in a letter that is only twenty-seven lines long. Sometimes, it appears only in the brief obituaries of a French newspaper. Then, a priest friend officiates at a morning service, where other friends gather to share the same pain. Here, there is no disregard for worldly concerns.

Responding to the call for a mass escape, a captain from the POW Corps of Engineers and an infantry lieutenant started studying the different possibilities for the excavation of a tunnel.[3] *Previously, tunnels started in a barracks under the floor, but since the Germans lifted the floors during searches, these two men looked for some other locations. They settled on the open-air theater, because of its proximity to the outside barbed wire, about one hundred ninety feet away. A study indicated that the nature of the soil would make digging a tunnel fairly easy. But it was under the constant surveillance of a watchtower and of the sentries' round inside the camp. They had to find ways to enter the shaft of the tunnel and remove the soil without being noticed by the guards in the watchtower. This first phase took a couple of month.*

In February, the Alsace and Lorraine group sponsored a seminar titled Alsace, A French Province, *to highlight and honor the resistance and painful sacrifice of the Alsatian population. Their leader gave an impassioned speech, reminding his comrades of June 1940, when they marched through Alsace and were generously encouraged by the Alsatians along the road.* "This Alsatian national longing," he remarked, "is the kind of resistance and endurance that prevented the Germans from integrating Alsace into Germany after 1871. Tragically now, everything French in Alsace has been obliterated, and the Alsatian youths have been conscripted into the German Wehrmacht despite fierce opposition."[4]

Jewish officers began hearing stories that their families were picked up by the Germans and sent to Drancy near Paris and from there sent to German concentration camps. The fate of their loved ones was very uncertain, even though the Germans and the Vichy government had signed an agreement stipulating that the families of Jewish French prisoners of war would not be subjected to the same treatment as other Jews, and would not be deported to Germany.[5] But how could anyone trust an agreement between the Vichy government and the Germans?[6]

My father continued his work of documenting his comrades' activities, determined to show how "they preserved their morale, energy, and will to live, in order to prepare a better future." In 1946 and 1947, he published books on *fly fishing, beekeeping, urban dwellings, car repair, and mountain climbing,* among others, using the hobby groups' activities. He also published a series on the folkloric dances representing many regions of France and some foreign countries, giving their history and complete instructions for executing each step. Tapping into the variety of occupational groups, he published books on physical education, woodworking, paper decorations, handyman work, and some elementary school textbooks.

Not forgetting what he liked best, i.e., literature, he envisioned a special edition of a dozen books for a series on "The Great [French] Novelists of the Eighteenth and Nineteenth Centuries," recruiting artists from the camp for the illustrations. He managed with his comrades to bring back the sketched illustrations begun in the camp, when they were liberated. These books were all published in 1946 and 1947.

17 February—Rout of the Germans in Russia. They have lost Kursk, Krasnodar, Rostov, Vorochilovgrad, Kharkiv. May the storm last even longer!

24 February—A heap of clay skeletons and their gaping crushed pipes, burnt and black, leak a sticky black juice like polluted blood. It piles up on both sides of the central alley and collapses in the ditches. Our little stoves have been sacked! May their scattered ashes rest in peace on the muddy ground for having kept us warm for a short time!

They have been condemned to death after being assessed by fire inspectors. But not all of them are surrendering. Their pipes, bent in convoluted ways, hang in the interior chimneys of the barracks like some kinds of thorns, bristling all over like giant cacti.

5 March—Small stoves and cupola [small furnaces]—enemies number two—are hunted down by teams of detectives. Greens! Green Beans! Twenty-two! Forty-four! Well-chosen cries give a warning signal. The appliances disappear even while they are burning, leaving behind telltale clouds. Many dramatic actions will remain in the shadows characteristic of this guerilla warfare rich in surprises. Well known is the heroic deed of an imitator of the famous seventeenth century pirate of Dunkirk, Jean-Bart. Defending a small stove still burning hot and already deprived of its pipes, he used it as a stool to the limit of his vigor. Only the extended presence of the suspicious enemy forced him to relinquish his seat.

12 March—The Germans relax the Giraud's sanctions, allowing the reopening of the movie theater. Unfortunately the film, *Le Coeur se trompe* [The Heart Makes a Mistake] is incredibly weak.

The newsreel, however, conveys news of great significance: the Germans are in trouble in the mud of Russia. Instead of hymns of victorious marches, we hear poetic stanzas on the heroic resistance and endurance of the German soldiers. The whole episode ends with fireworks of the Ferdinand, a tank known as the elephant, which is able to launch rocket propelled shells with its multi-barrel cannons. At his microphone Lieutenant P., our translator in chief, adapts the German text with rich innuendoes that are made delightful by the presence of the Chleuh.

13 March—The Russians take Wjasma back.

24 March—We wake up to a happy surprise; the sky is blue. With the very mild temperature there is no trace of snow and the ground is almost dry. Could it be an unexpected early spring? Greedy for air and sun we open all the windows. Wide-open suitcases dry out their moisture directly on the ground, while their contents, spilling out on blankets around them, give off a wintry humidity.

The groups of gardeners attack the poor soil with an eager spade in preparation for future sowing of radishes, lettuce and carrots....

But an elusive listlessness overcomes you and incites you to daydreaming. Shivering men, standing side by side against the inner walls of the barracks, which have been warmed by the sun, blissfully taste the intense pleasure of letting the slow gentle stroking of the warm waves penetrate their innermost core.

A number of films were the subject of much derision. Lieutenant P., an Alsatian, leader of La Maffia, *and friend of my father, was very adept at putting his own interpretation of the films while translating the German dialogues simultaneously into French;* "*the rich innuendoes, made delightful by the presence of the Chleuh," mentioned in the diary. (Regulations called for the Germans to sit in the front row at every showing.) In these incredibly weak, cheap erotic films, the men had quickly noticed that one of the actors would always and repeatedly lift the skirt of a woman to pat her on her behind. The moment had become so predictable from the sequences of the stories that, guessing when it would come, the men would shout, "Is the spanking coming?" As soon as the scene appeared on the screen, Lieutenant P. would shout "le geste à peau" (the action on the skin—close to the pronunciation of Gestapo). This allusion to the Gestapo would of course bring an explosion of laughter, particularly mindful that the Germans were sitting in front and did not understand French.*[7]

Planning for the escape of a large number of officers involved the total cooperation of the camp so it would not ever be leaked. It also required a large amount of equipment for the escapees: identity papers, civilian clothes, food, maps, and train schedules, etc.... They turned to La Maffia *team, who were regularly receiving many clandestine articles in the Diplomatic Pouch. To request such a large number of items from their French contact,* La Maffia *hid a sheet of very thin paper in the button of the jacket of an officer, repatriated because of his civilian job. He brought the button to La Maffia's contact in France, telling him that he had been asked to give him this button. When the button was pulled apart, it revealed a sheet of very thin paper with a long list of items written in very small letters.*[8] *In addition, some compasses and civilian suits were also created in the camp.*

The escapees needed official-looking German documents in the form of work permits. They turned to the POWs, who, working outside the camp, made frequent contacts with the French workers (six hundred thousand young Frenchmen were conscripted to work in Germany in 1942), forced labor which contributed greatly to the creation of the Resistance. After obtaining some French workers' work permits, they copied them for the would-be escapees. With a camera in the camp, a picture of the men could be affixed to the document, and according to post-war reports, the officer POWs possessed at least two stamps with the official geprüft *(approved) stamp.*

28 March—Thousandth day of captivity, they say. Noted only apropos this sentence by Descartes: "The time that we measure as a number on the clock, distinguished from the actual time passed, is nothing but a specific way of thinking about the perceived passage of time"

Time exists only in the mind of the one who measures it.... Alas! Doesn't our entire existence of captive gravitate around this measure in a desperate computation of the days, the minutes, and the seconds? The wisest does not escape this law. Were he able to avoid it, his circle would bring him back to it, knowing what anguished thoughts come to haunt his sleeplessness in the slow flow of the nights....

1 April—As of today there is no hint of a swift ending for this fight to the death of continents against continents. There is no doubt about the outcome but the end date is very uncertain.

Distraction at the movies: a forgettable dud film with a colorless name, baptized *Le Sous-Marin à pedales* [The Submarine with Pedals], reaches the zenith of ridicule.

Wienerblut, an operetta in the Viennese tradition, full of waltzes and lilting refrains, helps us recover from this silliness.

26 April—End of the "closures" and reopening of the theater with *Un soir au Grand-Guignol* [Guignol, a puppet character and theater specializing in grisly horror shows] and *Etienne,* two plays which receive a unanimous acclaim.

Opening of the Refuge in Barracks 14. This cabaret, decorated with young pines free of their bark, is more like a cage than *La Volière,* but it upholds the tradition: good cheer, humor, and sense of taste. Discovery: R. is a blistering singer full of spirit....

Sixty-one agricultural engineers, forty-six sick men, five Dieppois will be repatriated.

At the theater: *l'annonce faite à Marie*. The supporters and opponents of Claudel [playwright 1868–1955, prominent figure in the Catholic Renaissance of early twentieth century] open a dispute which is not likely to cool down soon.

Allied attack in North Africa.

Liberation of Tunisia: Keen satisfaction, doubled by the Allied capture of two thousand "colleagues" [German troops].

The men found a keen satisfaction to hear of the liberation of Tunisia,[9] doubled by the Allied capture of two thousand "colleagues." It was also the first time that the two sides of the French Army (Vichy and Free French) were reunited. It was, at first, a rancorous meeting. For the victory parade on 20 May in Tunis, the Free French Forces (FFL) opted to march with the British rather than joining their Vichy compatriots. The Vichy troops confronted the Gaullist Forces (FFL), calling them deserters and mercenaries, and the FFL called the Vichy troops collaborators. For the officers, it was bittersweet to find their old comrades of St. Cyr (the French West Point) on opposite sides.

The Tunisian population did not show such reservations. The New York Herald Tribune under the headline "Where Our Strength Resides," reported: "The wildest enthusiasm came as some bit of dusty tricolor, fluttering from a lorry, announced the Fighting French (FFL).... Is it possible to doubt any longer where the real strength and glory of our cause is to be found?"[10]

By late April, the plan for the tunnel was ready: The men would start the tunnel in the back of the open-air theater. To hide the hubbub of construction, they planned on asking the German Kommandant *for permission to dig a trench around the open-air theater to improve the drainage of water. The French Commandant agreed to the plan and suggested enlisting the director of the theater to make it more authentic. The three men went to the* Kommandant *and presented a comprehensive plan, showing how a trench would improve the open-air theater. They added their intention to build a couple of bridges over the trench to facilitate the entry and exit of the theater. It looked very professional. Impressed, the* Kommandant *congratulated them for thinking of everything and gave his seal of approval. The Germans were convinced that it was always good for the prisoners to be occupied and have fun, so they would not think of doing something bad, i.e., trying to escape.[11] The Germans gave them a few picks, shovels, and wheelbarrows, distributed in the morning and given back in the evening. A few may have disappeared.*

They had chosen to dig the entry shaft at the closest point to the barbed wire. That corner, however, was the most exposed to the watchtower. To hide the digging teams coming in and out of the shaft, they asked the physical education classes to conduct their classes around that corner. The lessons included moving in waves, playing games of attack and defense, rolling and falling. In the morning, the lesson ended with four or five fewer men and in the evening they had four or five more. In the barracks, carpenters prepared the necessary casings.

Work started in May with the underground team completing the shaft in one day, an encased 3.28 × 9.84 foot hole. They then dug a chamber for storage adjacent to the shaft and began the tunnel (20 × 26.2 inches) with a vaulted ceiling. The tunnel was to be 276 feet long. To guide the direction of the tunnel, they used a flashlight, a plumb line, and a sito-goniometer, vintage 1911. This was a pocket instrument contained inside a small aluminum box used by the artillery for the placement of guns. It measures the angles of a site and determines the distance to the goal. A can filled with ersatz margarine and a big wick, akin to a large candle, provided light for the workers. Work progressed quickly until the tunnel was over thirty feet when they met their first challenge; a sheet of gneiss rock. They had a couple of picks, but because their strikes made a loud noise, which could be heard above ground, the men asked the camp chorale to come practice in the open-air theater to cover up the noise of the picks. At the same time the aboveground crew dug the trench around the theater very slowly and began preparing the soil for the mounds that would serve to hide the excavated earth from below.

During that time La Maffia, *with the help of the POWs, had made contact with farms in the area and a few people from Vienna to Budapest who would help the escapees. They obtained maps and train schedules. Alsatians and Lorrainers, who had been conscripted by the Germans and served as guards, provided German money. Austrian guards, whom* La Maffia *had befriended, helped as well. In particular, when they knew that a certain barracks would be searched, they passed on a book to a member of* La Maffia *team, a seemingly innocuous gesture. But in the book was a blank page at the page corresponding to the number of the barracks to be searched.*[12]

30 June—Summer begins badly with torrential rains and violent storms, which uproot our fragile planting and even the soil of our gardens.

End of May: the Rally, an extraordinary game for big children, which lasted two days. Obstacle courses that *Polytechnicians, Centraux,* and *Agrégés* [All members of elite schools of higher learning and university graduates] flunked. Lots of energy.

The end of June saw *La Senaine de l'Enfance* [The Week of the Child], an exhibit in which the French children participated by using the works they had achieved in schools, which had been enclosed in packages. All the professionals in the camp support it by giving seminars on the psychology of children, the philosophy of pedagogy, all under the direction of B., philosopher and specialist. The viewing of two French films, *La Maternelle* [Kindergarten], and *le Mioche* [The Little Kid], fosters an intense emotion to meet again loved artists, the French landscape and the Parisian youngsters. At the theater, *Poil de Carotte* [classic book and film by Jules Renard telling the story of a family and a beloved little redheaded boy, named *Poil de Carotte*].

The regular activities continued in the camp. The exhibit, focusing on children, was sponsored by an active group called the Circle of Professional Educators, which included men of all levels of education and all regions of France with a common bond of developing the intellectual faculties and moral qualities of children. They had established many study groups, varying from teaching techniques and styles to discussing common problems with children. From the very beginning, the more experienced educators coached the younger inexperienced teachers.[13]

In a Canard *article, an officer wrote on a theme repeated on many occasions; regret that fathers, as prisoners, were "not present to raise their children, an imperative duty that a prisoner was not able to fulfill." In a sentimental mood, the writer added, "The charm of children with their big mischievous and affectionate eyes has inspired lullabies and paintings. Their mouths open to form a bright cheerful smile with the freshness of a fruit, which has just been picked. They spend their boundless energy loving and playing with everything, memory, and imagination."*[14]

2 July—A team of volunteers is enlarging the trench in the open-air theater to be used as a shelter, a project of civil defense that has been authorized by the Germans. What an odd idea!

10 July—6:00 a.m.—A pleasant hour, an hour of silence when we can in a subconscious state contemplate large pieces of an already bright sky from our straw mattresses.

Suddenly, a chest appears against the light outside the window. It is the well-known profile and voice of the "Baron" always hunting for the latest news. "Landing in Sicily," he shouts, "it is official." All at once the heads pop up from the bunks.

"*Popotier* [The officer designated as the cook], hot chocolate!" In a superb and generous motion he throws a powdery mixture containing 10 percent cacao.

13 July—At the "Refuge" last showing of *Les Cloches de Corneville* after thirty performances over a period of two months. It has engaged about thirty artists, wearing an incredible richness of costumes, backed by elaborate paper scenery. Staging created by P., the Napoleon of the spectacle, and M., the camp's feminine star and Lily Pons of the company, was the lead of the cast. Closure of the cabaret.

14 July—[French national holiday.]

Waking up to a brass band! The band is marching in an S-curve from barracks to barracks in a noisy exuberance of brass and cheers, impudent vibrancy that reaches beyond the barbed wire.

18 July—At the theater, *A Dix minutes près*, a detective play translated and adapted from English by Lt. R.

In early July the lack of oxygen stopped the tunnel excavation. The candle had stopped burning and the men could not breathe. One of the men had started building a blower using a dentist's drill, with food cans mounted on two crossbars. Powered by a hand crank and pulley system, the blower was capable of twelve hundred turns per minute [sic], blowing 2825 cubic feet per hour. The men gave it the name of Typhon *(typhoon). Just as the officer POW was finishing it, however, the Germans searched his barracks so suddenly that the men were not able to hide it. The Germans found it and took it away, apparently not thinking much of it. The officer engineer immediately set out to build a second one,* Typhon II. *This time it was installed, but the work had been delayed and the aboveground crew, who had been working as slowly as possible, was finishing the work designed to hide the excavated earth. They needed another reason to work on the open-air theater.*[15]

The French Commandant went to the Kommandant *to ask for permission to build a larger trench, arguing that the proximity of Vienna and other factories warranted building a shelter against Allied bombing, which had become frequent. Permission granted. Having lost over three weeks and with the looming deadline of mid–September for the completion of the tunnel, they doubled up the number of workers underground to accelerate the work.*

To maximize the time, they instituted a rigorous rhythm. Two men dug while another loaded the earth into a cart. When the cart was full, he signaled to two other men near the entrance to pull the rope attached to the filled cart, which was on rails. These men emptied the soil into bags, which were brought to the surface. When the cart was empty, a signal informed the men at the other end to pull the cart back. As it was very hard work, there was more than one team each day.

28 July—The German radio rolls out torrents of threats and denunciations. General atmosphere of glee! Badoglio,[16] who is now leading the Italian government, has overthrown Mussolini.

11. The Great Adventure

1 August—Our terrible enemies, the fleas and lice, overactive because of a heat wave, have unleashed their annual offensive. These bugs, more abominable and formidable than their sisters, progress methodically from east to west occupying each year new blocks of barracks. Some bunks are so infested that their occupants sleep on the tables or even on the ground. Every morning hooded in their meat sacks four to five thousand specters chase the vermin.

Much rankled by the women censors, the Anastasies, *for blocking expressions of love from their wives, some men decided to take revenge, concocting the idea of using fleas to send a message. They made a few small boxes, and after catching the over-abundant bugs, put them into the boxes instead of killing them. The POWs, whose job it was to clean houses for these women, took the boxes and opened them while making the beds, letting the fleas and bed bugs out.*[17] *This stratagem was repeated a few times. The men would never know for sure whether the women got the message, but some thought that, after repeated applications, the* Anastasies' *pens were a little more cautious in blocking out expressions of love from their families.*

10 August—The Russians advance near Orel. *Le Comité d'Alger* [French Committee of National Liberation (FCNL)], names General Giraud Supreme Commander of the French armies and General de Gaulle, President of the Provisional Government[18] [an important political move].

After over a month of work the trench-shelter is only sixteen to nineteen feet long. On the other hand the open-air theater is quickly covered with earthen seats resembling couches. We are told the excavated earth from the trench is being used for the creation of a solarium.

Strange! The volume of excavated earth seems much larger than the hole of the trench.

At the theater, *Trois, Six, Neuf.*

19 August—We bask in an almost Mediterranean sky with a blue of such intensity and such radiance that it dazzles.

This is the peculiarity of this country, given to contrast and changing from one minute to the other, from the cold wind of the east to the hot outburst of the south, from the hot summer to the harsh winter.

In the gardens of the *Vorlager* the mad buzz of insects populates the insolently bright colored flowerbeds with feverish life. In the greenhouse the snake belonging to V., the biologist, bumps his tenacious head into the wire fence that imprisons him, just like the men looking for the hole in this arachnid enclosure crueler than a wall.

26 August—A very busy week starting on the 20th with the opening of the swimming pool: The swimming pool! A big hole full of muddy water equipped with a diving board.

The 22nd, opening event of the Week of the Sports in the open-air theater.

The 23rd, Bull Run, a slapstick comedy of irresistible clowning, made spicier by the wriggles of Dudule jerking with a hysterical laugh.

The 25th, camping exposition brings an acute nostalgia....

The 26th, boxing match under the bandstand attracts three thousand spectators in an atmosphere similar to the *Palais des Sports* in Paris.

The 27th, gymnastic demonstration by Captain H.'s team.

The 29th, interregional athletic assembly in the stadium and parade of regional costumes. Alsatian men and women with their red vest and large black knot headgear [Alsatian ethnic hat] march in the procession while the band plays "*Vous n'aurez pas l'Alsace et la Lorraine*" [You will not get Alsace and Lorraine]. A Chleuh officer, seeing the crowd saluting, does the same and salutes [Similar to response from the Germans 23 February 1941 with *La Marche Lorraine*].

8 September—At 6:50 p.m.—Shouts of joy at the capitulation of Italy, [by the Italians] announced in the middle of the shows: at the theater and the movies.

9 September—The communiqué reports a new breach in the European Citadel. The Allies have landed in Southern Italy at Salerno. The German radio stigmatizes the perfidy of their allies, as only they know how to do. During that time the Russians liberate the Donets basin.

We have observed a strange activity around the solarium for a few weeks. Three rollicking rascals seated side by side near a culvert, their legs dangling in the ditch, which borders the open-air theater, are engrossed in a new game, consisting of passing from hand to hand an object hidden by the bank of the trench.

As soon as they are finished, a fellow casually steps forward pushing a wheelbarrow. He removes a few shovels full of earth from the bottom of the ditch at the end of the human chain and walks away to pour out his load on the flat strips of the solarium.

The ditch progresses only a few inches each day.

14 September—Two hundred eighty nine senior officers coming from Wiesbaden arrive at the camp after a tough journey of eighty-two hours. Many of them had been in Oflag XVII A from July to September 1940. They crossed many trains of Italian prisoners, treated with brutality and contempt by their former companions in arms.

11. The Great Adventure

The Russians recapture Novorossysk, Briansk, Poltava, Kremenchug.

Undoubtedly, the activities in the open-air theater during the week of 26 August were covering the coming and going of the underground team.

The engineer officer supervising the excavation came into the tunnel almost every day to make sure that the direction and level were correct, and always left an assignment for the team coming the next day. On 14 September the underground team found the assignment to dig the exit shaft, break through the ground, and install a sort of trap, which would be lifted at the time of the first wave of escapees and replaced for the second wave, and third wave. Two hundred men had signed up to leave. In four days it would be the new moon.

15 September—A team of the *Abwehr* [counter intelligence unit], equipped with long iron rods, painstakingly probes the ground for hours around the open-air theater. Spectators, looking very worried, pass by again and again.

17 September—It is not a secret anymore for anyone. Two hundred have registered to leave. Exit: the underground passage of the open-air theater. Departure: tomorrow.

Everything is ready. The entrance to the tunnel under one of the culverts in the ditch is camouflaged by a lateral shoring, which gives access to the departure chamber. The gallery, three hundred two feet long, passing under the barbed wire fence, will open about sixty-five feet away from the patrol path and an equal distance from the road to Edelbach. Supported by some flooring marked by a candle, a piece of sod twelve inches thick still blocks the exit hole. Started in June, an enthusiastic team spirit brought the work to fruition, spreading the excavated earth in broad daylight for the solarium. The trench? A pretext. Oh! A masterful hoax, fully worthy of success. Preparation for *la Grande Aventure* has been meticulous. Workshops of cartography and compasses, a clandestine printing office and a photo studio have provided maps, materials, and false identity papers.

Our Camp Exchange Service has supervised the creation of civilian wardrobes pooling together the tailors and designers, who cut and fitted the garments. The bunks are buzzing like beehives.

In these final hours, a lively haggling to join *la Grande Aventure* [known now as *la Grande Evasion*] has taken place, but the organizers of this monster escape exercise a rigorous selection of the competitors. In the lead, all those who have worked to carry out the completion of the underground tunnel followed by those who have already participated in similar projects or escapes.

There are stringent instructions for those participating; the plan is to utilize the metro [the tunnel] a few days in a row, if possible. Everyone must follow an assigned itinerary, and in case of capture, be silent for at least twenty-four hours.

18 September—Since access to the fields is prohibited after 6 p.m. the bags of the travelers were placed in the gallery in the morning in the order of departure. The seventy-three prospective escapees began entering the underground at 12:30 p.m. The first was Tonton [endearing name for uncle], the miner and the last was Captain P., the two master overseers. They entered one by one, lying down on their back with their legs spread out and their bags on their stomach, and overlapping one another the even numbers placed the back of their head between the thighs of the uneven numbers. During the eight hours of waiting the ventilation provided by the blowing mechanism proved to be inadequate and five dropped out after fainting. Tonton settled for punching a hole in the exit plug despite the danger of being found.

At 8:15 p.m., Tonton sawed the grass of the escape hatch and carefully let the board slide on the grass.

8:30 p.m.—The searchlight crisscrossed fully on the network of barbed wire, creating the impression of broad daylight. A pull up! Tonton was outside and crawled toward the road when he heard the noise of voices; two sentries were chattering with each other. Anxious wait! The sentries parted from each other. Tonton began crawling toward the road only five feet away. Two shadows emerged from the ditch; it was a couple. Cold sweat! After long kisses the lovers left holding each other. Phew! Tonton threw his bag in the ditch to scout the terrain and check whether there were any ambush armed with a machine gun and ready to fire. One never knows. Finding nothing, he went back to his bag. Forward!

One by one, the sixty-eight men exited and glided in the dark. Captain P. closed the trap door. He would leave tomorrow. It was exactly 9:30 p.m.

Placing the escapees' bags in the tunnel required some planning, since it was in full view of the watchtower. The men enlisted again the help of the physical education trainers, who planned movements on the ground using blankets. Each officer came with his blanket or the famous cape, and with his backpack wrapped in the blanket or the cape, dropped the backpack in the hole during the carefully controlled movements of the physical education class. The packs were then lined up in the tunnel in the order of the escapees' number.

The entry of the men in the shaft was handled differently. First, as a diversion they organized some sports event in the stadium in the morning, which was far away from the theater. At the appointed time small groups of walkers began crisscrossing from different directions, every three to four minutes, providing a screen between the sentries in the watchtower and the hole. At the same time

11. The Great Adventure

three men sat in animated discussion at the edge of the ditch near the hole. One of them would take the opportunity of the screen to disappear into the ditch and then into the shaft.[19]

19 September—Today is Sunday, when there is no roll call in the morning. Everything is absolutely quiet. The success of the first wave arouses a wind of optimism and immerses the camp in joy. One seriously envisions a third wave. This evening the next batch will be using similar procedures as yesterday.

10:00 p.m.—Total quiet. Complete success; sixty-four men have left!

20 September—8:00 a.m.—The roll call takes place in the barracks where we pass from one room to the other through the lavatories. Thanks to the set of traps installed in the ceiling some devoted accomplices, following the example of the extras of the Chatelet Theater are being counted several times. The roll call comes out rigorously exact. All is well.

8:30 a.m.—Something has happened and we are called to a general roll call. Guards in full gear surround the barracks. The Viennese police have announced the arrest of several escapees by telephone.

10:45 a.m.—The traps that had to some extent functioned as planned continue to conceal ninety of the one hundred thirty-two departures. The Chleuhs explore the ground but are still unable to discover the mysterious exit.

11:15 a.m.—It is all over. The wolf pack has located the entrance hole.

7:00 p.m.—A roll call, which has lasted since 3:30 p.m. ends with a tally that reflects high fantasy. Orders from our leaders: buy time, at any cost, in order to give the maximum chance to those who are still at large.

The general roll call, which forced the men to come forward with their POW number to the designated guard for their barracks, revealed that perhaps as many as one hundred twenty men had disappeared. Incredulous, the Germans asked the prisoners to stop the joke and come out of hiding. But soon they had to admit that a large number of men had escaped. The local police blocked all the roads and bridges of every village. The frontiers to Hungary, Czechoslovakia, and Yugoslavia were blocked. A rumor spread that paratroopers had landed.

21 September—The busses of the Viennese Security Force pour out their usual riffraff with their badger furs. These Messieurs want to count us individually producing a quaint session that ends in the way of a quadrille and multiple incidents. Only our weariness and hunger eclipse the general verve and liveliness.

In the evening, a truck drops off a bunch of escapees. Alas! There are already twenty.

26 September—Only thirty-six vagabonds are now officially on the lam. Almost all the others are already back. In the absence of a large enough prison they are immediately returned to their bunks and are welcomed as prodigal children. Each tells his story, all day long, a luscious collection. The speed of the German reaction, which declared the entire region in a state of alert, as you would for an invasion by skydivers, made the escape very difficult. There were roadblocks everywhere, and patrols of civilians armed with shotguns. The pipe dreams of freedom got caught in the mesh of this wide net. We can summarize almost all the accounts in this way; after walking nine to twelve miles on foot across the countryside, you came nose to nose with the *Warten* [warden] or the *Landsturm* [local police]. You were then incarcerated without glory in the prison of the village, where onions, hanging from the ceiling, are left to dry. There were few hostile acts from an often-sympathetic population. We are told that a few chosen ones got hearty soups and even some café au lait!

A few of the most unique adventures worth telling:

First, the picturesque escapade of about twenty rascals who had been gathered in a military base in Horn; quite a few Alsatians were working there, having been pressed into involuntary service by the Germans. Our twenty Frenchmen with the help of their Alsatian compatriots literally took over the command of the post. After occupying the guardhouse, they lived there as pashas being served by the German soldiers, whom they pestered with orders, complaints and invectives.

In Vienna, X. could not resist the charms of a pretty woman. A brunette, sympathetic, she spoke such correct French that he presumed, it could only be a French woman. She told him so and he made the mistake of believing her. Above all, he accepted a date. Alas! When he arrived there he found only her friends, two guardian angels, who carted him away on the spot.

Tonton's adventure, the miner, ended in Salzburg. Brought in front of the local Gestapo, he was subjected to a meticulous search before entering the municipal jail. The search yielded all his possessions spread out on the table, including his faithful companion of many attempts, a midget compass and an irresistible attraction to grab; he snatched it. Pulled out of the pen a few minutes later, he was subjected to a second search, even more intrusive than the first, followed by a storm of imprecations during which the word *Kompas* kept coming up again and again. No compass could be found; Tonton had carefully placed it under his tongue. Returned to the pen, he was again removed from it an hour later, and was subjected to the same treatment. The operation was repeated several times, but the interrogators suddenly announced that they would screen all the detainees; a joke that was not to the others' liking and nearly turned sour for our hero, as soon as the Chleuh-guards turned their backs. Brought one more time in front of them, Tonton, innocently, took the compass out of his pocket, as they were getting ready to start their sinister investigation again and said to them: "Is it what you are looking for? Why didn't you ask me earlier?" Tonton remained silent on the last act of the comedy.

Finally, the odyssey of Solange, a young lieutenant with innocent blue eyes, who owed his name and celebrity to the roles of an ingénue he had created on the stage of the theater. His civilian clothes consisted of a feminine outfit that looked gorgeous on him. After walking for about nine miles, he reached the access to a train station around 5:00 a.m., and having changed in the bushes he was able to take a seat in a train departing for Vienna. Unfortunately, the circumstances changed at the next station when a young woman, accompanied by her beau on leave from the Wehrmacht, took a seat across from him. The soldier immediately showed great interest in Solange. This attitude seemed to exasperate the "Gretchen," who, from then on, continually stared at her rival with dagger eyes. Yet, the poor fellow tried only to be ignored. The train finally arrived at the station in Vienna. Everyone stood up to get off, when a sudden jolt thrust our Solange, his breast forward, into the real young woman.

"They are made of cardboard!"

"What?" says the man.

"Her breast!" Able to count only on a swift flight, our athlete, in his get-up, shoved the couple aside, leapt unto the platform and in one hundred dizzy meters reached the gate, which he crossed with springiness. Chased by a howling wolf pack, he managed to get out of the station and hail a taxi. But in vain, and it was accompanied by a policeman that he wound up in the station of the Security Forces, where, for hours and still in the same outfit, he endured an interrogation according to the classic methods of the Gestapo. A few days later, in a train from Vienna, one would see a charming young woman, flanked by guards, her cheek bristling with the beard of a tramp.

29 September—The success of this escape, the most important since the beginning of the war, seems to have rattled the innermost layers of the civilian police and of the *Abwehr*. Every day, civilian and military investigators, following one after the other, take pictures, collect measurements, and jot down notes. The German officers charged with our custody are marking time with anxiety. It is rumored that the General and his primary deputies will be brought in front of a War Council.

7 October—Glorious summerlike weather; an especially mild day is marked by the visit of the Viennese Security Force. Search of barracks 6 and 7. The amiable henchmen are welcomed by a fiendish ruckus. Losing his cool the German general gallops behind the demonstrators yelling out in the wind: Cowards! You are attacking a thousand to one.

No kidding! Where are our machine guns?

14 October—The last glow of a late summer peters out in the mist, the cold, and the mud. Again, the monotone march of days without history returns. About ten escapees are still running in the fields.

According to one report—exact numbers are hard to come by—one hundred sixteen men were caught within a few days. Two were brought back in mid-October. They had been caught in the high mountains between Hungary and Austria on the Hungarian side. Two Polish officers/escapees were killed when apprehended. Twelve officer POWs who made it to Hungary were taken as prisonniers d'honneur. They eventually broke their pledge and joined the resistance group in Slovakia or a French resistance group in Yugoslavia. One is said to have traveled to Turkey and from there to Africa, where he joined the French Army, which landed in Southern France in 1944. He was killed during the liberation of Alsace. One stayed in Vienna for almost a year and returned to France, where he was living as of 2010.[20] La Grande Aventure was the largest escape of World War II.

12

Wait: Leitmotiv of the Prisoner
Late October 1943–15 April 1945

In early 1943 a number of officer POWs may have originally turned to General Giraud, whom they knew well as a prominent military leader since World War I. As the political situation evolved, however, they became acquainted with General De Gaulle's actions and success in continuing the fight. For many who had shown so much patriotic fervor in facing their captivity, the clarity of General de Gaulle's call to re-establish a republican government was a clarion call full of hope and an incentive to continue their resistance.

24 October—An exposition closes its doors: the Hunting and Fishing Exposition. Today, gala day: sale of paintings, drawings and even a bag decorated with the *Tapisserie d'Aubusson* [well-known tapestries starting in the sixteenth century]. The atmosphere reflects "very old France." Captain H., President of the Saint-Hubert-Club [Club de chasseur] conducts the gathering.

27 October—Heavy fighting resumes in Russia, where one expects the evacuation of the bend of the Dniepr by the Germans. The fall is mild and foggy. A new exposition in progress, the Engineering Show: remarkable work, particularly the mock-ups of the dams of Laigle and Kemps, and of the gas factory of Saint-Denis.

At the Refuge: a prestigious adaptation of the *Coups de Roulis* [operetta by André Messager, 1928] by the operetta troupe with R., as Sola Myrrhis brimming with sex-appeal. At the theater a genial and very much appreciated symposium: *La Vie facile* [the Easy Life] by Lieutenant L. R.

16 November—The Russians have taken Kiev again. Humid and cold fog: once again mud, grime. Winter!

30 November—Snow. Tehran meeting.[1]

The German General and his staff are relieved of their commands and replaced by a new team.

31 December—The year ends with official festivities. Almost every barracks have organized their own spectacles and created distinctive motifs at the price of general chaos. In one, we can see venerable sheiks smoking their long pipes under a tent of a very local color. Further on, it is an opium den and the highest of anachronism: Richelieu and le Père Joseph in search of the exotic have come there to relax for a moment.

Barracks 8 has become a street in Montmartre, with its bars, its nightclubs, and its salacious attractions.

At the 15, one serves popular soup. Required dress: the most repulsive possible. The repulsion spreads to the organizers.

Barracks 24 has transformed itself into a movie studio with a pub, movie stars, script girls, flood lamps, and merry company.

At the theater: Fanny.

At le Theatre des Hommes, a lavish recreational feature which lasts almost four hours with the Orchestre Musette of B. [band] and an amusing staging of the *Chanson du Maçon*.

Scattered everywhere: revues, skits, and music. Buffet and feasts when the resources of the *popotes* [kitchen groups] were pulled together.

Around midnight, the chaplain R. who came to spend the last day of the year at Oflag XVIIA passes through the joyous crowd. Are they really joyous?

Despite all this explosion of spectacles and the remarkable orchestration of general jubilation, one detects an artificial and false je ne sais quoi.

Despite all the promises that the future holds, the wait, the inhuman wait, slowly wears away faith, and kills enthusiasm.

1944

10 January—Quiet on all the fronts.

13 January—Discovery of an underground passage in Barracks 7: one hundred forty-five feet of a planned six hundred fifty-five-foot subterranean gallery, dug up in less than forty days. This tunnel, beginning from the eastern edge of the barracks, would have come out on the road to Edelbach after wandering under the 2nd battalion's field. The removal of the earth was accomplished by means of small bags, dumped in the cesspools of the *Maisons Brunes* [Brown Houses, the lavatories]. Three "miners" are caught in their hole. The opening plug, hidden under a stilt, has not been discovered.

15 January—The least harsh winter we have known. The temperature

12. Wait: The Leitmotiv of the Prisoner

is close to thirty-two degree Fahrenheit. But a slow succession of muddy days adds to the firm hold of an ever more profound listlessness, sickly sweet opium, which slowly kills all desire to respond.

17 January—Arrival of the new Herr General, a huge and heavy Saxon, carrying his stomach in suspenders and his jowls on his shoulders: A Teuton and a boor.

23 January—Allied landing at Nettuno [city on the Italian coast, just south of Rome].

2 February—Sudden change of temperature: fourteen degrees Fahrenheit. The small stoves come out of their hiding places and their convoluted pipes are hooked on the chimneys.

The Russians attack Leningrad.

10 February—The least incident in this huge village draws together a crowd of onlookers, eager for any action.

Draped in an ample khaki cape, even at the peak of the most torrid days, one spectator always sneaks to the first row.

The cape opens halfway for one second, showing the round eye of a lens. C., the hunter of pictures, takes a clandestine photo. [Some of the photos were published in an album in 1954.]

The photographer had been taking pictures for quite a long time, but apparently sensing the end, the diarist felt confident enough to mention it. The camera was enclosed in a case, which looked like a big Larousse *dictionary, akin to the* American Heritage Dictionary *in the United States. A hole for the lens was carved from what looked like the back of the dictionary and what would have been the front cover opened like the cover of a box. No Germans would stop him for holding a dictionary under his arms.*

The films were developed at night in the camp. A clandestine picture shows how one of the men had transformed his bunk into a darkroom with a plank serving as a table, working under a lamp covered with red cellophane paper. A blanket covered the front of the bunk/alcove so no one would know what he was doing. Another picture shows two men carving the heels of the wooden shoes to hide the developed films. They were then shut with a plug.[2]

The photographer had also obtained a movie camera and was filming a clandestine film. The officer POWs had written a script for the film, depicting the daily life of the men and some of their tricks, but without sound. They obtained the reels in clandestine packages, and on one occasion, one of la Maffia *members got a reel from an Austrian sentry, whom he had befriended. When the sentry brought it, the officer POW asked, "How much?" The sentry replied, "It is free." When he opened the reel, he found a note saying, "gift from the Austrian* resistance."³ When the reels were complete, they hid them in a recess made in the seat of the stools on which they sat.

While they filmed the scenes in a barracks a team of sixteen men stood watch all around the camp for an unexpected search, or a visit by a guard wandering around snooping. As soon as one of them noticed a guard walking in the direction of the barracks/studio, he would shout, "Besnard is needed in the kitchen," a call repeated by the others all the way to the barracks. They had practiced hiding the equipment so well that the camera, the lights, and the accessories, everything in the studio would disappear within seconds. By the time the German(s) came in, they were sitting on their bunk reading or around tables playing bridge.⁴

15 February—Five degree Fahrenheit and a snow storm, long icicles flow from the roofs.

25 February—One degree Fahrenheit and washed-out shimmering blue sky.

10:00 a.m.—Finally, the Festival of Ice, delayed for four years always for lack of ice the day it was to take place. Forbidden by the *Abwehr*, it still takes place: Hockey match, Dance Exhibition by captain H. and lieutenant B.

1:00 p.m.—Two loud explosions: Long and erratic white contrails in the sky. Allied planes! A disabled machine dives in a tailspin, leaving behind a vertically meandering long tail of black smoke.

Our sky is coming alive.

28 February—As usual on Tuesdays, showing for the German personnel at the movie theater: male censors, female censors, officers, non-commissioned officers, and *Mannschaft* [enlisted men] enter directly into the auditorium through a reserved door which opens to the road to Edelbach. At the time of exit two imaginative officer POWs, disguised as women, manage to slink among the women. Misfortune! A too enterprising Chleuh, who teases them with his flashlight, discovers the deception.

15 March—After a foretaste of spring the return of winter; the wind blows with fury, scattering a fine and light snow, which glides at ground level like steam.

The cold comes through the wooden walls, the ceilings, and the floors. We receive very little coal. The little stoves play hide-and-seek with the guards. Everything which burns and offers an accessible prey is torn down, cut, and transported: interior walls of the *Maisons Brunes*, log pathways, and even the inner barbed wire fence posts which have collapsed in the snow.

The snow piles up to such height that the roll call is done in the barracks and most often in the bunk cubicles. The consummate art consists of spending it in bed.

12. Wait: The Leitmotiv of the Prisoner

31 March—Packages arrive two or three months late. Is it the consequences of increasingly heavy bombardments? Their absence demonstrates even more so the inadequacy of the rations. The diminished allocation of potatoes is "compensated" by dry peas—tough and full of weevils—a brew of barley and millet which has been split in clear water, cabbages, or dried rutabaga.

Every Saturday, most fortunate distribution of *singe* [monkey—tins of boiled Beef, the standard meat ration during World War I, called monkey because it carried the name of a Madagascar brand. Thereafter, the French Armed Forces called all tin-canned meat *singe*] and biscuits, sent by the French Red Cross.

11 April—In the middle of the night, one of the chimneys of Barracks 7 crashes to the ground, burying the newest dream of premature liberation. The molehill, from which new underground tentacles had spread out toward the road to Edelbach, slumped down as a result of the thaw and infiltration. And yet, what a fight! Ninety-two cubic yards of water, drawn bucket by bucket, and siphoned into the lavatory of the barracks. A long week of wading, day and night, in freezing water, which reached to the chest, continually interrupted by the presence of the suspicious Chleuh. Ultimate satisfaction, the heavy cube of masonry has covered the traces of the work under it and once more "they" do not understand!

With Germany under pressure, both food and fuel were in scant supplies. The men dismantled anything made of wood, transporting the pieces by attaching two ropes at the end of the piece and carried it as close to the ground as possible so the sentries would not notice it. The latrines, the Maisons Brunes, *which were big rooms with forty toilets, each separated by open partitions, the interior walls noted in the diary on 3 September 1940, took on an unusual look. When the men removed the partitions for fuel, the room became one big room of forty free-standing toilets side by side, all in full view. The removal of the logs of the pathways transformed the paths into mud streams.*

With the thaw in April, some roofs started leaking, pouring water into the bunk beds. A lieutenant in another camp recalled, "The system in vogue consists in finding the biggest can and hanging it where it is leaking. If the can gets too heavy and overflows, you may wake up drenched. Woe to those who sleep all night!"[5]

Sometime during the winter my father met Armand Oldra, who had arrived from another camp. Oldra, an active duty officer, was also an artist. My father engaged him to illustrate Rabelais' Gargantua and Pantagruel, *which he planned to publish upon their return.*

16 April—While the Russians throw the Germans off the shores of the Black Sea and recapture Odessa, Herr General has fun with new methods of counting. Each field is divided in two halves by a barbed wire fence, with an opening wide enough for one man to go through. The battalion, enclosed in one half-field has to pass unit by unit to the other half. The cattle rebel: pulled out posts, hecklers coming and going over and under the barrier. Intervention with bayonets: crowd on edge. Four officers [POWs], who are lightly wounded, go to the gniouf as punishment. Reason: "They have forced the guards to use their weapons."

20 April—Yesterday, search by the Viennese Criminal Police unit. Usual methods: acrimonious and numerous incidents followed by arrests. Today, there is some semblance of return to calm. The length of the roll calls "in the new way" extends to the point that it compromises the theater's shows. Advertisement on posters: At the refuge, *Donogoo*, adapted by *les Cyrard* [graduates of Saint-Cyr/French West Point]. *A la Douze* [théâtre des homes]: *Musique en tête*, grand spectacle musical revue: fourteen scenes, one hundred twenty costumes. At the Dix-huit: *Au grand Large*.

One must consider giving matinees.

Plays for the trimester at the 18: *Maître Bolbec et son mari. Le Voyageur sans bagage, Bichon, Le Cyclone.*

22 April—The fourth spring of captivity is ushered by sudden and vivid openings in the sky, uncovering a bright hot sun, and bottomless blue.

On all the fronts: dead calm.

Endless weight of oppressive futile months and years without substance: growing apathy after too many exaggerated raised hope, and too many precipitous falls into reality. The last act of the war is near, but having expected it too early and too often, we do not allow ourselves to believe in it right now.

Prognoses, opinions, considerations are cloaked in reticence. Only a few great strategists still raise some bold speculations. In a memorable conference, which borrowed from Wells and Jules Verne, they contemplated and figured out a foolproof landing on the coast of Cotentin [The Cotentin Peninsula juts out into the English Channel from Normandy towards England forming part of the northwest coast of France].

26 April—Curiosity aroused. Some barracks and watchtowers are under construction at the four cardinal points outside the camp under the protection of trenches and barbed wire fences. The sentries will soon occupy these four points of support, placed about six hundred fifty-five feet from our enclosure. A second line of surveillance keeps watch on the first. Emblematic image of the Great Reich!

6 May—Frail green seedlings born of the April plantings break through the heavy soil of the small gardens.

There are no operations in progress on the fronts, but intense bombing, especially in France. Today helped unload the meat for five thousand men: one calf not skinned, one head of a horse, a few cow's ribs, and one very skinny sheep. They all look very bad.

29 May—Rhythm of the seasons: It's the turn of the plane trees lining the road to turn green in the radiance of spring. The earth also decks itself with tender green. Big June bugs, heavy and clumsy, fall from the meager shrubs planted along the central alley.

But the gorgeously blue sky is filled in turn with new life. About thirty airplanes, metallic and bright dots fly over us at high altitude. Every day an alert around 11:00 a.m. Destination: Wiener Neustadt.

By 1944 the camp resistance apparatus was so complex that the French Commandant took the lead and created a number of offices, staffed with senior officer POWs to direct the various clandestine activities. With the help of the POWs, La Maffia *had established contact with other groups of POWs in the region and with the Austrian resistance. It enabled them to sketch out some of the war industries in the area and to draw maps, which were transmitted to the resistance group* La Défense de la France. *This information was turned over to the British in London and the French in Algiers, as was reported after the war. They had particularly zeroed in on the military activity of Wiener Neustadt, which was just bombed. Tongue in cheek, they called the barracks of the Commandant* La Maison Blanche *(the White House).*[6]

The intense bombing, especially in France, as noted in May, were anxiously followed, particularly by the many men whose families lived in Normandy (an estimated twenty thousand French civilians lost their lives in the bombing of the Normandy campaign, and another sixteen thousand lost their lives by the end of 1944), fearing for their lives and unable to do anything about it. There were many Normand officers in the camp. An active community within the camp, they commissioned a few to write a book about their province, called Normandie, *which my father was preparing for publication after his return.*

June 4—After heavy combat the Allies entered Rome. Bombing from the air continue on Germany and France.

We receive very few packages; long delay in the mail. Despite the ruins and the grief, the letters from France abound with hope and confidence.

Edgy nerves in the suspense of major events.

The *V.B.* [German newspaper] and *Das Reich*, a movie of current events, artfully demonstrates the significance of the invincibility of the Atlantic Wall.

One longs to be part of the action, to know and to serve. The daily enumeration of the towns being bombed in our provinces adds to the anguish and impatience.

June 5—Rain, wind, deadly passing of the hours.

At the cabaret, *Mam'zelle Nitouche* has been showing for almost three months while at the theater *Azaïs, Jupiter*, and *Tovaritch* follow one after the other.

The stadium will not be open this summer, our masters estimating that the benches, which enclose the basketball court, create dead corners that could give shelter to the digging of a tunnel opening. A temporary stadium is set up in *Petite France*.

June 6—At 9:30 a.m.: announcement of the landing of the Allies on the coast of Normandy. The news is so momentous that it is received with calm and almost silence.

We look everywhere for ways of creating or completing maps of France; waiting anxiously for the 9 o'clock evening news.

Such news, even though expected, was hard for the officer POWs to believe. Recalling that day, two years later, an officer from Normandy, a prisoner in Oflag XVIIA wrote, "6 June 1944.... You, my comrades in captivity, have this date engraved forever in your memory. Certainly, you see again the appearance in your barracks of the one who came to announce the landing we had anticipated so much. "They have landed!" Was it possible? You could hardly believe it, and yet it was real."[7]

Momentous events have a way of being etched in a person's memory, bones, and blood for as long as one lives. There is an element of the sacred about an event that changes the direction of human life on earth; our hearts grasp it in unspoken ways for the ages.

On 6 June 1944 I was nine years old, living in France. Like the men in Oflag XVIIA I have the announcement engraved in my memory. What I remember, however, is not calm and silence, but hope and confidence mixed with much anxiety. For both the men in the camp and the families in France it was the joyful promise of an end to the misery of the past four years, but also a fearful expectation of the devastation and death of the coming shooting war. For the families, as active participants on the ground, there would be some terrifying experiences, but at any particular moment everyone was together and knew that they were alive. For the men in the camp it was quite different. They were far removed and impotent. They may have been in less danger at the time but were gripped by the anxiety of not knowing what happened to their families, a fate they would not learn about until their return a full year later.

12. Wait: The Leitmotiv of the Prisoner

I remember these few minutes of the announcement with a sensitivity that still brings me to tears today. I was with my mother, the wife of another prisoner and her daughter, my age, sitting in the kitchen of their house in a village, listening to the clandestine radio broadcast from London, likely the same broadcast the men heard in the camp. It was hard to hear, but it came through that the landing in Normandy had begun. I have no recollection of what was said, but the atmosphere in the room was so charged that what stayed with me is an overwhelming moment of joy and excitement at the promise of a return to normal life, mixed with equally charged feelings of anxiety. We were on the other side of the lines, subject to being caught between two fighting armies, and knowing full well the scorched earth policy of retreating Germans. "Sometimes the euphoria of liberation and the horror of killing were very close together," wrote a British historian.[8] Then, after the first exhilaration of the news, there was the anxious wait for the next news, and the next. The landing was an incredibly risky endeavor. What if it did not succeed?

I remember few events of my life during the war; the mind blocks what is continually hurtful. But that particular moment of joy is special. After four years of occupation, a father captive far away for as many years, normal life destroyed, the world that day suddenly changed in ways my child's mind could not comprehend, but my intuition grasped. It was by no means the end of our plight. Scary circumstances were yet to come, but it was a ray of light, a promise for the future.

June 30—The events have happened at such a pace, the facts are so complex, the development so many-faceted that one must give up the details.

The beachhead has held: fall of Cherbourg. In Russia, offensive on the middle front, liberation of Vitebsk.

Feverish days marked by suspense, which are nevertheless full of daily incidents. At first tentative, the conviction takes hold that the end is near, and from pessimism or measured prudence one passes little by little to optimism. One envisions again and again the possibility of return and one goes so far as devising one's plan of re-entry. Some dilettantes, who had pursued their favorite pastime with satisfaction or nonchalance, tackle with childlike fervor difficult works of professional endeavor they are anxious to finish. One hears T. moan frequently, "Hopefully I can finish my project!"

Meanwhile, the vegetables in our gardens grow in strength and height. In the absence of a variety of seeds one sees only the undulation of the leaves of carrots' stalks, broken here and there by a big green blob of lettuce. Radishes are rare so that these two emblematic announcements have adorned the exchanges: "Fifty radishes to be harvested immediately, for one pack of cigarettes," and "fifty radishes to be harvested immediately, in exchange for fifty radishes to be harvested in a month."

Usual misfortune; a tunnel has been discovered. Leaving from Barracks 16, it was already three hundred ninety-four feet long. From the technical viewpoint, it was the model of its kind: electrical ventilation, tub mounted on wheels hoisted by a steel cable; security signals with lights of different colors and vibrating electric bells; a full-fledged entanglement of false galleries and false traps to confuse searches in case of the discovery of the opening, a web of precautions, which a series of unfortunate accidents has rendered useless.

A young Alsatian in a German uniform, conscripted under duress, murmurs to us in passing during a patrol: "When they are busted, do not leave me behind!"

July 14—[National Holiday].

Waking up to a fanfare, sports festival, and beginning of the Exposition of the Book in the library, sponsored by the publishers and technicians of the camp, and interpreted in lectures. It is very successful.

In the evening, all along the central alley, accordions, saxophones, and violins, standing on improvised platforms decorated with flags and paper banners, uplift a wild crowd, which bursts into a chorus of some old popular songs.

15 July—After a time of stalling on the beachhead in Normandy, the battle resumes southeast of Caen. Russians attack in the direction of Kowel.

20 July—At 8:00 p.m. the loud speakers in the central alley announce with snarling anger the attempt against Hitler's life.

31 July—These last few days, torrents of specific Russian communiqués: capture of Dunaburg and Brest-Litovsk. Their advance places them at 360 miles from Berlin.

Again, expectations erupt. Bets are made on when the war will end which is predicted between three to six months [They will, in reality, be liberated ten months later]. At this point, no one is preoccupied with the methods of return, and the discussions focus more intensely on figuring out whether it will take place by geographical zones or by class. Last minute news: the Americans may have liberated Avranches [Normandy].

After the D-Day landing, fierce battles continued in Normandy during June, July, and the beginning of August. Nostalgic for the home they knew, a region now trampled by war, the Normand officers wrote the preface to their book Normandie *during these two and half months, choosing to tell a moving story of four imaginary days of traveling through the countryside as they remembered it.*

12. Wait: The Leitmotiv of the Prisoner

They recalled, "The smell of the fresh air in the cheerfulness of the coming spring and the morning fog; the sun rising over the Town Square of Dreux, the waters of Nomancourt, and the ramparts of Verneuil." They passed by the beach, and in late evening reached "a canal lined with poplars glimmering in the moonlight, where a single yacht was sailing." The next day they entered a town, where "fishermen calmly waited for the pull of a fish, and the crowd—white dresses, a bright scarf, and a dark-color coat thrown on the shoulders—stayed in the shade. A Sunday in August: the regattas in Ouistreham. The sea is always near and ever-present."

Four short days fulfilled with dreams of a region of Romanesque and Gothic art graced by the powerful Gothic arches of le Mont-Saint-Michel, a region of special people, whether merchants, sailors, or farmers, of succulent food and liquor, creamy Camenbert, bountiful fruit and Calvados. "Our goal for this book," they concluded "has been to create an atmosphere, which introduces the life in Normandy. We hope that you become intimately connected to a peaceful valley, the crossing of paths in the forest, a small village or a well-known city. And then, you will love Normandie." Signed: Normandie, June, July, August 1944.

They concluded, "This book was composed by Normands who far from their province have never before felt so desperately the deep and loving connections, which attach them to these images, to their rivers, their meadows, their forests and their ruins. While every day the names of Caen, Thury-Harcourt, Sainte-Mère-Eglise, or Saint-Lo, and many more were painfully made famous, these Normands recreated for themselves and you, the smiling and prosperous face of Normandy, their testimony to find solace and hope."[9]

Two years later, just before the book was published, they wrote an additional chapter, telling the story of the battles of Normandy, and ended with these words: "All of you, free citizens of America, children of Texas or Missouri, Canadians of the Great Lakes, descendants of our families from Dieppe, Britons, with whom we have a common ancestor in William, and all of you, friends, who died on our soil, whatever your flag is, sleep in peace. Sleep in peace in our rich soil of Normandy under our apple trees, and in the shade of your white crosses. We will never forget you."[10]

1 August—An electrifying day of extreme nervousness, tension, and stupefying news; our radio service is befuddled by the discrepancies and contradictions between the official communiqués and the announcements of the wire services.

Pontorson reached and bypassed, beginning of an encircling movement [of Paris], which excites the strategists. We finally reached the evening with our head on fire, our tongue dry, and worn out by the chitchat and the controversies.

15 August—The incredible news and a similar state of mind continue. The heat is scorching, which contributes to increasing the tension. At 1:00 p.m.: announcement of the landing in Toulon. The incoherence of the dispatches, the exuberance of the war correspondents, the silences from the official channels, and the abundance of our deductions end up in absolute confusion.

18 August—Where are they? The American tanks may have reached Chateaudun, Pithiviers, and Chartres.

Following from a distance the advance of the Allies, not knowing the fate of their families who lived in the cities mentioned, was excruciating. My father knew that my mother and I were in the proximity of Pithiviers, where some combat took place, and that the Germans engaged in a scorched earth policy, gathering men and young boys as hostages, shooting them indiscriminately.

The landing in Toulon was also exciting news. General de Lattre, leading the French Army B, attached to the American 7th Army of General Patch, landed east of Toulon (Southern France). General De Lattre, looking ahead from the landing craft, said, "France is there.... A few more hours and her sons, who came to liberate her, will throw themselves in her arms.... As our flags are hoisted on all the ships, La Marseillaise [national anthem] bursts out, the most moving I have ever heard it.... Eyes misty with tears, the heart seized by emotion, every man looks at the land which brings them the first smile of France with which they are reunited."[11]

20 August—Competition sportive: close to two thousand sports certificates are awarded following the various competitions which have engaged a larger number of older men than younger ones. Love of physical culture or self-esteem?

Yachting is replaced by a new game. Squadrons of "scale models" crisscross our air space. The graceful gliders brush by the roofs, and full of irony glide beyond the barbed wire fence. This week, Exposition of the scale models at the 17 west. The *Kommandatur* forbids a huge release of these harmless devices.... A question of security!

21 August—Versailles is seized, capture of Toulon. March toward Draguignan. The Russians expand their offensives.

Oppressive heat, the thermometer reaches eighty-eight degree Fahrenheit in the bunks.

23 August—1:00 p.m.—Special communiqué: Digne, Gap, Sisteron, Grenoble. [French Army B marched north very quickly, parallel to the Rhone Valley.]

12. Wait: The Leitmotiv of the Prisoner

1:10 p.m.—Collective madness: Runners dash in and out, shouting full throated: Paris is taken … Paris is taken…

From one window to the other one yells, Paris is taken … Paris is taken. An immense echo rolls, bounces back, and swells up. Paris is taken … Paris is taken…. The barracks shake with a furious tremor. Frantic, a horn sounds the "Hallali" [the kill]! Sirens: alert greeted with a chorus of cheers. At 1:20 p.m.: reading of a brief official communiqué, followed by a call to calm.

Calm is brought into being, little by little, within the waves of a profound joy. At 5:00 p.m. gathering in formal uniform, and facing west, salute France, and to show our independence make the 5:30 p.m. roll call last only a few minutes.

5:40 p.m.—They can't believe it!

8:00 p.m.—Sudden and phenomenal blossoming of flags: the flame-like paper strips with the colors of the Allies hug the somber and black barracks with a shimmering incandescence.

24 August—Touching solicitude of our temporary masters: our Jewish comrades leave for the camp of Lübeck [reprisal camp]. We are sure we will see them again soon, but liberated.

At 11:00 a.m., alert. For the first time an immense air fleet flies over. Hundreds of shiny arrows glide in the transparent sky, as tight as sardines. Frenzied Hurrah!

Around 4:00 p.m. the exuberance falls and is replaced by a dreary anguish: one fights in the capital.

25 August—The anguish intensifies: Le Crillon [a leading hotel in Paris on the Place de la Concorde] is burning. Street combat: L' Hotel de Ville [town hall] is in flames as well as the Pavillon de la Reine in Versailles. Huge damages. One fears that Paris will suffer the fate of Warsaw. Consternation not dispelled by the passing of a powerful air fleet, flying from north to southwest.

26 August—Everything quiets down. General de Gaulle has entered Paris. Yesterday's news was exaggerated by the alacrity of the American correspondents.

Slow return to joy.

At the time of the men's exuberance about the ins and outs of the battles, a bitter sarcasm in the entry on 24 August struck a cruel note, of their Jewish comrades being sent to the Lübeck camp. The Germans pursued tactics of revenge in the camps as they had in France, as witnessed by the diarist's sour note, "touching solicitude of our temporary masters."

Everyone knew that Lübeck was a reprisal camp, and the possibility of being killed was high. Attempting to ignore their bitterness, some wishful thinking follows:

We are sure we will see them again soon, but liberated. In addition, the Germans sent two of the leaders of La Maffia *to Lübeck, torturing one of them in October.*[12] *At the same time, these men also learned that their wives and children, who had been incarcerated by the Germans in the camp of Drancy in France, had been moved in July to a concentration camp in Germany.*

An insurrection and guerrilla warfare in Paris from 10 to 19 August threatened to break up the French Resistance and facilitate the take-over by the Communists. After General De Gaulle's intervention with General Eisenhower, General LeClerc entered Paris with a division of seventeen thousand Frenchmen who had taken part in the Normandy campaign, supported by an American Infantry Division. Leclerc obtained the capitulation of the German Kommandant, General von Choltitz. On 26 August General de Gaulle walked down the Champs Elysées, acclaimed by the crowd.[13]

31 August—Marvelous unfolding of the news; fortress Europe is a sieve according to the common majority opinion. Updating the maps takes a large part of the day, and for the rest of the day, their thrilled contemplation is followed by lengthy commentaries. All the fronts are moving. In the West, Amiens is taken, Mezières, Charleville, Saint-Dizier reached, fight over Valence. In the East, Romania has signed an armistice. Revolt in Bulgaria.

Christmas at home! Why not!

20 September—Balance sheet for the month: Liberation of Luxembourg and Belgium, siege of Aachen, and liberation of Brest. Finland stops fighting. Bulgaria declares a state of war with Germany.

Arrival in the camp of 400 officers [POWs] coming from Montvy.

1 October—The Paymaster does not pay out our military pay anymore. Real reason: the Lager-mark, ersatz currency for use by the POWs, has a higher value than the Reich-mark. It has an official standing outside of the camp and is used by the good German bourgeois, hoping to be reimbursed after the defeat, at the actual rate of the Mark.

Will we be left without money?

Error: a French bank is organizing for our internal payments—transfers, checks—when a checkbook?

30 October—Again, walls of mist in our sad horizons, and one after the other our expectations die....

Inexorably, the fronts stabilize. Fall has a hold on us, already cold drizzles and fog, and winter lurks, as we are poorer and more destitute than ever.

With the lack of packages, our reserves are depleted despite the ruthless rationing of the *popotiers*. We are reduced to the German pittance: potatoes, three times a week, barley and dry cabbage.

12. Wait: The Leitmotiv of the Prisoner

Thanks to the crop of the groups' gardens and of the nearby fields, cultivated by courageous volunteers, one throws oneself ravenously on the brew of vegetables cooked in a carrot base.

No coal or so little: thirty-seven pounds per day for two hundred men. No more distribution of wood; raids on everything that burns. The music kiosk, beheaded, shows only a few posts pointing toward the sky. The Chleuhs finish it off. The log pathways smashed and dissected are in turn dismantled by the Germans, but the wood disappears from the carts before they arrive at the *Vorlager*; heroic scenes, fights. Many are thrown into the gniouf.

Resignation! We are so used to it. Actually, isn't it a dream? Was it possible that this would finally end?

26 November—Sudden warm spell before winter. Strasbourg is taken, and Alsace is partly liberated. The Siegfried line [Siegfried Line refers to the World War II defensive fortifications, built by the Germans during the 1930s opposite the Maginot Line] is crushed. Slow advance toward Köln.

Dreary weather! Engulfed by a wave of lifeless melancholy, it is difficult to express any joy.

It is taking too long....

No more individual packages, but distributions one after the other of American packages. A few days of abundance are followed by meager days.

An average *popote* actually possesses in reserve: five or six servings of beans, the same of noodles, a little bit of sugar and flour enough to hold about fifteen days, fasting every other day.

On 12 September a group from General Leclerc's Division, which had advanced east, and one from General de Lattre's Army, coming from the south, met about one hundred miles southeast of Paris. A captain from de Lattre's Army remembered, "I can never forget the immense joy of seeing the first armored vehicles of Leclerc's Division coming to meet us. This meeting personified a great victory of the French Army over Nazism and the end of the dark years of the occupation."[14]

12 December—At the theater, *Un petit ange de rien du tout* [*A Little Angel of No Importance*] closes a spectacular season, marked by daring ventures such as the staging of the *Grand Poucet* and *Electre*, and the repeat performances of the great successes of the *boulevards* with *Les Amant terribles* and *Les Vignes du Seigneur*. At the Refuge, variety shows and coffeehouse—including an excellent retrospective *Du Chat Noir à l'A.B.C.*, and *Pérette*, an operetta by Marc.

Between the shows, cabaret with orchestra—there are about ten in the camps—and the jazz of R.M. and Marc. There are numerous meetings of the most diverse organizations, punctuated by skits, reviews, even folkloric songs and dances.

December 20—Frost, glistening grid of the barbed wires, dressed in a shimmering of crystals. Heavy bending of the electrical cables pulled toward the ground, and which break in a final vibration.

No electricity, no light, no water. One replaces the former by *loupiottes*, made of a piece of cloth rolled tight and dipped in fat, the latter by melted snow.

No electricity, no news, except for those of the *V. B.* which proclaims the success of the German attack in the direction of Malmédy [Battle of the Bulge].

Our wardens resume some degree of smugness. It is necessary to have strong nerves.

December 31—Dreary holidays for Christmas: midnight mass. Saint-Sylvester: turning off of the lights at 9:00 p.m. sanction taken as a result of the theft of wood.

It is impossible to break the heavy listlessness which smothers the last jolts of this dying year. For having promised too much, it leaves us disillusioned, stung by doubt and forlornness.

Today: thoughts that fly toward France where one had fervently hoped to be at this date. Tomorrow: waiting for letters, packages.... The blues, cold, hunger.... There is nothing to hope for before we get out of this enclosure of misfortune. When? But when?

1945

Cold and snow: the same scourge that always recurs on the same dates. The Germans' attack in the Ardennes is finally stopped. Domestic preoccupations: letters and packages: nothing from France. From time to time, we receive an American, Argentinean, or Canadian package to be split between five or six men.

12 January—Ray of hope: launching of the Russian winter offensive. The German pocket dwindles in the West.

17 January—Today is a good day. Three things: a Russian communiqué announces the fall of Warsaw; the German front is pierced in the direction of Eastern Prussia; and arrival of French packages mailed in July and August.

The university, theater, and cabaret are closed. It is too cold. Withdrawn life in our cubicle, where the hunt for the little stove begins again: doleful lethargy in the shelter of blankets.

12. Wait: The Leitmotiv of the Prisoner

5 February—Liberation of Colmar after a ten-day offensive [last pocket of resistance in Alsace liberated by General de Lattre and the First Army, which then crossed the Rhine and took Stuttgart fighting in Germany to the end of the war in Europe]. The attacks on the Siegfried Line have resumed, and a Russian quick-paced advance is reaching the Oder River at Kustrin and Frankfurt an der Oder.

Around 5:45 p.m. order to immediately go back into the barracks. In fifteen minutes the stragglers will be shot. Reason: theft of wood.

Rumor: the dog of one of the sentries has been clobbered and prepared as a stew. The truth: a few starving men eat rats that some trap and sell for cigarettes [In the middle of March a fresh rat was worth five cigarettes. By the end of March it was worth ten].

1 March—The weather is very mild. The Russians have reached the Baltic Sea at Rugenwald. Renewed theft of wood: it is forbidden to leave the barracks after 5:30 p.m. The electricity is cut off at 9:00 p.m. The sanctions will last for two weeks.

Almost daily alerts: Bombers, escorted by fighters, fly over the camp. Their target: Vienna.

6 March—Snow storm and glacial wind; cold that penetrates deeply into the cubicles.

Increasingly meager food, which V., the biologist, estimates at eight hundred calories per day and not one grain of salt for many weeks. Vehement protests by our Commandant to the Red Cross in Geneva.

March 8—What a wonderful day! We receive collective packages from France, and the Allies succeed significantly in the West and take Köln [Cologne]. The Rhine River is crossed at Remagen. We immediately forget all our deprivations and a vertiginous optimism rises; radiant smiles, and a growing excitement, which becomes enthusiasm. It is impossible to go to sleep.

15 March—The Third Army crosses the Moselle River. Coblenz is taken.

New tightening of the rations: Doctors point out many pernicious anemias; skeletal weight loss, beards that do not grow anymore, low temperature of ninety-six degrees.

Our friend F., five feet nine inches tall, weighs only one hundred three pounds. Odd feeling: seeing a fellow man grow skinny. First, the cheeks hollow out, then the neck is emaciated; suddenly the ribs protrude. We stare at each other with surprise, astonished to see a stranger being born at each new stage.

22 March—Glorious spring efflorescence: a few white, round clouds sail softly in the blue sky. Alert as usual: one hundred or so fortresses, trailing long white contrails, which hang on the clouds behind them, fly in the direction of the north and after a wide turn head for Vienna. Bombing continue on all of Germany. Profusion of news: it seems to indicate that the French troops have entered Germany and the Russians are marching toward Danzig.

We receive neither letters nor packages.

24 March—No one engages in sports activities anymore. Only a few fanatics, untouched by hunger pains continue to frequent the Barracks of the Sports. There are only a few activities left at the university as a result of the harsh universal law of starving. It has, however, a new student, who generates a most spirited anticipation: a young rabbit picked up inside our wire fence [what was it doing there?] is the object of the jealous attention of V. the biologist. It will not be a matter of vivisection.

27 March—One loses one's bearing in the complexity and abundance of the communiqués. Capture of Frankfurt am Main. Considerable excitement about the Germans' alleged request of an armistice. A chaotic optimism reigns in our community, always ready to extreme oscillations. A month ago, we contemplated the end of the war, possibly in June; a week ago, we predicted it in May; the day before yesterday, it was in April; this morning, in about ten days; this evening, in four to five days at the most. All the possibilities are considered to mitigate the expected German collapse: requisitioning, finding provisions on the premises, billeting in the villages and the hotels of Vienna etc. The flock of sheep, which grazes peaceably the rare grass of the nearby fields, is apprised, weighed, and already portioned out [All work of La Maffia. In 1944, the French Commandant had appointed a special staff to direct the operations in case the camp was left to fend for itself after a German collapse]. In sudden flashes we think of our return; it's not a vague daydream anymore, in which a treacherous play of mirages, at times gives rise to hope, and other times takes it away, but it has become a quasi-mathematical certainty. One tries to imagine what this return will be, this arrival in a country, in a town, in a house, left almost six years ago, and one contemplates this undeniable liberation as a logical event that will come very quickly.

29 March—No electricity, meaning no news. Some calm. Endless daily alerts. There is nothing to do. In the absence of materials, and owing to the almost constant shutdown of electricity, it has become impossible to put on a show. And then, try to give a performance on an empty stomach in front of spectators tormented by stomach cramps.

1 April—The Russians occupy Danzig; the French cross the Rhine River. It seems that the German opposition tries to stiffen on a line parallel to the Rhine. One hundred ten miles from us, the Russians resume their attacks in the direction of Vienna. A squadron of Allied airplanes flies over our heads and dives to attack the Göpfritz train station. Success! An enormous jet of steam: locomotive hit. At about 4:00 p.m. attack of a German encampment located one mile or so toward the west.

3 April—A magnificent white truck stops at the camp gates. Packages! The magic words fly to the four corners of the camp and penetrate into the heart of the barracks. Shipment from the French government, via Switzerland: sardines, soups, nougats, jams, gingerbread.

Toward evening, a red glow in the southeast and the rumble of faraway cannons.

4 April—The German resistance is falling apart. The Russians are approaching Magnio Rova, Bratislava, Wiener-Neustadt. All of a sudden this advance revives the flame of our worries of a forced departure, on the road with a backpack. In their advance on the western front, every day the Allies find camps of roaming POWs, thrown out into the countryside by their frightened guards. Until now ours protest, but the arrival at the *Vorlager* of four old field kitchens and their repair gives us something to think twice about.

5 April—Sudden rise of fever: we estimate that the Danube and Morava Rivers have been crossed by the Russian push. Since this morning the road from Edelbach to Göpfritz offers the classic spectacle of displacement behind the line.

A long line of peasants, creeping along following carts piled up with common house furnishings, is moving toward the west fleeing from the battle. At intervals, a convoy of ancient cars passes full of hay, accompanied by Romanian or Hungarian contingents dressed in khaki.

This spectacle, the stupendous evolution of events, and the fever that predominate here, suddenly lead to the idea of an imminent evacuation of the camp.

In all the cubicles a frantic flurry of packing: a bed of torn papers already covers the floor. We stuff our bags, adjust the strap, cut, and sew. We carry the packs and unload them. Notebook on hand one flies to friends: "Address? Phone number?"

Some say it is insanity to abandon notes, work, books, clothes, and the few possessions we hold in order to walk in circles and be liberated in ten to twelve miles in morass and destitution. Be aware, others think, that we may come back faster thanks to the chaos, even if we have to forge ahead.

The 9:00 p.m. communiqué brings glorious news: the Ruhr is encircled, Münster, Karlsruhe, Arnheim, Osnabrück, Gotha, Kassel, Mülhausen are taken; Bratislava is occupied by the Russians. Hungary is liberated. Neither the Danube nor the Morava Rivers have been crossed.

6 April—Rain hits the windows with full force.

Similar psychosis of departure; intensified by an escalation of rumors.

No idleness for the camp exchange office, whose secretary Toto G. passes along "confidential" information from time to time. "Above all keep it quiet!"

The "confidential" tip of the day; we will leave in the direction of the northwest, two battalions at a time, ten miles per day.

One hour later the whole camp is "confidentially" informed.

7 April—We continue to prepare for our departure with the same contagious zeal. Some possess an overabundance of goods, which others lack and vice versa. Therefore, business flourishes in the camp exchange services. Simultaneously with the official camp exchange services, X. holds an unauthorized bureau where, at less controlled rates, one can obtain anything that is lacking in the official market. The most asked for items: bags, straps, satchels, shoes, socks. Food is unobtainable.

The wind blows and heavy snow continues to fall.

8 April—Our Commandant, General G. pays us a visit and speaks of the possible evacuation of the camp.

He especially mentions "the poor state of health of the enlisted men and officers [POWs]" and consequently requests that "the necessary measures be taken for emplacement of the encampments, supplies along the way, moderate length for each segment of the march. A sufficient advance notice must be given before departure." He gets a harsh non-response from the adversary: "It has been studied. I have nothing to tell you." [The French organized for their protection.]

Afternoon medical visit of a German doctor to list those unfit for the march. From a list of fifteen hundred to two thousand, two hundred fifty are authorized to stay put. Formation of battalions in case of departure: a French hierarchy is established. It will assume control in case of the failure or disappearance of our guards.

"Confidential" tip from the camp exchange office. Arrival point: Salzburg, via Krummau, Gratzen and Passau.

Altogether one hundred fifty miles, provided the passage of the Danube is not cut before we arrive.

Several towns are taken in the direction of Vienna: Hildesheim and Essen are occupied.

9 April—The mass of refugees now forms an uninterrupted column, which moves slowly toward the west. It appears from the edges of the plain, which borders the horizon beyond the road to Edelbach. It flows forever renewed, carried by its own energy, as if it were to never end, intermingling military men, civilians, livestock, and vehicles.

12. Wait: The Leitmotiv of the Prisoner

Women in red dresses, their head tightly covered with a bright-colored scarf, walk next to peasants dressed in black dragging their kids by the hand.

The German sentries gaze at the spectacle with bovine impassivity.

10 April—The Russians have entered Vienna, where they occupy the Town Hall, the Opera, the gas plant, and several garrisons. A battle rages in the St Joseph train station. This time the imminence of departure seems inevitable even for the skeptics. It is their turn to rush into the madness of preparation. Letter from our Commandant to the German General:

"You are taking a heavy responsibility. We do not want to leave. You are forcing us. Weigh well all your actions." No answer.... We have not had any bread since yesterday. In its place we get one pound of raw potatoes.

From the east an interminable stream of refugees continues.

11 April—There is a constant lack of electricity, which means a matching lack of water. In the absence of bread, the *Verwaltung* [administration] empties its silos of potatoes to which we adapt the best we can. Breakfast: potato soup. Lunch: potato stew. 3:00 p.m.: potato crepes. Dinner: mashed potatoes. Nothing else and our stomachs give up. There is nothing to report. Having finished our preparation, we resume our almost regular life: in the evening, lecture by the contemporary *Cercles d'Etudes*. Subject: town-planning.

The sky is amazingly pure and immutable for a pleasant and warm day.

12 April—New outburst of energy: birth of the small luggage cart, a box mounted on wheels creating a handcart. Everything that can roll is used as wheels even lampshades made of enamel sheets. They are tested with their loads in the central alley, clogged up like a Chinese back-alley. The back of a minuscule cart bears a red, white, and blue flag painted directly on the planks, and this inscription: 41st R.I. 3rd Company, 2nd battalion.

13 April—The death of President Roosevelt throws a veil of mourning on the day. Fall of Vienna. An oppressive calm reigns.

14 April—Rain. Storms. Sky full of clouds. The Allies reach the Elbe River, which they encircle around Magdeburg.

The Austrian people have welcomed their liberators "with great joy...."

A green ripple runs on the fields and young growths suddenly appear on the firs. Spring is blossoming. The sky is crystalline blue.

Vertical fall of the excitement: sliding toward a new belief: "If we were to leave, we would have done so already."

There were different opinions about the evacuation of the camp. The German guards were anxious to leave and go west. They did not want to be taken prisoner by the Russians. While the French worried about their poor conditions to walk, the stronger sentiment for leaving, certainly from La Maffia, *including my father—was the worry about being liberated by the Russians. This stronger desire to leave was expressed in the diary,* "vertical fall of the excitement," *when they thought they would stay in the camp. As my father told me later, it was particularly crucial for the Alsatians, who often were taken as Germans by the Russians and incarcerated in Russia. The avowed protestations from the French Commandant, mentioned as their poor conditions to walk, while well-founded, may well have been a way to put pressure on the Germans for some material support during the evacuation of the camp, raising the specter of their responsibility in case of deaths of the POWs on the way.*

13

Trekking Eighty Miles to Freedom

16 April–11 May / 19 June 1945

16 April—8:00 a.m.—Departure tomorrow at 6:30 a.m.! The order bursts like a thunderclap. We immediately resume the rush of activities.

Big fires consume letters and personal papers. Our suitcases and trunks bearing our painted names are sent down to and stocked in the *Vorlager* in case the future occupants of the camp would forward them. Fully outfitted walkers train in circles in the fields. Suddenly they stop, put down their backpack, empty it of some of its content, put it back on their back and move again in great strides, the shoulders pulled by a weight still too heavy. A little further they do the same thing again. They line at the infirmary in front of the single scale, which is used to weigh luggage. The inexorable needle continually shows an excess of weight!

A last minute communiqué announces that the Russians have taken St. Polten: thirty miles as the crow flies and one of the crossings of the Danube.

Exhausted by fatigue and overwrought, we climb in our cubicles, and motionless the eyes wide open, we try to imagine the promise of this magic word: departure tomorrow morning!

17 April—3:00 a.m.—Get up in there! A stubborn cigarette lighter scatters its sparks; a vacillating flame zigzagging in the night attaches itself to a little grease lamp, which lights with difficulty. Dazzling return of lucidity: we are going! We are going to go! Five years have been consumed waiting for this moment, sixteen hundred nights dreaming of the dawn of this day. It will happen in a few hours. We will cross the gate which has separated us from life, leaving behind us the flea-laden barracks and the fields worn by the scraping of our clogs. Our happiness is so intense that it hurts. A completely new feeling and yet, crowded with recollections D. cries out, "It looks like a departure for vacation!" Yes, that's it: an anticipation of the splendor of the sun and of play after the interminable school year. A sudden patch of light: live forces for too long contained, which erupt at the call of freedom! Freedom! We feel it so inevitable and near. Aren't we leaving toward it? Where will we catch it, on what road, at the corner of what woods, along which brook?

Still no electricity; the feeble light covers in half tones a messy sight. L. busies himself around our little stove and the brisk fire which throws tongues of flames and places a black bottom kettle full of the last beans. Silent, "the Ten" buckle up the straps of their bags. Our group walks together toward the cart, on which M., who built it, fastens the load. The box of provisions: three and a half pounds of pasta, two sausages, sugar, a gingerbread loaf, together with a large aluminum pot, a big tin can, a few tools, a piece of sharpened metal which we use as an axe, and ten individual satchels.

6:00 a.m.—Miserable day that seeps through the windows and spills over on the floor strewn with rubbish. We are ready. A last look at what was our home and prison. An unusual resonance reverberates through the torn sheets of cardboard dividers. On the table lay dirty dishes, old socks, torn sweaters, and one wooden shoe with its nails upward.

9:45 a.m.—We cross the gate. Stop on the road which runs parallel to the camp toward Edelbach. The weather is oppressive. Strenuously the sun, ringed by a peculiar halo of luminous haze, rises slowly in the east.

Sitting on the back of the embankment we contemplate in silence this ghastly square, bristling with barbed wire, against which our hope and expectations were dashed for so long. In a quick glance we embrace the long row of barracks, connected together by strings on which stretched rags are drying. The kitchens, piles of graying buildings, spit up black smoke. A gruesome sadness emanates from this geometric and ugly compound. Would it be better to carry away an image as proof, or suppress it in order to forget? A number of motionless groups, also silent, are facing us from the other side of the barrier. Our gazes cross. They are our friends. Identified as unfit for the road or hiding at the time of departure, they are staying there to wait for the liberation on the premises. A different adventure! Movement: time again to carry the backpack. It feels heavy. A last glance at the bare ground: the bowling lane and the open-air theater, some kind of luxuriant island with its wild grass. The cemetery.... Head turned to the right, hand on our cap we salute those who remain prisoners of this hostile earth and for whom no one is waiting anymore. Good-bye M., old buddy.

Edelbach, which yesterday we still caught sight of as the Promised Land

13. Trekking Eighty Miles to Freedom

with its red-roof houses and stone church, is already behind us, a deserted hamlet and a village without joy. On the right, suddenly the Camp still spreads its entire horrid monstrosity behind the top of the hill that seems to slide slowly in order to discover it better. But in front of us the road opens up, broad, between green fields that undulate softly and melt away in the firs. The cart rolls cheerfully, pulled by two men.

At noon, quick lunch on the go between Allentstein and Zwinzen in a verdant glen, close to an encampment of demobilized Hungarian soldiers, fleeing toward the west. Army of another time, living evocation of the hordes of Arpad, with its coarse covered wagons, in which also sit women with thigh boots, dressed in worn-out furs, gaunt with weariness next to the warriors with heavy mustaches,

Heavenly stopover in the grass of a completely green meadow—grass! Tall and new!

The road is a tough ordeal for men who have been enclosed for five years in a square measuring sixteen hundred feet by fifteen hundred feet.

From time to time, a comrade, overcome by fatigue, slides to the bottom of the ditch, his bag on the ground, waiting to be picked up by the medic's cart. Smart-alecks choose the proximity of a village or an isolated farm as a calculated dropping-out place, hoping to stay there, in relative security until the liberation. Another aspect of this adventure!

5:00 p.m.—Krosskainraths: fifteen miles from Edelbach. The cart has just lost one wheel. The lampshade, which was used as an end plate and hub, has given up under a too-heavy load. Parked in the center of the village in front of the porch of a farm, we watch the stream of battalions pass us under all kinds of jibes. Two images superimpose one on the other. One, already ancient, of a doleful herd pushed toward the east by young, passionate, dynamic victors. And this other, all-thrilling under our eyes: the same men walking in the reverse direction, prevailing over their puny bodies with all their utmost will, and dragging along their guards like dogs on the leash: Endless and odd throng, which takes on the picturesque look of the nomadic migrations. Fancy bags, and triumph of the do-it-yourselfers and of improvisation. Suitcases balanced on two long branches resting on the shoulders in the manner of Chinese coolies; proliferation of carts from a scaled-down model for one person to four hundred forty pounds pulled by five men in front. All of this passes at a good pace in a cloud of dust. Meanwhile our chief and C. barter from a farmer a few planks and some nails for cigarettes, and from the farmer's wife three fresh eggs for a bar of chocolate. Skimpy pittance for ten hungry stomachs! Before we left, we received one loaf of bread for two and three and a half ounces of cheese. There are only two field kitchens for three thousand men. Worries about dinner deepen a furrow on the cook's forehead.

A few retrospective notes while we wait for the repairs to be completed. As we passed through villages, we were stunned to rediscover attractive houses, women in light dresses, and children. No hostility, but a sort of lifeless stupor. The French are leaving! Why: seeds of a muted anxiety.

We pass along the morning news to the men of a Panzer regiment, waylaid in the woods while waiting for the Russians: St. Polten occupied, the British at the outskirts of Hamburg. The morale of the troops is very low; the German combatant is waiting for the end and does not understand anymore this foolish resistance that reduces the Great Reich to a field of ruins.

"Let's go: D. and P. at the yoke!" The repairs finished, the little cart starts, squeaking, dragging along the Ten, who hang tightly all around it and embed themselves in a break of the column.

Allentsteig, a small commercial town with schools and a hospital, had been spared the expulsion of the villages for the military reservation in 1938 and became its headquarters. It is dominated by its castle, founded in the early Middle Ages and enlarged in the sixteenth century in Renaissance style with a large two-storied courtyard, graced with an arcade around a pathway. Surviving the chaotic times of the Thirty-Year War, Allentsteig flourished in the subsequent years. With the building in 1870 of the famous Franz Joseph Bahn (railroad), eventually linking Vienna to Prague, it became an important commerce center. The line has recently been electrified, but in 1940 the French officers took the original train, pulled by a steam engine.

From Allentsteig the men went straight west, following secondary roads and sometimes going on paths cross-country.

18 April—5:30 a.m.—A cold mist treacherously penetrates through the blanket and chills us to the bones. In the still drab morning light the gray smokes of the bivouac rise toward the sky, and the outline of the encampment reveals itself. We slept under the stars, directly on the ground of a plowed field sloping down to the bank of a fast flowing river. Sleep of a brute, interrupted by the yelling of the guards and the constant running around of those with dysentery, who put down their pants at the edges of the field, where we have pitched camp as the last arrival. There is no canopy. The wind blows a swarm of defiled papers and waves of stench over to us. We wash up in the river, and water duty. A fire of vine shoots between two stones warms some tea.

8:15 a.m.—Departure of the battalion led by the French Colonel O.,

13. Trekking Eighty Miles to Freedom

stocky and energetic. On the German side a captain of the Flack [anti-aircraft unit] in a purple uniform, tall and with a fairly open face, commands the battalion. He seems animated by human feelings, an amazing thing. On the other hand, his lieutenant, a creepy little ball with the mug of a bulldog, showed himself savagely bitchy as soon as we left. The sentries, old men or creeps picked up by the Wehrmacht's expansion, show glaring signs of fatigue and laissez-faire. One of them openly declares himself a social democrat; another, past director of a school in Vienna, carries at the end of his arm a minuscule school bag which contains all his belonging. They all drag their feet and groan, "*Ach die Füsse!*" [Oh! My feet].

We march on an extremely rugged, stony path in the direction of the northwest, following the choppy, lurching rhythm of the cart. Valleys covered with meadows and firs, reminiscent a little of the Monts du Beaujolais. We cross large villages, where some bold companions sneak in to exchange American soap, sweaters, and socks for food. At a crossing on the side of the path, our Commandant, General G., straight and steady, looks at the passing column. A few minutes later, a motor vehicle passes us: the German General drives under a concert of imprecations and catcalls.

We are soon in full view of Kirchberg.

Around 2:00 p.m. we enter an immense "ranch" enclosed by barbed wire. Oh! The sinister feeling! We receive one loaf of bread and a chunk of sausage for two days. There are no field kitchens. The march, the exertion, and the hunger plague our weak bodies. Small fires. Menu: baked potatoes, dandelions, and sausage. It feels good to stretch on the grass keeping an eye on the kettle.

4:00 p.m.—The potatoes, baked just right, are steaming in our mess kit. Call to assembly: stormy grumbling, another invention to get on people's nerves. A message flies: sleep in town in a barn. For crying out loud! We fit the top of the mess kit on the perfectly warm potatoes and fresh dandelions. Dinner is for later whenever possible.

19 April—A barn, which could hold four hundred men, swallows eight hundred. Eight hundred aching bodies so entangled one into the other that any movement brings a violent reaction. And always those with dysentery! In order to reach the door they wander in the dark, stepping with their soles on a hand, a head, or a stomach. Just like the warning of a lighthouse signaling a reef, a barking voice makes a human presence known with the refrain: "Mister, pass on the left," a pre-emptive and commanding admonition.

Finally, daybreak and the bright sun of a spring morning.

A stop does not offer surprises anymore: the fits and starts, the stops,

Map of the Trek, 17 April–11 May 1945: Trek of some of the officer POWs over the mountains in northern Austria to what was then Czechoslovakia and back to Austria to meet the American Army (Jacqueline Vautrain Collins).

the false departures, the congestion of the little carts, all of that is now familiar. This time, however, serious news; the guards have received the order to prevent barter, and the inhabitants are forbidden to open their doors. By redoubling our cunning we still manage to pick up eggs, potatoes, and bacon. In this way, we pass through Waldenstein, and Hormanns. The wind is blowing violently.

The scenery is greener and more mountainous. On our left a wide-open valley dominated by a medieval-looking building, perched on a mountain peak. We climb a steep slope to Altweitra. Bivouac. In the east, a forested butte rises above a meadow. Halfway to the top, a railroad track: at the bottom, a swift river with willow trees along its banks. Campfire for the ritual boiled potatoes. The field kitchen distributes a few tablespoons of a clear brew of barley. R., a fanatic and master fisherman, whose luggage includes a fly fishing line, catches a trout, followed by an admiring and terribly jealous crowd.

13. Trekking Eighty Miles to Freedom

20 April—The meadow, so welcoming yesterday, is now reduced to a rutted field, where a few burning ambers smoke. The night was so cold that the water froze in our canteens. Shivering shadows stay close to the big fires. It is 8 a.m. We are told that the day's march will be thirteen miles. We know what that means: aching muscles, and our bag feeling as if they are loaded with stones. Spreading along the line, the news, heard on the portable radios, circulates: offensive in northern Italy, siege of Berlin, capitulation of Düsseldorf, occupation of the Ruhr. Nothing is happening in our sector. At the outskirts of town, where the houses are uniformly closed as ordered, we meet a company of women auxiliary of the Flack, strong young women in blue pants tightened at the ankles. Their commandant, Frau Hauptmann, wearing a very short blue suit and silk tights, walks to her car preceded by a heavyweight, her assistant, carrying a rubber tub under his right arm and a bag made of gaudy canvas at the end of his left arm. That is the new look of the Wehrmacht.

Last houses: a door opens partway. A woman lays down a basket full of potatoes and disappears. Gesture of silent greatness! We are at the boundaries of Czechoslovakia.

And the exhausting march resumes, in the wind, the sun, and the dust. Unserfrau, Schagges, Heinreichs, Pyhrabruck [villages along the way].

We climb an interminable hill crossing over a pass, which used to be the old frontier of Czechoslovakia, and descent toward Gratzen [now, Nove Hrady]. There will be an extended stopover: one after the other, each battalion breaks up to its respective encampment, nearby farms, where it will stay for a few days. Ours has to travel another five miles, generating vociferous protests, which naturally get nowhere.

Gratzen: a neat little town with its middle-class houses behind iron gates and hedges, but without doubt, a Nazi stronghold with men in uniforms of every shades, from a pale blue to a canary yellow, covered with insignias and medals; a few good mugs of Chleuhs. An incident for a futile motive becomes violent with an edgy guard; bayonets point and are then lowered. We climb up again a very steep slope, and on a fairly pleasant plateau surrounded by hills, which are already fading in the mist, we discover on our right a square of large buildings with brown tile roofs topped with a small steeple. Pause. We unbuckle our bags, and lying on the aromatic grass which grows along the road, we feel the cool air flow like fresh water on our burning faces.

The entire region was settled in the thirteenth century with small villages, usually less than one hundred inhabitants, scattered a mile or so from each other. They were bound together in municipalities of about one thousand, which provided governmental oversight. The villages often carried the name of the aristocratic family who built a castle with the exception of Pyhrabrück. It was named as the bridge (brück) over the Birken.

In addition to a castle, each village had a church, either in gothic, baroque, or rococo style, with a tower topped by an onion-shaped structure, more akin to the Orient. Pyhrabrück, a larger village, prided itself of its bell tower of the nineteenth century. More consequential was the seventeenth century pilgrimage to the Nativity of the Virgin Church in Unserfrau-Altweitra, where there was a medicinal bath.

At Altweitra they turned mostly north toward what was at the time Czechoslovakia to reach Gratzen, a small town in southern Bohemia, surrounded by deep forests, picturesque valleys, and meadows. It, too, was settled in the thirteenth century with a castle protecting the trade route. After a stormy history in the seventeenth century, it flourished in the eighteenth century, known for its glasswork in Venetian style. The new castle (Nova Hrady) was built in the early nineteenth century in rococo style, called the "Czech Versailles."

The men will now walk full west, just parallel to the Czech borders, on a regular road.

21 April—As we step out of the dark barn we are almost blinded by a light too bright and the vivid blue of the sky. In the center of the farm courtyard is an enormous pile of manure and all around it, many carts and agricultural machinery. Here and there, a few small fires already burn with the wood crackling. From the courtyard, we can reach a big meadow, from which we discover a vast panorama of round hills, crowned with firs. In the hollow, major villages are tucked away. One seems dominated by a huge church with two bell towers. Along the buildings huge chestnut trees intermingle their branches to form a deep arch over a grassy alley. They resonate with birds...

Foretaste of freedom: a sentry gazes casually at the walkers, who stray beyond the pond shining under the sun.

3:00 p.m.—The weather breaks up. Heavy clouds, pushed by a raging wind, which scrapes the roofs of the farm, and snowflakes begin to fall. Squatting near the fires, the cooks warm their numb fingers near the flame.

22 April—We huddle in the barn. A treacherous wind penetrates through the tiles and rips through the porches. Last evening was enlivened by an extraordinary event: commotion around 10:00 p.m. with the unexpected arrival of a Red Cross truck loaded with food supplies. Wild joy! On the other hand, we learn painful news. Some say that Lieutenant P. has been shot for having wrung the neck of a chicken during a stopover. Fortunately, a refutation comes almost immediately. Lieutenant P. is in jail in Gratzen. Our

Commandant is trying to get him out. We receive a French package for two: noodles, cigarettes, gingerbread loaf, jam, cookies, chocolate and a few American foodstuffs. What a windfall! Since the Heaven-sent truck could not reach Leipzig, the goal of his trip, it was eventually redirected to our farm. The team, a Swiss driver accompanied by a Canadian prisoner, speaks of an enormous traffic jam on the roads, but they do not think the war will end before summer. We are happily persuaded that they are wrong. We celebrate Mass under a shed between bales of hay.

23 April—There is no end to the wind, rain, and snow and still no field kitchen. We have to cook under the rain and stay in the barn. The smart ones manage to sneak into the stable where there is the good warmth of the animals. But space is scarce.

Communiqué: the Russians are said to have reached the suburbs of Berlin, the French, Constance, the Americans, the outskirts of Munich. We take note of the Germans' intentions to resist in the Tyrol. It would really not be very smart to go there with them.

24 April—The bad weather continues. Many are sick with dysentery. The Red Cross truck has fortunately brought a few medicines. We learn in the evening that we have to return to the road tomorrow at 10:00 a.m. in the general direction of the southwest. Four days should bring us to Freistadt on the road between Prague and Linz.

25 April—After two miles of a steep slope we reach Strobnitz [Horn Stropnice], a big town that seems to be half rural half craftsmen. We cut across the whole length of a large rectangular square. Our passing attracts a curious and silent population. Policing is coordinated by the *Volkstürmer* [Territorial Army] in khaki overcoats, coming from the Czech ex-army. Here and there, a few big bellies in yellow uniforms and a flat cap with stripes.

We follow a relentlessly strenuous road, passing by wide plateaus, interrupted by woods of firs until we reach Deutsch-Reichenau [Rychnov]. The village appears empty with doors and windows shut, and every fifteen hundred feet a man from the *Volksturm* [territorial army] stand in civilian clothes with an armband. The chief wears a hat with a plume. Honor guard? NO. We are told that they are waiting for the Russians. Air alert: Loud detonations toward the south. Caught a glimpse of a few Allied fighter airplanes very high in the blue sky, playing with the round and stationary clouds.

We speed along the miles with an empty stomach, but nourished by encouraging news. The Russians are at Potsdam. Soon, the Allies, coming from the east and the west, will meet. Patton advances southeast of Pilsen, and the Americans reach twenty-four miles of Passau [sixty miles away]. The crossing of the Danube will be cut soon and the wrench is closing on us. Good day, the end cannot be too far away, and if it is true that the Germans have asked not to observe the clause of the Geneva Convention, which stipulates that POWs should be kept away from combat zones, we will be found encamped in some surrounding farm. We reach Deutsch-Beneschau in the evening, the goal of the day. The day before, a German deserter was hung on the village square. Wounded after having killed a *Volkstürmer,* who wanted to arrest him, he was brought on a stretcher to the place of torture and hung on a tree. We quarter in the barn of a windmill. The night is gorgeously starry and peaceful. Stroll along a torrent that tumbles down a series of obstacles a few hundred feet downstream. No restraints: The guards are sleeping.

26 April—We leave Deutsch-Beneschau at 8:00 a.m. following the main street. The shops reveal windows empty of merchandise but adorned with portraits of Hitler and posters of the party. As everywhere else, a silent and intent crowd with garish and unexpected colors. The weather is stormy. The road climbs in switchback to a pass twenty-three hundred to twenty-six hundred feet high close to the village of Radischen. Stop in the fir trees, in the direction of Pflanzen. Long stop in front of Kaplitz (Kaplice). We enter it after passing on a bridge already mined. The stores are empty. There are several hospitals and the population, which we sense hostile, is mixed with many wounded or maimed German soldiers. After Kaplitz we follow a national road, clogged up with convoys, which pass us, cross us on the other side, cut in front of us, and push us into the ditch. The pace is slow and painful. We are extremely tired, and stop increasingly frequently.

At 5:00 p.m. we reach Einsiedl, some kind of village, consisting of a bunch of big farms.

The men had arrived in the proximity of Freistadt, their last stop, where they will be meeting the Americans. From Gratzen to kaplitz they walked through the southern part of the Sudeten area, a sliver of land, which was part of Czechoslovakia until 1938, when Hitler was allowed to annex it to Germany in the treaty of Munich, under the guise that a large number of Germans lived there. Hence the German names of the towns, which reverted to their Czech names. It had been part of the Austrian Empire until World War I.

As on the other side of the border, Deutsch Reichenau was founded in the thirteenth century, and when the men passed by, it was a prosperous large village. After the war the German population was thrown out, leaving the newly named Rychnov a very small community.

Deutsch-Beneschau, also a Middle Ages settlement, became a small town with the establishment of a brewery in the sixteenth century and a town hall in

13. Trekking Eighty Miles to Freedom

Renaissance style. A secondary and an agricultural school were built in the nineteenth century. The town was a farming and trade merchant center. The Germans were expelled after the war.

Kaplitz—Kaplice, a prosperous mid-size town on the main road between Prague and Linz, located at the foot of the Novohradské Mountain, was on the trade route used for the transportation of salt. As the officer POWs crossed the large central square, they passed by the typical onion church tower and administrative buildings, seat of the political and judicial district. Right after World War I, even though Kaplice was part of Czechoslovakia, Kaplice remained mostly German, although they co-existed with the Czechs peacefully. After the Munich Agreement the Czech minority left for the interior of Czechoslovakia to return after the war, when Kaplice became again a Czech town.

27 April—The battalions are distributed in the farms near the road. These old buildings are too small for the excess of human livestock that needs to find shelter in it. It is impossible to fit all of us in a barn of two stories made for straw, into which we climb with ladders. The smallest nooks of the building are scoured and settled in. F. sleeps in a cart full of straw while C. and M. bunk between the wheels. P. and G. have adopted an empty nook for pigs of which they pulled down the trap door on themselves. Unruffled campers, loving fresh air and moonlight, sleep outside the walls in shelters made of branches, or what is more attractive, under a tent.

Still non-existent provisions; we must continue to live on barter, which forces us to find unoccupied farms, therefore at a distance. Early morning, scouts leave with their backpacks and satchels slung over their shoulders in the pursuit of lard, eggs, and potatoes, which they exchange for cigarette or American soap.

We gravitate toward two poles: the road and the river. The road leads to Prague in the north and Linz in the south. Vehicles pass one another nonstop, from the sumptuous staff car packed with [German] officers to wheezing trucks, made of scrap iron and bristling with gigantic gas tanks. No organized columns, but an uninterrupted ebb and flow, which exudes a feverish state and incoherence.

The river flows at the bottom of a deep ravine with steep and rocky sides planted with firs. Its banks are covered with a thick and dense grass. Clear water races very fast on a rocky ground. We wash our clothes and wash up naked in the sun. A few fishermen, followers of R., throw a fly with a hazelnut pole, a ten-foot line with a bent pin. Here and there, lying on his back, his cap on his eyes, a wise fellow sleeps.

28 April—Yesterday's news reports the encirclement of Berlin, an Allied advance toward Regensburg, push beyond Passau –which has not been confirmed.

The roll call this morning turns to comedy. Absolute prohibition to leave the farm; the guards have received the order to shoot. Will they obey? To be feared more are the SS, who lurk in the surroundings as well as a few elements of the Vlassow Army stationed in the vicinity. We are reminded of the ordinance against looting, requisitioning, and individual trading of food, items punishable by death. It is becoming more and more difficult to obtain something to eat but fortunately, the German guards, fond of cigarettes, indulge openly in the black market. With a benevolent payoff they find it a supplement to the ordinary. The French provisions, received at Gwendt, are rapidly dwindling.

The weather turns suddenly to rain and cold. It is quite difficult to find a dry place and a shelter from the wind.

29 April—The layover oddly drags out. Regensburg and Passau have been reached. The Russians and Americans meet on a sixty-mile front. Berlin is close to being occupied. In Italy: fall of Turin and Milan.

The sky remains cloudy and showers follow one after the other. We celebrate Mass in the hall of the farm. Lunch under the shed, with wind blasts sweeping through. We warm up our hands holding our mess kit.

The coming and going of cars on the road is increasing, and the exodus of the civilians is beginning in the direction of the south. In the evening, a German truck plows into a column of Hungarians. Two are dead and one is critically wounded. The driver does not even brake and continues his course hitting a steer on his way, killed it on the spot. Lying in the barn, we learn around 10:00 p.m. that Himmler has sent a request for surrender to the Anglo-Saxons. We are skeptical. Another announcement excites us much more: we will try tomorrow to collectively buy the meat of the steer and of a slaughtered mare in the neighborhood. Something to dream about all night...

30 April—Showers follow one after the other, heavy, unceasing, and freezing rain. We walk from porches to porches and from stables to stables, looking for a shelter, while waiting for the potato stew, embellished with a few pieces of lard. The courtyard of the farm is a big cesspit of mud and manure. The nearby fields, ploughed by our trampling, have become a big slough in which we sink to the ankle.

We hear loud bombardment of cannons in the direction of the northwest.

1 May—It is still cold and it snows. The communiqué confirms the negotiations between Himmler and the Russians via Stockholm, but it is reported

13. Trekking Eighty Miles to Freedom

that Stalin has insisted upon the cessation of all resistance as pre-conditions. Italy collapses. Mussolini might have been killed by the patriots. It is also said that Hitler may be dead.

Attempt to have a roll call at 8:00 a.m. under the snow. It ends in chaos and confusion. In their farm, on the other side of the road, the colonels refuse to participate. Sanction: they will stay locked in the farm the entire day.

The road is more and more jam-packed and shows complete disarray. We observe army detachment passing by on foot. They are not very lively. A corporal, limping, shouts in our direction: "Sleep and wait for peace!" To the driver of a truck, which stays for a long time in front of us, we shout: *Zu spät*! [Too late] After thinking for a long time, he responds: "Are you telling me that we will get busted!" Hungarians who are coming from the south assure us that Linz has been taken; a civilian adds that it has not been defended. Other pieces of information locate the Americans at fifteen miles from us. Fleeting joy: a Red Cross truck with a Swiss insignia emerges at full speed. Deaf to our yelling the driver motions that he is going further. Consternation! We have only one day of food left, and it is almost impossible to get any.

2 May—Hitler is really dead. Admiral Doenitz takes command. Reaction of the Germans: some do not hide their satisfaction and others deny the news and blame the enemy propaganda. And some get together for long consultations.

Still more snow. It covers the fields clinging to the trees; from the distance they look like they are covered with flowers. The access to the farm is a lake full of silt. We receive seven ounces of bread—pretty much the daily ration— thin soup with a few grains of barley, which amounts to about five hundred calories. The strain, the wait, and the uncertainty of what the next day will bring subject our nerves to a severe endurance test. Courtesy, politeness, and even friendship peel off like a too fragile veneer.

3 May—It snows. The water puddles are covered with a layer of ice.

The news is passionately interpreted: on-going negotiations between the Allies since 24 April. End of the Italian campaign and capitulation of the armies south of the Danube. The Americans are nine miles from Linz.—It was, then, not captured?—The resistance in northern Germany collapses. Doenitz is said to have declared, "We can surrender; our honor is intact." Isolated from these momentous events we have at times the distressing impression of being forgotten on this lost plateau.

The road shows the disarray. A detachment of the Vlassow Army passes. "Where are you going?"—Home. Still armed, these pirates live by robbery. To two wounded men of the *Gross Deutschland* Division, who are evacuated from Kaplitz and going toward Salzburg, they shout, "You will not get there!"—We are going back home. Our Führer is dead. We are released from our oath.

4 May—A very difficult night; forty-one degree Fahrenheit, and again, blue sky. Need to wash up, to shave, and to clean our nails. Around 10:00 a.m. an Allied squadron flies over the farm, followed by the dive-bombing of the railroad a mile away in the southwest. We quickly lay out three blankets on the ground—red, white, and blue—to indicate our presence. The planes turn to the north. Sound of bombs in the direction of Kaplitz. Some civilians pretend they have seen the Americans about six miles away. Around 2:00 p.m. a very brisk cannonade, which seems close, appears to confirm the hearsay.

The *Verwaltung* [German administration] makes an effort to increase our rations, following vehement complaints by our Commandant, who places the responsibility of the precarious situation in which we find ourselves specifically on the German General. They will get ten tons of potatoes at Strobnitz. Despite the restrictions, intrepid scouts, greeted by numerous gunshots, leave to personally find food. Nobody is hit. The guards do not seem to aim carefully. A *Feldwebel* [Sargent], however, almost hits a runaway with two shots from his Mauser, discharged at less than one hundred feet.

In the evening, odd rumors circulate. A peasant is said to have reported that the guards would leave during the night. Another said that they were to stand by in a state of readiness. It is true that all day long the sentries have huddled together for mysterious chitchats. Snippets of sentences were heard that talked of departure. In the evening in the straw, we indulge in bold speculations. How sweet it would be to be finally alone tomorrow!

5 May—Error, they are still here! And once more dark clouds glide in the sky, pushed by a very strong westerly wind. At 10:00 a.m. reading of an impressive communiqué. The BBC announces the annihilation and capitulation of the armies of the north. There remain only a few small islands of resistance: Norway, Denmark, and Czechoslovakia. Alas! We know it very well! Toward 4:00 p.m. an announcement by our Commandant: "In the probable eventuality that our guards leave us, I will take command. Stay calm and disciplined. No provocation! The requisition will be done collectively. We will organize the encampment, while we wait for the Americans." Diverse bureaus are already forming, and we are put in companies and battalions under French command. Used to counter-orders and disenchantment, we note all this with some detachment. In the evening we locate the Americans at Freistadt [14 miles]. Our entire sector all the way to Kaplitz is said to be in a state of "tank alert." At the last minute the radio announces that Prague has suddenly stopped its broadcasts and has sent appeals to the population that we unfortunately have not understood.

6 May—Dark night ... La Marseillaise! [French anthem] Is it a dream? Bodies emerge, one after the other, from a straw that crunches.—"What is it?" "What's happening?" A powerful voice yells: "The Chleuhs are gone!"

They are gone! All the voices unite and join in unison: "*Allons enfants de la patrie*" [Let's go, children of the fatherland—beginning of the French anthem]. Then total silence followed by a sudden and tumultuous outburst: Free! We are free! It has come to an end. What patience to come to this moment. It's done. It has already passed. It is 4:45 a.m. The last sentry has left the premises at 4:30 a.m. Impossible to go back to sleep. The day creeps slowly between the tiles of the roof. Many can't stand it anymore and get up to see, to look at what liberty looks like.

Outside: an immense quiet. There is no one on the road, and no one to prevent its access. It feels good to take it and hear it ring under our steel heels: fast walk, cheerful, and without any goal other than to go straight ahead. Intense pleasure to stop, to start again, jump a ditch, go through a field, and come back to the starting point without any other guide than one's own will or one's own delight.

The French flag flutters already on all the farms. How vibrant are its colors against the dark pines. Also everywhere; the Czech flag. How could all these flags slip through the Gestapo searches for so long?

At 8:15 a.m. salute to the colors. The flag is hoisted to the top of a great mast in the presence of the General.

We embrace this happiness little by little. At first, cagey and timid, it becomes affirmed by the deliciously warm chocolate whose precious blocks have been collected with some difficulty. From now on, our Commandant exerts his authority. The requisitions are beginning. We will soon get fresh meat and bread, baked by the locals. At around 9:30 a.m., we learn of the good-bye communiqué addressed to our Commandant by the ex–Kommandant of Oflag XVII A. It is exquisite.

Monsieur le Général,

Following our meeting yesterday, I am letting you know the situation at this hour. Some American troops have reached Freistadt and Oberlaid yesterday afternoon and we expect their arrival at Unterhaid. The advance of the American troops is not encountering any resistance, so that there should be little combat activity along the road. It is therefore not necessary to recommend moving the French officers away from the road. However, we have some information that the train lines have been seized by Czech insurgents who were in front of Kaplitz and who have the intention of occupying the railroad of the old Czech territory to Unterlaid starting this morning. Accordingly, it is absolutely necessary for our guards units to leave in order to avoid combat actions in our encampment. By 4:00 a.m. I will leave at Einseidl the provisions, which were prearranged by the administration for the coming days: two field kitchens without a horse team and cooking utensils to prepare the food for the encampment. At the German emergency post of Einseidl, you will find a large box of medicines for the head physician. You will be able to ask for cars from the mayor to transport the provisions. I am asking you, to the extent possible, to take under your command the protection of the civilian population. I would like to ask this as a special request and take leave from you and Captain Koeller. Unfortunately, other tasks prevent us from seeing you in person. I convey all my sincere regards of soldier to you and your officers, and considering the hard times that you have endured, we wish you a quick end of your sufferings, which will probably begin for us, as well as a happy return to your families.

Signed: Ridell

Captain and Kommandant of the Camp

The cooks, who want to produce a grand lunch, empty their sacks completely. Never mind the limitations! No worry about the future! At 11 a.m. we feast with gusto under a warm sun. But at about 12:15 p.m. a soldier in green uniform, followed quickly by many others, scrambles up the embankment of the road. They point their submachine guns on the peaceful and cheerful crowd. Again these bastards! So it is not finished. This incident takes a funny turn. A sick kid of the *Arbeitdienst* [labor force] had stopped on the side of the road to throw up. During that time his rifle and helmet have disappeared. The Kommandant of the detachment wants to find them. One unit comes toward us and surrounds us. They ask for five men. Five come forward and are immediately taken away. We wait in silence and dismay. At about 1:00 p.m. our five volunteers come back: if the gun and helmet are not found by 4:00 p.m. they will be shot. Our Commandant devotes himself to calming these maniacs; charged anxiety and dreary wait. Freedom is bought dearly. By 4:30 p.m. nothing has happened. Little by little the uneasiness subsides. These unwelcome invaders have disappeared. For fear of new incidents our flags have been lowered.

Important communiqué: the encircled German armies capitulate everywhere. Linz is finally taken, and uprising in Prague. Order to the prisoners:

remain calm and disciplined. Around 8:00 p.m. in the direction of the southwest, some brief shelling causes isolated glows and detonations. We rush toward the edges of the field: "The Americans! The battle! They are here!" but everything already falls silent in the serenity of dusk.

It certainly will be for tonight! State of alert; we bring our luggage downstairs to the courtyard. Will sleep fully dressed, which means without taking off our shoes.

7 May—Bitter disappointment; nothing has happened. We occupy the place that these Messieurs have vacated and organize the encampment. A French office takes the place of the German office in the kitchen of the farm. We meet no difficulties in making requisitions. The promised rations are tremendous: ten ounces of meat per day and bread in abundance, etc.

The distributions will start as soon as tonight. Long stroll in the countryside and along the river. We hear a cannonade that seems far away. No echoes of fight nearby, even though the local information announces that the Americans are in Kaplitz and Unterhaid [four miles]. At 6:15 p.m. the news is like a thunderclap; the armistice has been signed. Being understandably instinctively cautious, we wait for a confirmation. It arrives at 9:00 p.m. The armistice will be effective as of tomorrow. 8 May 1945 will be the day of Victory.

8 May—10:00 a.m. 8 May will be the day of Victory.[1] To persuade ourselves we have to strain our imagination and instill in ourselves a blind faith, as no precise event has happened until this moment to color this day with a brighter light, a day begun with the usual tedium of uncertainty.

What can Victory mean to us? Other than the material control we can exercise over our masters of yesterday, holding by the neck, those who were for so long our jailers. Massed along the road, we wait. Nevertheless, the sky is happy, the sun, bright and warm. A light fever intoxicates us, born of the completely new spring and of the still undifferentiated promise of an immense joy to come.

Suddenly, a funny open little car, an enormous toy, driven by men in khaki, their faces scarlet under their helmet, appears at breakneck speed; a "Jeep!" The Americans! Crazy cheers! They are going to meet the Germans massed around Kaplitz. Enthusiasm bursts out, irresistible and wild. The funny little car has reconnected us with the world.

At their posts, the stoic cooks stoke fires which sparkle, cheerful under the kettles. Oh! The foodstuff is not lacking. Yesterday evening, with the help of a truck requisitioned on the road, the supplies of the commissary of Unterhaid has been emptied. Cheese, bacon, dried peas have been widely distributed, and for the feast that is being prepared the food reserves have definitively been raided.

We learn that yesterday our Commandant sent a representative to the American General staff. In return, a car came to pick him up, and at this hour they must be discussing the means of our return.

A huge cry is rising from the road, punctuated by the backfires of motors and the clinging of tracked vehicles. A unit of the Flack is heading south preceded by the little jeep, which passed by a few hours ago in the other direction. The German Army is entering captivity. It is exactly 11:00 a.m.

7:00 p.m.—Vehicles form a continual stream from the north. Heterogeneous convoy in which all the army units mix, civilians and military personnel are next to one another in the chaos of the debacle. Instructed by the American Army, French NCOs and officers proceed to disarm the captives. Three check points have been erected, at the exit of Kaplitz, of Einseidl, and of Unterhaid. The captives of yesterday welcome the captives of tomorrow. Return of just deserts!

At about 10 p.m. the column, immobilized by the checkpoints, forms a compact and ugly heap two miles long. The men sleep in a heavy slumber in the cars and in the trucks on the side of the road. We know from experience that they must be full of nightmares.

Some four hundred young officer POWs had formed so-called "Groupe-Francs." Common during World War II, Groupe-Francs *were front line units, formed to scout German lines and storm positions. When they arrived on the front line of combat, they looked for potential danger and took action to protect the units in a dangerous war zone. As soon as the armistice was signed, the Oflag's* Groupe-Francs *were anxious to repay the Germans' actions in 1940. Before leaving the camp in April, they had volunteered to help their comrades along the way: distribution of food and control of movement of the three thousand men on the back roads of Austria and Czechoslovakia.*

According to a La Maffia *account,*[2] *the leader of one of the* Group Francs, *pulling out a concealed pistol, pointed it at a German colonel, and said "American vanguard!" The colonel relinquished riding a "magnificent Mercedes." Then, twenty-four French lieutenants in impeccable uniform, kept for this kind of occasion, arrested the entire regiment. The* La Maffia *account concluded, "The Allied trucks were able to pass and the supply of food was assured." Upon his return my father told me a similar story; one of his friends secured a Mercedes and then ordered the colonel to sit on the hood, and as they were driving, he had him shout to the mass on the road to get off the road to make way for the American trucks, getting the road cleared.*

13. Trekking Eighty Miles to Freedom

9 May—The road! ... is a hodgepodge of vehicles and men jerked by momentous jolts. The ditches, fields, and woods are strewn with debris: rifles, revolvers, grenades, equipment, Panzer-Faust, gutted boxes, and stacks of papers blown by the wind spread in nose-dives.

Man to man contact with the defeated enemy. The [German] officers, truly impudent, act with contempt, while the troops are fearful and compliant. The Mausers on our belts keep the distance. Current question caught on the fly: "Sir, Americans, to not take us prisoners?" and this unexpected one from a blond of the *Arbeitdienst*—at the most sixteen years old—"Will I be able to return to my parents' home?"

Is he innocent, naïve, or already needs to hope?

The entrance to Unterhaid is a roadblock, where the French with armbands take the weapons. The cars are summarily searched.

"*Die Waffen*" [weapons], the car doors are slammed in a bitter recollection, still vivid of 1940 [Retribution of when the Germans did the same thing to the French. See diary entry 24 June 1940].

After a while: a sickening feeling.

Snack on the Village Square. Ham, bread, eggs, soaked in cognac, generous gift from the disarmament teams. Lieutenant T. empties a bunch of trucks of its occupants for our use, in case we will camp out in the vicinity for a while, as we have been told.

But suddenly we are seized by the wish to sit down at a table in one of these rustic houses whose open windows disclose walls painted with fresh paint and newly waxed furniture. An old woman welcomes us. A Czech citizen, who likes France, she gives us two big bowls of fresh milk, which we slowly sip.

8:00 p.m.—Return to the farm. Ecstasy! The Americans will take us tomorrow in trucks to the airport in Linz. On the same day: flight to France. My God, is this possible?

The night is cheerful with a sky full of stars. Joy too deep to bury it in the dusty darkness of the barn.

Sleep catches up later, laying under our blankets at the edge of a wood of pines, kept awake by the humming of our thoughts and the rumbling of the road, where to forget their wait, the Chleuhs burn their stock of missiles in a furious fire work.

10 May—8:00 a.m.—Here they are! Opening the crowd that overwhelms "our road," about forty six-wheelers arrive in an impressive line at thirteen feet one from the other.

Noon—Standing, forty-five per truck, we hold on tightly to the side rails, or on the rope, which divides in two our rolling crate. It is impossible to move. Thrust forward at the sudden application of the brakes, thrust backward at the lightning startup, and thrown from one side to the other by the briskness of the steering wheel, we pass twenty-four miles of a shapeless throng. We reach Freistadt, which holds a human river, choking in between its Middle Ages houses, bristling with white flags.

1:00 p.m.—Stop! The airport! We drove the thirty miles from Freistadt to Linz at top speed. We have lunch on the grass, generosity of the American PX. The sun burns in a sky without a cloud. On the runway, the Boeings, one after the other, take off in the thunder of their motors.

4:00 p.m.—Missed! About a thousand are left on the tarmac. They will leave tomorrow. The Boeings have absorbed only a fraction of our impatient crowd. One more night sleeping anywhere on the cement of the hangars, or the grass of the airfield. Absolute prohibition to get close to certain buildings; some miserable deportees are dying of typhus or the plague.

11 May—Anxious wait for the squadrons coming from London. Part of the group is already divided in teams of thirty-two passengers, waiting quietly in line in front of the runway. The sky is slightly foggy through which we search with eager looks.

10:20 a.m.—One—two—three—ten—fifteen—twenty planes spring out of the bright mist and after a wide turn land on the runway and taxi toward the first groups waiting to load…

11:05 a.m.—The duralumin body of the airplane vibrates under the fury of the motors. Squatting on the shaking cargo floor we feel the power grow, irritate, and go through us until it hurts. Light shock. Through the porthole the hangars subside and look warped. After a change of command we can see the hard-surfaced runway flow like oil and suddenly sink. The vibrations stop. A very soft sway carries us to the sky. The big starboard wing tips slowly, then straightens out. In a wide curve, the plane turns toward the west. Linz is already only a gray clump fading away. Silent and bent toward it, we look at this inhumane soil slide, disappearing in the misty distance.

Five years have also slid like shadows and have been lost in the night.

The American Air Force flew one hundred twenty B 17 Flying Fortresses to repatriate the over three thousand men who finished the trek. On this remarkable day of ready-to-burst hearts, these men found themselves back on French soil in Orléans in less than two hours after five years of exile and one year of war. How to imagine or express the emotional shock?

None of the men knew what had happened to their families in the past year, as war was raging on French soil. Had their families survived the Allied

A B-17 on the tarmac of the Charleston Executive Airport on the occasion of the Liberty Foundation's Memphis Belle flight in October 2013 (Jacqueline Vautrain Collins).

bombing, or the scorched earth policy the Germans practiced before leaving? Even where the destruction of war was minimal, families had changed; over six years they had lost some members and their children had grown. We can only imagine the pang in these men's hearts, when, arriving in Paris, the center for discharge; the Parisians dialed their home phone number, not knowing what they would find on the other side of the line, and for those living outside Paris, who sent telegrams, the uncertainty continued. Who would be there to welcome them?

Postscript

On 11 May 1945 the majority of the officers and enlisted men [POWs] of Oflag XVIIA, those who could sustain the trek from Edelbach to the vicinity of Kaplitz, touched the French soil. But...

... But close to two thousand men were not part of this happy group, either because they stayed in the camp, or they abandoned the march.

The section of the B-17 where the officers sat on their way home to France (Jacqueline Vautrain Collins).

Thanks to notes which were gracefully given to us, you will find here a short overview of their adventures.

I. *Those in Edelbach*

After the departure of the column, there remained in the camp about 600 officers [POWs] and enlisted men [POWs]. Two hundred fifty had been declared unfit and three hundred were resisters.

17 April—Suddenly the camp seems immense. The last men of the column have disappeared behind the houses of Edelbach, and with trembling hearts we wander in this almost empty rectangle, where trash piles up and the ashes of pieces of rubbish still smoke.

The entire section of the camp, located below the kitchen and barracks 20, was evacuated. We are grouped in the upper section.

18 April—The camp is guarded by a division billeted in this sector. The sentries occupy the watchtowers as before, showing a similar attitude toward us. Composition of the contingent: very young recruits and old vets, all anxious

13. Trekking Eighty Miles to Freedom

to end the war quickly, whatever the circumstances. Food is provided by the division. The rations are more generous than with the old command, particularly for meat and bread.

The vacated barracks are emptied. Teams of Serbian prisoners throw all the filth we have left through the windows.

As soon as yesterday, stragglers began to return. They came back home in trucks or on foot. There are already about one hundred.

23 April—Nothing special to report: flat calm, interrupted only by the daily communiqué, heard from the radios left behind.

But now fear of departure resurfaces. Visit of doctors to select those who are able to leave "with luggage" or "without luggage." Suddenly rumors spring up: imminent evacuation of the camp.

24 April—Return to known practices: building of little carts and one begins again to stuff backpacks, weigh them and weigh them again. Food increases thanks to contributions of local supplies, allowed by the Kommandant of the camp. Under the nonchalant eyes of the sentries, copious harvest of dandelions in the open-air theater empty of its public, as well as between the barbed wire.

No one travels on the road. A few German planes fly in the sky.

6 May—Still dead calm: no incidents, but some vague worries about our comrades on the march. According to some rumors that we cannot verify, there have been crude executions along the way.

7 May—2 p.m.—Our guardians abandon their weapons, piling them up in the *Vorlager*.

3:30 p.m.—We learn of the unconditional surrender, signed in Reims at the Allied Headquarters. Our passive guardians let us go out, and on the road to Edelbach we assist the headlong flight of vehicles toward the west.

8 May—The gates of the camp are wide open, an amazing sight. The German retreat is swift as always in front of the advance of the Russians.

Around 3 p.m. explosions toward Göpfritz. The Germans disable their planes and destroy the runways.

5 p.m.—The guards leave the camp. We are alone.

8 p.m.—Absolute calm.

9 May—Around noon, Russian advance detachments are seen in Göpfritz and at 3 p.m. two Russian officers arrive in the camp. One is a drama author. We gather on the square: speeches, clapping. The French flag is raised at the main entrance and at the chapel. The German Eagle is lowered with rifle shots.

Abundant provisions from the Russians and local resources: feasts which last late into the night.

10 May—Incommensurable feelings: to be able to go freely through these gates, which were immovable for so long! We visit the neighboring camps. Beds, mattresses, utensils are brought to the barracks as if we were to stay there for a long time. A train of provisions which stops in Göpfritz is unloaded of some of its content for our benefit. No contact with the Russians.

9 p.m.—The TSF [French radio] broadcast the speech of the Representative, given in France at the arrival of the first men repatriated from Linz. We are happy and terribly disappointed at the same time. We were told that our departure would be today toward the east [the opposite direction from France].

14 May—Our group, counting the successive arrivals of officers brought back by trucks, numbers now 800 men. Still, low morale: we have few contacts with the Russians. However, Commandant C. has obtained a pass allowing him to contact the Americans.

15 May—Saved! It is the end. Commandant C. has succeeded. Departure tomorrow morning in American trucks in the direction of Linz and repatriation probably by planes.

16 May—7 p.m.—Stormy journey. On several occasions Russians sentries tried to block our passage, but thanks to the cleverness of the Commandant of the column, all obstacles were overcome and passed.

No planes on the tarmac. We have to wait for two or three days.

Taking their turn, "those of Edelbach" touched the French soil on 19 May 1945.

A more detailed story was told by Armand Oldra in his recollections after his trip to Vienna in 1996. A brief review follows.

Armand Oldra, declared too weak to make the march, was among these 800 men. At some point, he managed to walk out of the camp in search of food, but, quickly exhausted, knocked on the door of a nearby farm. A woman and her adult daughter answered the door, invited him in and gave him some food. She was acquainted with the camp, as she regularly went to the cemetery adjacent to the camp, to put flowers on her father's tomb, often seeing the officer POWs through the barbed wire rehearsing in costumes in the open-air theater. She sometimes gave food to the POWs who worked around the farm. She and her daughter gave Armand a bowl of soup, some sausage, and bread. Unfortunately, as he was eating, two local policemen came to the door to requisition food. When they saw Armand, they forced him to go back to the camp.

But now the Germans, very jittery of all the different bands roaming the area, confined the men to a barracks, enclosed by a network of barbed wire guarded by dogs. They were there for two days without food, until all the guards disappeared and so did the dogs; the German had capitulated. The French officers immediately entered the German administration building, took some of the pistols and organized parties to find food, most notably seizing a large amount from a supply train stopped in Göpfritz. Finally, the Russians arrived at the camp, gave them some provisions, and asked them to stay in the camp, saying that the countryside was in chaos with German units, Russian Regiments, and many groups of foreign workers, walking in all directions. Armand decided to pack up all his possession in a military trunk, which he had found in the administration building, and placing it in a wheelbarrow took it to the farm. He asked the woman to keep it and said, if he did not come back within a year, she could dispose of it as she wished.[3]

Left were those of Gratzen [Nove Hrady].

II. Those of Gratzen

On 25 April when the main column continued its journey to reach the region of Kaplitz about 25 miles southwest, about 700 officers, either sick or tired, were gathered in a farm near Gratzen. As fate would have it, the farm where they stayed was included in the sector occupied by the Russians at the time of capitulation, while the region of Kaplitz was included in the American zone. That resulted in a return to France one month later and a whole series of adventures.

8 May—Capitulation of the German Army: a huge French flag is raised in front of the farm and at 7:45 a.m. parade and salute of the colors. Mass: Te Deum. Our guards assist with a lifeless acceptance of the reversal of the situation. Colonel L.B, who commands the detachment, tells them that at 1 p.m. we will consider that we are free.

3 p.m.—We wander in Gratzen. The shops are closed. Some Czechs in local costumes, gathered on the square, sing patriotic hymns, but the sudden arrival of a regiment of SS scatters the crowd. The mayor and his assistant, who had taken down the Nazi emblem from the town hall, are hung from the second floor windows. The SS advise us to get back immediately in our encampment.

5 p.m.—A lieutenant of the French Army, widely cheered, gets out of a "jeep" and disarms the sentry post. He gathers our mail and promises to do everything possible for our prompt return.

9 p.m.—The German Army in rout flees toward the west, trying to get

to the American lines. In passing, a German officer entrusts us with four Alsatian-Lorrainers, who had been conscripted by force.

9 May—The German columns continue their rush toward the west.

10 May—The Russians: a horde of wagons draws by two horses rush toward the south. Two or three men in each car are accompanied by women in uniforms. There are no visible weapons. They are hidden under a bed of hay, which covers the materiel.

11 May—According to the clauses of the armistice, the Americans push back all the Germans, who were in the Russian zone at the time of the capitulation; long faces and bitter lips.

16 May—We leave Gratzen in columns, accompanied by wagons drawn by requisitioned steers or horses. At least, we are not carrying our luggage. The Russians are directing us toward the southwest. They promise us, tomorrow the Americans, the day after, France.

Bivouac under the stars in Scheiben near an immense camp of Germans and Hungarians.

17 May—Thanks to the requisitioned provisions in Gratzen and bread given by the Russians, our food supplies are guaranteed for a few days.

Stopover at 10 miles, but this time we are going in the direction of Krems [meaning they are going east, away from France].

In the Austrian farms we exchange our tired steers for fresh teams.

18 May—Stopover at 14 miles in Rudman, bodies of German soldiers along the road.

20 May—Stopover at 13 miles in Lichtenau: we are free to organize our own encampment, stopovers, and rights of requisition from the farmers. For the first time we savor an excellent Perry.

We have just learned that American trucks came to Gratzen to pick us up forty-eight hours ago. Fate, definitely, haunts us.

21 May—Senfstenberg, large village, stretching as a long street, nestled in the valley of the Krems River near the ruins of an old castle. Great climate! We are in a rich and hospitable land; the cherries, already ripe, hang from the branches. A sympathetic population invites many officers in their homes.

22 May—We have reached Krems, but the Russians enjoin us to continue heading for Vienna. Disappointment! We definitely thought that Krems would be the end of our misery; encampment at Engabrun, about six miles from Krems.

New disappointment! The goal of our journey is not Vienna anymore but Bratislava [in today's Slovakia, just east of Vienna]. The distance which separates us from France increases every day instead of diminishing. Colonel

13. Trekking Eighty Miles to Freedom

L.B. decides to go to Vienna, where Marshall Tolboukine resides, and ask for a meeting in person.

27 May—7 a.m.—In accordance with Marshall Tolboukine's promise, about thirty Russians trucks, American made, take us to Gmund, where we arrive at 1:30 p.m.

5 June—We are still in Gmund. The Russians have thrown the inhabitants out so we can stay in their places. Our group grows to three thousand from Kommandos, who join us. But it diminishes every day, due to numerous individual departures by Czech trains via Budweis and Pilzen.

We have our meals in the camp built by the Russians for that purpose. We receive abundant rations and unlimited bread.

An American liaison officer informs us that trucks went to Engabrunn to pick us up 24 hours after our departure. Again this hellish bad luck!

9 June—Finally! The last eighty officers, who were left, leave in trucks for Linz, accompanied by the enlisted men of Oflag XVIIA. A last disapointment! The Air Force Division has moved two days before. The Americans decide to repatriate us in trucks to Metz [French town in Lorraine]; a thirty-six-hour trip without interruptions through the Great Reich.

And those from Gratzen finally crossed the French borders on 10 June at 6 p.m.

Epilogue
by Jacqueline Vautrain Collins

In the late spring and early summer of 1945, waves after waves of men returned to France. In a country of forty million people, there were over one million men prisoners of war, up to six hundred thousand young men coming back from forced work in Germany (STO, *Service du Travail Obligatoire*), and thousands of deportees from concentration camps (Jews, members of the Resistance and political activists). Families did not know at what exact time their loved ones would be back. Some never returned.

The officers coming back on 10–11 May were taken from Orléans to the *Gare d'Orsay in Paris*, which had been set up as a discharge center for the returning men. According to a lieutenant, they first met nurses, who "sprayed on their clothes a great amount of powder, which (they) knew to be DDT."[1] After taking a shower they saw a doctor and filled out forms. They were then free to go home. There had been no communications between my father and mother for over a year. She did not know the conditions of his camp, and he knew that, in case of the landing of the Allies, we would go to a place, which happened to have been in a heavy combat zone between the German and the American Armies.

My father called home and probably took the metro (subway) to get home. My mother, perhaps under the shock of hearing his voice, told me that my father "might" be coming home. I remember it as something still very uncertain. My father had the good fortune to ring the bell of the same apartment he had left six years before. My mother opened the door, and there he was. I remember him hugging my mother, and he certainly hugged me, but my first recollection was his emphatic comment: "She is so tall," with an inflection in his voice I cannot quite place, but struck me enough to remember it. He had left a four-year-old child to find a ten-year-old girl.

The second disconnect was a very French habit. As a child before the war, I would address my parents with the formal pronoun "vous" for you (rather than the familiar form "tu" for you). With the war formalities were bypassed, and I was addressing my mother with "tu." When my father heard me addressing him with "tu," he immediately corrected me, prompting my mother to tell him, "We don't do that anymore." That was his first lesson of a changed culture. Since there were limited communications with the camp, except for a few letters, the returning fathers of children my age and younger were complete strangers to their fathers and vice-versa. Six years older, the children looked very different.

Armand Oldra was among those arriving 19 May. They were transported from Orléans to the demobilization center in Paris by trucks. Later, Armand recalled his first surprise: the trucks were driven by Blacks. At the center, he went through what he called "a serious disinfecting, which lasted half the night." He then sent a telegram to his wife—it arrived days after his return. Allotted a taxi free of charge, he was driven to the train station from which he could take a train to his hometown of Vernon in Normandy. Directed to the special wagon for returning POWs, he found a highly tense atmosphere, both joyful and anxious. As the train pulled into the Vernon station, he first noticed a large number of people on the platform. Anxiously wondering whether his wife would be there, he stepped down out onto the platform, and with immense relief spotted his wife waving at him. Not knowing when he would arrive, she had waited for each train every morning and every evening for the previous six weeks in the hope of seeing him. As he entered his house, he met his son for the first time, five and a half years old, born while he was on the front in 1939–40.[2]

In his memoirs, a lieutenant from another camp wrote of his landing at the Paris airport: "The door [of the plane] opens and we touch the French soil. That is it. It is really true: we are in France ... and free. It is impossible to describe our emotion." As they were driven to the *Gare d'Orsay* in the center of Paris, people lined the roads to welcome them, waving their handkerchiefs and scarves. He waved back and added, "The clothes and the hairdo of the women have changed, one of the many changes we would discover in this new world as the days went by. We were like big children who had to relearn everything." Wanting to thank a female captain, who welcomed and helped him during the disinfecting, he wrote, "How should I address her? It is the first time, I see an officer in a skirt."

There were no trains to his hometown until the next morning, and all available lodging for returnees, hotels or private homes had already been taken, as two Oflags had been liberated at the same time. Having received one thousand francs, he decided to go fend for himself and find a hotel room. After many disappointments he got a room, and exhausted tried to sleep, waking up early to catch his train. As he paid for his night's lodging, he had another shock; it cost him six hundred francs for a room, which he thought would cost a fraction of that amount. Life in 1945 cost many times over what it cost before the war.[3]

Like Armand Oldra he went to the wagon reserved for returnees, his anxiety of whether his wife received his telegram intensifying as he got closer. He happened to be the only returnee to come back to his small town that day, but many hopeful families were waiting on the platform. Scanning the crowd, he suddenly heard his wife shout, "There, he is!" His wife, parents-in-law, and old friends surrounded him. After this initial welcome his wife pointed to his son, sitting on the shoulders of a family friend. He recalled thinking "He is looking at me with his eyes wide open. It looks like he is saying to himself, 'So this is the one who calls himself my dad.'" He continued, "I wondered how he would take to me. In fact, I did not know him. He was six months old when I left and he was six and a half when I came back."

The officers came back ready to engage in France's future, convinced that they would be her leaders. An officer wrote, "Our hope for a bright future and dreams of what we could build, when we came back, had sustained our survival.... We dreamed of behaving in a more reflective, more balanced, richer, and more productive way. We all joined in a strong will to transform our lives to do "better" than in the past."[4] While in exile they created activities that replicated a French atmosphere with the ultimate goal of improving their abilities to rebuild France. A group of political science intellectuals had even begun preparing a draft of a new constitution to re-establish a republican government.

But France had suffered a repressive German occupation for four years, becoming a country different from the one they had left five years earlier and very far from the one they dreamed of during their captivity. For five years, family life had existed without them, leaving the women in charge and completely on their own. The technology of 1940 did not allow much contact between the men and their wives. Adding to the predicament, France had been liberated eight to ten months before the men's return, and already had a functioning Provisional Government planning the re-establishment of the Republic. The right to vote had been granted to the women in 1944, and one election had already taken place. For many months civil society had resumed a basic normal daily life without them. Many men returned in poor health in a country with few resources, where rationing was still in force.

The jobs for the men on salary had been given to someone else and despite regulations that the returning men should get them back, they had to fend for themselves. Farmers and craftsmen fared somewhat better, but many businessmen had to start from scratch. They had received part of their officers' salary while in captivity, but it was in Lager Marks, money which did not exist except for the camps. What they had saved was duly recorded, when they were discharged, but it took seven years to pay it to them, and they received it at the exchange rate of the old francs, worth a small fraction of the new francs, whose value had escalated in rampant inflation.[5]

They were celebrated and warmly welcomed at the time of their return, but they felt disoriented and like strangers, and it did not take long for the undercurrents of the conventional opinion to surface; they were the soldiers who reminded everyone of a crushing defeat. The memory of World War I was still very much alive with the French population, holding in reverence the men who fought in the trenches and not acknowledging that the conduct of the war had dramatically changed. The World War I veterans shunned the World War II veterans, discounting or not aware that in 1940 over ninety thousand men were killed and over two hundred and thirty thousand were wounded in forty-five days of combat.

In addition, France had new heroes in the men and women of the Resistance. The returning prisoners receded in the background, prompting some pushback. In a magazine article of December 1945, an officer from Oflag XVIIA recalled those in the camp who had been sent to reprisal camps, isolation, and torture for leading clandestine activities (some of the camp Commandant and leaders of *La Maffia*). He concluded, "During five years, under particularly difficult conditions in the heart of the enemy's country, some French officers did everything in their power to either rejoin or help those who, free, had an opportunity to figh.... They can be proud of what they have done. I hope that we do not forget those who inside barbed wire had only one ideal: to serve regardless of the price.[6]

Opinion about the prisoners had evolved over the five years. In the first year of captivity, the French population tried to help and coddle the prisoners of war, their captivity seen as expiatory for the disarray in France. Marshal Pétain called them his children, whom he continually thought of. He was working to liberate them, he said, while the Vichy propaganda told that the men were in good conditions with adequate food, lodging, and even wine, specially requisitioned (as noted in the diary the men never got that wine). In 1942, a collaborationist weekly newspaper went so far as to declare: "The prisoners put France to shame. They should have let themselves be killed rather than accept *'une vie de chateau'* (a plush life) in Germany."⁷ Taking the activities of the oflags out of context, it was easy to spin life in the camp as a pleasurable, relaxed life.

My father broached this myth in his introduction to the book on Nuremberg. Acknowledging that everyone had experienced distress and a deep abyss that had marked them, he went on to assert that their sense of decency prevented them from repeating their destitution at infinitum. He continued in part: "But anyone with a critical mind who says that after all the prisoners had a tolerable existence, *'une vie de chateau,'* so to speak, would be unjust. Do not be misled; we have deliberately wanted to ennoble our lives, to show our energy, our thoughtful will to think, to live in order to prepare a better future for our families, despite our bereavements and personal misery."⁸

Their vision of France's renewal included a country which would have grown from its ordeal and would form a unified front. They had gone through that transformation in the Oflag and were prepared to lead that unity. Instead, they found a country as divided as ever and still reeling from the politics of the war in an atmosphere of retribution against the participants of the Vichy government and the collaborators. Marshal Pétain's trial took place a few weeks after their return. (After a short trial he was condemned to death, with a commuted sentence to life imprisonment. He was 89 years old.) They also thought that the world would now want a lasting peace. Instead, they were faced with the possibility of nuclear war.

Some pursued their career with great success, notably an Alsatian who became the *Préfet du Haut-Rhin* (somewhat similar to a governor) in Strasbourg. Three scientists became well-known. Jean Leray, a mathematician, was elected professor at the *Collège de France*. He made fundamental contributions in fluid dynamics and algebraic topology, among other subjects. Etienne Wolff, a biologist, a pioneer in research of vitro culture and fertilization, including changing the sex of an embryo, was well ahead of his time. Worried by this work, he declared, "It allows us to hope a little and fear a lot." He wrote two books while in Oflag XVIIA, was elected professor at the *Collège de France* and later *L'Académie française* (an institution founded in 1635, which regulates the French language). François Ellenberger, founder of the *Comité français d'histoire de la géologie*, published a comprehensive history of geology. While in the camp he gathered rocks and samples from the soil and created a laboratory of petrography in the Oflag, using a microscope fabricated in the camp. He and his students examined three hundred thin blades, glued to the glass taken from a window. After his return he published his findings in a unique book about the *Waldviertel* region of Austria.

A life, such as these men endured during five years, is a defining experience which changed them forever and can never be fully understood by those who did not experience it. They came back to a country, which had also lived a defining but different experience. They remained silent during their lifetime, finding comradeship only with the men which whom they had survived. Immediately after their return, they organized the Oflag XVIIA Association, publishing a newsletter every two months originally titled *Notre Canard*. It included many announcements of births, marriages, deaths, numerous books written by their comrades, and many advertisements for a variety of businesses of their members. My father had an ad promoting his collection of children's book for Christmas. They continued the meetings of "the Circle of the Child," started in the camp with the same goal: trying to know the child better, in order to raise him (her) better. Their lost relationship for six years with their children was an obsession. They advocated for a better treatment of POWs in general and for the widows and orphans in particular: promises made and not kept, money due to them and not given, and difficulties with the bureaucracy and health services.

1955

Ten years later, the October-November 1955 issue of *Notre Canard*, now titled *Le Lien* (The Connection), reported on a couple of officers who went back to the camp, taking advantage of the departure of the Russians from Austria. The Russians had taken over the maneuver ground around the camp during their occupation of Austria. These two men were able to successfully reach the camp right after the Russians left and before the Austrian military took it over. They reported that the Administration buildings and four adjacent barracks had burnt down, and seven barracks at the other end of the camp had burnt as well. That included the library and the chapel. Russian soldiers had been stationed in the remaining barracks. Edelbach was destroyed, having been used as target by the Russian troops. The cemetery was full of weeds, and most of the tombstones had been removed.

The officer concluded, "Without any life the camp looked very sinister, giving a much sadder impression than when the solidarity of our comrades, and the intense intellectual activities succeeded in making this spot of exile a center, which had become a corner of France." One of the officers found the barracks he had occupied still standing and discovered, tears in his eyes, the trap he had built to hide the famous makeshift stoves. After the departure of the Russians, the local population, in dire need of materials, dismantled the wood of the barracks, leaving only the foundations.[9]

1985

A small delegation of officers went back to Edelbach, to return to France the few remains of those who died in captivity and were still in the cemetery. To honor all their comrades who died, they planted a very small tree, placing an inscription on a large stone: "This tree was planted on June 1985 by French officers, prisoners of war 1940–1945" (the inscription is in German). In 1989 an officer wrote in his memoirs, "Even though we talk about it [captivity] very little, we think about it often. It disrupts our sleep. Fortunately, POWs' associations were created which have extended our fraternity. Some of us, however, want to erase the painful memories of captivity.... Let us always remember that the officers of the oflags lived a painful adventure and an extraordinary social event without precedent."[10]

1994

Reflections on the Fiftieth Anniversary of D-Day (June 6)

Fifty years ago thousands upon thousands of young soldiers boarded ships and airplanes to invade France and reverse the tide of fascism. Acting fearless but fearful inside, they listened to Dwight Eisenhower's send-off. "The eyes of the world are upon you. The hope and prayers of liberty loving people everywhere march with you.... Good Luck."

Young soldiers, full of life, anxious yet courageous, apprehensive yet feeling invulnerable, waited for the hour, the minute they would hit the sand of the beach. Momentous moments when no one could predict the outcome, but everyone believed it was the right thing to do and was committed to make it succeed.

Back home in the U.S. on that morning, people heard the announcement of the landing and Franklin Roosevelt's prayer for the troops. "In this poignant hour, I ask you to join with me in prayer.... Let our hearts be stout, to wait out the long travail, to bear the sorrows that may come, to impart our courage unto our sons where so ever they may be."

Many anxious moments, and then grief! So many young people cut down before they had a chance to live. Parents, wives, sweethearts, friends felt the overwhelming burden of the task.

A great sacrifice had been expanded by an entire nation in order to restore freedom.

On the other side of the line, I, too remember D-Day. I was very young but that day, one of the most intense days of my life, is etched in my memory. Nothing has ever surpassed the intensity of hearing the news of the landing, sitting in the kitchen with my mother, a family friend and her daughter my age. We strained to hear the words over the clandestine radio, jammed to the utmost. Did they really say, tens of thousands of troops had landed, five thousands ships patrolling the sea, we asked each other? Would they succeed?

The tenseness of that moment held all the past and present suffering and sacrifice, human courage, steadfastness, perseverance, all the future grief, mixed with joy and gladness.

Recalling those moments this week and seeing rows upon rows of white crosses marking the American cemeteries in France sent chills up my spine. So many human lives cut off in their prime so that freedom would prevail.

Two other scary months passed before I actually experienced freedom, welcoming the tanks and soldiers who had rolled down the beaches, and eight more months passed before my father was liberated and returned home.

War is a human tragedy that knows no boundaries of race, gender, nationality, intelligence, wealth, or poverty. It never ends for those who have been part of it.

May humankind learn how to keep peace in the world.

Spoken in the Unitarian Church in Charleston, South Carolina, June 5, 1994.

1996

On a mid-February morning in 1996, Armand Oldra answered the phone.

"Mr. Oldra, I am calling you from the Central Archives in Caen [a large town in Normandy]. A piece of luggage which belongs to you has been found in Austria. Would you like to get it back?"

All of a sudden a flood of feelings rushed through Armand's body and overwhelmed him with great sadness. All the hunger and cold, the isolation and fear of a period of his life which he wanted to forget and had never talked about with his wife and children, came back to him. In a daze, he heard the woman ask again, "Would you like to get it back?" In an almost mechanical way, he answered, "Madam, this happened fifty-one years ago. Keep it. It reminds me too much of a period of my life I would like to forget."

Hearing of this, his wife and sons convinced him that he should retrieve his piece of luggage, a military trunk. A few days later, when an Austrian radio station called him, inviting him to come to Vienna to officially take possession of his trunk, he accepted. Lieutenant Oldra had been one of five thousand French prisoners of war in Oflag XVIIA. In May 1945, while waiting to be liberated, he had put his few precious belongings, family pictures, books, drawings, and writing in a trunk.

On November 20, 1996, Armand Oldra and his family arrived in Vienna, welcomed by a historian of the University of Vienna, Rolf Kleinschmidt, and his associate with bouquets of flowers for him and his wife.[11] After a short stop at the hotel, they were taken to the French Institute in Vienna for a reception, where they met embassy personnel and Austrian personalities of the area. The walls of the reception room of this elegant mansion were adorned with copies of pictures of the content of his trunk. Oldra remarked, "Looking at this exhibit, I was overcome by a great sadness." The reproductions would later be placed in a suitcase deemed easier to carry back to France for Oldra.

Armand learned how his trunk had been retrieved. With the arrival of the Russians in May 1945, the Austrian farmers, the Kohl family, buried the trunk on the ground of the farm. Sometime in the early '90s, the son-in-law inherited the farm and began works of renovation during which they unearthed the trunk. Noticing the name and address on the trunk, they realized that it belonged to a prisoner of war in the camp and took it to the small local museum, founded after the ceremonies marking the fiftieth anniversary (1988) of Hitler's invasion of Austria, to document the tragic and tormented forgotten history of this area.[12] It recounts the history, and exhibits artifacts of Displaced Persons in the *Waldviertel*.

A traveling photographer, interested in World War II and intrigued by the trunk in the museum, tried to find more information and noticed that it was not mentioned in the catalog. He turned to Rolf Kleinschmidt, who had been studying the *Waldviertel*'s history. Using the address on the trunk, Kleinschmidt inquired about Oldra and found him at the address on the trunk.

Oldra's visit was a special occasion for the Austrians of the area. To be able to talk to one of the prisoners was "a sort of apparition from the past," wrote Oldra. He and his family were driven to Allentsteig, the small town just outside the military zone, the headquarters for the military, housed in the ornate sixteenth century castle. All the dignitaries of the town were there to welcome him, including the children of the town, wrote Oldra, "impressed by this live man from another time. Then, a woman in her seventies stepped suddenly forward from the waiting crowd and hugged me. It was the daughter of Mrs. Kohl, who had given me something to eat in 1945." Under the klieg lights of a full crew of the Austrian radio and TV, one speech followed another in quick succession to which Armand Oldra responded with his own remarks.

When the speeches were finished, the mayor of the town invited Oldra to go to the trunk, which had been set on a table in the center of room, covered with a deep blue cloth. As they walked toward the trunk the band played, first *La Marseillaise* [French national anthem] and then, the Austrian national anthem. In his diary, Oldra wrote about the opening of the trunk. "I took in my hands objects that I had touched half a century ago: letters, photos, course notes, drawings, books, dry tubes of paint, and a sewing kit, the mockup of a book I was going to illustrate to be published upon our return.[13] To relive the past deeply upset me." A reception followed.

From Allentsteig they drove a few miles to the Kohls' farm but did not enter, as it was under construction, and continued to the location of the camp. It was somewhat confusing for Oldra. He spent a quiet moment of silence in front of the stone and plaque honoring his comrades who died in captivity. Expressing the depth of his feelings, he wrote, "Ever since our arrival in Vienna the sun was shining brightly. Now, the sky darkens and a cold wind begins to blow. The landscape becomes sinister again, just as in the past."[14]

After a couple of days visiting Vienna, Oldra and his family hosted a dinner for the men he had met, "his Austrian friends with whom he felt an emotional connection." He also realized that for the historian, organizer of the trip, and the local Austrians, he was a live witness for all the POWs, political deportees, men and women of the concentration camps, foreign workers, and refugees, who had tread the Austrian soil.

2010

Joining a group of French families whose fathers had been POWs in Oflag XVIIA, two daughters, a son-in-law and I visited the location of the camp. An ammunition depot occupies the left side of the camp. On the right side the foundations are still there in a row along what was the central alley, still marked by some of the old trees, planted by the officers. One can see the configuration of the camp on Google's satellite view, which shows the rows of barracks and some of the entrance roads. The village of Edelback has disappeared. The area is still a maneuver ground for the Austrian military and as such off limits. The group had obtained special permission and was the guest of the Austrian military, who welcomed us warmly.

The officers of Oflag XVIIA, as all prisoners of war, deportees, and displaced persons who survived their captivity, understand freedom in a heartfelt way. Reflecting ten years after his liberation, an officer explained that freedom was not a principle without substance such as giving rights in superficial regulations, but it was the reality of a personal choice made by the entire person, the body, the heart, and the mind. He wrote, "In the night that was captivity, we practically lost all physical movements, while our intellectual and spiritual freedom was the only light shining, a weapon against tyranny, as we totally possessed the freedom of our opinions despite our jailers."[15] These men made the choice in my father's words "to unite in a moral effort to transform their lives with an inner radiance ... that would encourage others, he hoped, to find more energy and trust."

An inner radiance and common effort led the officers to the unflinching solidarity of their last three years of captivity, fostering relationships "of independence and respect," an attitude I felt most strongly from my father, particularly special for a girl and a young woman. Their ideal was a tall order that a few may have found in their families, but which did not exist in the nation as a whole or the world in the form they had dreamed of. Altogether, however, their models of relationships and advocacy contributed to the growing consensus of the international community; to uphold the supreme value of the human person that led to the draft and enactment of the Universal Declaration of Human Rights in 1948. By striving to uphold this supreme value we honor the ideal of the officers, the prisoners of war.

As U.S. troops have come home from Iraq and now from Afghanistan, let us remember that experiencing war directly is a defining experience that is difficult to fully understand for the rest of the nation, those not touched by it. But we can strive to attain relationships of independence and respect, that foster the value of human connections in our daily life. We can honor our returning warriors and their families by letting our hearts accept, trust, and value the dignity of every human being.

Background

The officer POWs followed what was happening in the world passionately as an important antidote to their isolation. It was crucial for sustaining their morale. Diary entries noted briefly or implied whatever they knew of the war and politics outside the barbed wire. I have added these background notes to the entries and grouped them chronologically to give a better perspective of the events.

Chapter 5

Two responses to the defeat, which will divide the French officers (1940)

Marshall Pétain: The deputies, aware of the country's high regard for Pétain, agreed to give him full power to revise the constitution, allowing an abrogation of the French Republic's constitution. This event marked the beginning of the *Etat Français* (Vichy government/regime) of 1940–1944, replacing the French Third Republic. Pétain became "Head of the French State," using his power to institute an authoritarian regime and promulgate the *Révolution Nationale*. The government was located in the town of Vichy, hence the name, Vichy government/regime (free zone until November 1942).

At the time of the armistice, Marshall Pétain declared that "he would remain in France whatever happened, even if the conditions proved unacceptable, in order to share the fate of his compatriots." Casting himself as the protector of the country, he announced that he was offering France "the gift of his own person in order to attenuate her misfortune."

In October, when he met with Hitler in Montoire, France, he declared, "I enter today into the way of collaboration." He justified his action by assuring the country that its suffering would be lightened, "the fate of our prisoners ameliorated, occupation costs reduced, and the demarcation line made more flexible." (For a full analysis see Robert Paxton, *Vichy France*, chap. 1, "The French Quest for Collaboration").

General de Gaulle: In the *Appel*, de Gaulle said, "The honor, good sense, and superior interest of the fatherland command all the free French to continue the fight wherever they are, and however they can." And added, "Whatever happens, the flame of French resistance should not go out and will not go out," and he called on anyone able to do so, to join him in England (speech of General de Gaulle June 18–22). The speech can be heard at http://www.charles-degaulle.org/dossier/18juin/temoignages/son22j.htm.

Charles de Gaulle started his military career a few years before World War I as a young lieutenant in the 33rd Infantry Regiment commanded by Colonel Pétain. Colonel at the beginning of World War II, de Gaulle was promoted general on the battle field in May 1940. Because of his past political connections, he was then asked, in early June, to take up the post of Under-Secretary of State for War and National Defense, a post which removed him from the military. General de Gaulle, not being in the military when Marshall Pétain called for a cease-fire, would be freer to choose his course of action.

Editor's note: My grandfather was a major in the 33rd Infantry Regiment on Marshall Pétain's staff before World War I and was connected to both Marshall Pétain and General de Gaulle. He died early on during the Battle of the Marne.

Mers-El-Kebir: The French fleet was the fourth largest in the world with ships in many ports. Many of her ships were anchored in Oran (Algeria was under the control of the Vichy government), having escaped capture by Germany. Admiral Darlan, the French Secretary of the Navy, had given his word to Churchill that the French fleet would never fall into German hands, but there was not much trust between Darlan and Churchill. In addition, the English translation of the armistice was ambiguous and led to misinterpretations.

On 3 July Churchill gave orders to the Royal Navy Senior Commander to present the French Commander in Mers-el-Kebir with four options, all involving being decommissioned, or put under British control, and failing that, being destroyed by the British. The British Commander and the French Commander were on very good terms, but had to communicate through emissaries. An American sailor wrote, "The situation was ripe for disaster. Within the time constraint, miscommunications and pride, both sides had boxed themselves into a corner from which there was no honorable retreat," leading to the British Navy sinking the French flagship, two battleships, a number of destroyers and submarines. One battle cruiser managed to leave the port despite the mines and sailed to Toulon on the Mediterranean coast to rejoin another part of the fleet in the free zone of France. Almost thirteen hundred French sailors were killed or missing (http://www.militaryhistoryonline.com/wwii/articles/merselkebir.aspx).

Chapter 7

Africa: The Free French Forces organize (1941)

The Free French Forces: While the officer POWs learned of some of the campaigns of the war, they most likely did not yet know the political implication for the French. The armistice of 1940 had left the entire French colonial empire, which included a large part of Africa, under the administration of the Vichy government. General de Gaulle, recognized by the British as the leader of the Free French as early as August 1940 and keenly aware of Africa's strategic importance with a substantial number of colonial troops, tried to rally the French colonial governors and troops to his side. He succeeded in Equatorial Africa (Gabon, Cameron, Chad, Congo), a campaign led by Philippe LeClerc and General Koenig, but failed in the West African and North African colonies, which remained solidly loyal to Vichy. By October 1940 General de Gaulle had established the Empire Defense Council to oversee what became known as the Free French Forces (FFL, Forces Françaises Libres), at that time a force of seventeen thousand troops, twenty-four ships and one thousand airplanes.

Koufra: The FFL, divided into five battalions, took part in the campaign of Eritrea and Somaliland with the British, which started in the fall of 1940. While the British occupied Libya along its coast beyond Benghazi, the Free French Forces in Equatorial Africa entered the Libyan Desert from the south. In March 1941 the Italians surrendered the Fort of Koufra, in the desert of eastern Libya about one hundred miles from Egypt and famous for the oath of Koufra, taken by the participating troops. They declared, "We will stop only when the French flag flies over Metz and Strasbourg." In fact, General Leclerc liberated Strasbourg in December 1944, fulfilling the oath to the Free French Forces.

Chapter 8

Battles in the Levant (1941)

Syria and Lebanon: The Free French Forces, led by General Catroux, joined the British. General Catroux, who had been the governor general in Indochina before the war, went to London after the signing of the armistice, and tearing three of his five stars from his sleeve reported to General de Gaulle, who wore only two stars (*Time Magazine* August 4, 1941.) *Time* wrote, "It is no easy thing to be a Free French man in 1941. It is the most brutal, the most difficult choice. Most of the leaders have been condemned to death in absentia. Smaller fry that are caught get fifteen years at hard labor. Most of the Free French have families living in France, subject to retaliation."

After the British won, they signed an agreement with the Vichy government which turned Syria over to them. De Gaulle relentlessly confronted the British until Churchill relented and allowed a French administration under de Gaulle, who promised to give Lebanon and Syria their independence. (He did.) *Time Magazine* reported that de Gaulle flew to Beirut to congratulate the troops. "In the street, he stopped his motorcade, stepped out of his car, and gravely saluted the Lebanese flag. At this gesture the Lebanese went wild, and flocked around de Gaulle cheering" (*Time Magazine*, August 4, 1941).

Chapter 10

El Alamein and Operation Torch: The Germans invade France's Free Zone (1942)

Bir Hakeim: Recognizing that the FFL resistance greatly disrupted Rommel's offensive and facilitated the success of El Alamein, Winston Churchill wrote, "Holding back Rommel's offensive for fifteen days, the Free French in Bir Hakeim contributed to save Egypt and the Suez Canal's destinies."

The official German radio, however, announced that the Germans had taken Bir Hakeim by storm, omitting the fact that the fort was mostly empty. As the first direct engagement between the French and the Germans since the debacle of 1940, it became a source of pride and restoration of honor for the French, while it was a thorn for the Germans. When a journalist described to Hitler in detail the combats at Bir Hakeim, he shouted, "this shows again that the French are still after us, the best soldiers in Europe. After this war we will definitely have to set up a coalition that can militarily control a country of such impressive military feats." (For details see Dominique Lormier, *C'est nous les Africains*, 132–135.)

Consequently, the Germans announced that "the white and colored Frenchmen made prisoner at Bir Hakeim, since they did not belong to any regular army, would not be subject to the laws of war and would be executed." An hour later, De Gaulle put out an announcement on the BBC in all languages, "If Germany were to dishonor itself as to kill French soldiers fighting for their country, General de Gaulle would regrettably feel obliged to inflict the same fate on German prisoners." That same day, the Germans announced, "On the subject of the members of the French forces, who have just been captured in the fighting at Bir Hakeim, no misunderstanding is possible. General de Gaulle's soldiers will be treated as soldiers." (See Charles de Gaulle, *Memoirs*, 299.)

After the dismal news of the Russian front, the battle of El Alamein was a decisive victory. Seeing the battle of El Alamein as the turning point in the war, General Auchinleck, recognizing it in a communiqué, wrote, "The United Nations owe it to themselves to be full of admiration and gratitude towards these French troops and their valiant General" (de Gaulle, *Memoirs*, 300). The challenge for de Gaulle was to keep France at war, and by offsetting the Vichy Government's collaboration, make it possible for France to participate in the Allied battles and victory. (See "Les forces françaises libres" mai-juin 1942 à Bir Hakeim, pdf. at http://digitool.library.mcgill.ca/R/?func=dbin-jump-full&object_id=33900&local_base=GEN01-MCG02.)

Operation Torch and political maneuvers—Giraud: The Americans had enlisted General Giraud to command the colonial troops, believing that he was known by the colonial army and would facilitate a peaceful landing. The day before the operation was to begin, Giraud, who had been restricted to his estate in Southern France, was picked up on the Mediterranean Coast by the British submarine *Seraph*, which brought him to Gibraltar, to meet General Eisenhower. During his clandestine contacts with the Americans, Giraud had understood that he would be the overall commander of the Allied Forces. On learning that he would "only" command the French forces, he punted in Gibraltar for a day and reached Algiers after the landing. In the meantime, the Americans were forced to deal with Darlan.

Darlan: The diary note, "Darlan dissents," is a condensed version of the facts on the ground. The historian Rick Atkinson writes: "Darlan [who first gave the order to fight the Americans] appeared to have capitulated twice and reneged twice under the countervailing pressures from Vichy and Major General Clark [the American go-between]. Giraud's influence in North Africa seems to be nil. Three days later the Germans entered the free zone of France, Darlan, seeing the writing on the wall, ordered the French troops to stop fighting.

Roosevelt-Pétain: President Roosevelt sent a letter to Marshall Pétain to ask him for the cooperation of the French Authorities in North Africa, reminding him of the friendship between France and the U.S., and assuring him that his greater aim was the liberation of France (http://www.presidency.ucsb.edu/ws/?pid=16191). Roosevelt did not receive a direct response, only a statement that said, "We are attacked, we shall defend ourselves. This is the order I am giving." Pétain sent a note to Admiral Darlan, his would-be successor, who happened to be in Algiers, saying simply: "I am glad you are in North Africa. You may act, and inform me." When the Americans and the British landed, the French colonial troops, who had kept their allegiance to the Vichy government, started fighting the Americans.

De Gaulle: The other player in this drama, General de Gaulle, had been kept in the dark of the pending landing, reluctantly by the British, who followed the American lead. On 7 November de Gaulle, guessing after listening to radio broadcasts that the landing was imminent, immediately contacted Churchill and Foreign Secretary Anthony Eden, who informed him of the Allies' plan to work with Giraud and Darlan. He told Churchill that he was willing to join in, but knowing Darlan too well, warned that he would do it only if "the Vichy government and its supporters were expelled from Algiers. The resistance movement as a whole would not tolerate their maintenance in power" (Charles de Gaulle, *Memoirs*, 351). De Gaulle then spoke by radio to his supporters in North Africa, enjoining them to join and help the Americans, which they did effectively, until blocked by the Vichy Forces.

Occupation of the free zone by the Germans; Hitler: Officially, the German radio broadcast of Hitler's letter to Marshall Pétain announced what everyone had been concerned about: the occupation of all of France. In his letter, Hitler, excessively deferential to Pétain, put the blame for the war on Great Britain and America and assured Pétain that he would remained completely free, but that the circumstances had forced the German troops to invade the free zone of France. While this action clearly voided the armistice of 1940, Hitler declared that the occupation was only "a precaution that did not end the armistice and would be lifted as soon as circumstances permitted" (http://www.der-fuehrer.org/reden/english/42-v11-26.htm).

Pétain: In France, as the Germans occupied the free zone, Marshal Pétain ordered the Armistice Army to be demobilized. (The armistice allowed France to have 100,000 men as a military force in the free zone of France. They were, however, deprived of tanks, armored vehicles, and most guns.) General de Lattre, who commanded one of its sectors, had secretly put in place a defense plan to resist the Germans, should they occupy the free zone. He was "immediately repudiated and forsaken by all" (Charles de Gaulle, *Memoirs*, 358). He was captured and thrown in prison.

De Lattre: General de Lattre had done as much training as possible with the Armistice Army, emphasizing athletic activities to prepare for an eventual fight with the Germans. He was condemned to ten years in prison by the Pétain government, but fortunately remained in prison in France. He contacted de Gaulle with the help of his wife and Resistance friends. After escaping from prison in September, he was able, with the help of the British Secret Service, to rejoin de Gaulle in Algiers in

December 1943. His wife and teenage son, who would have been deported if found, lived secretly, until they too rejoined him three months later—March 1944—after an amazing journey (Simonne de Lattre, *Jean de Lattre: Mon mari*).

Marshall Pétain declared to the French people, "You have only one duty: to obey. You have only one government: the one I have empowered to govern. You have only one country: the one I embody, France" (as quoted in Philippe Burrin, *France Under the Germans*, 165). It was now very clear that the sentiment that Pétain was playing a double game had been a total illusion. The officer POWs had to come face to face with Pétain's betrayal, however painful. "The biggest risk of loyalty is to be deceived," the sportscaster Frank Deford declared recently on NPR, speaking of a head coach in college sports who had ignored beyond all evidence the misconduct of another coach and childhood friend.

Political aftermath of the landing: In the aftermath of the landing in North Africa, Darlan, after much bickering, became High Commissioner of the French North African colonies and Giraud became the leader of its armed forces. Darlan, alleging that he had received a secret telegram, declared himself "head of the French State in North Africa in the name of Marshall Pétain," and proceeded to create an Imperial Council consisting of Vichy administrators. President Roosevelt decided to make a deal with him, as a "temporary expedient," acknowledging that he was "walking with the devil" (American Foreign Policy website, Operation Torch and http://www.personal.ashland.edu/-jmoser/usfp/poling.htm). The leadership of Darlan in North Africa with the support of the Americans provoked general indignation. Wendell Willkie wrote: "Shall we in America be quiet, for instance, when our leaders, after promising freedom to the French people, put into control over them the very man who has helped to enslave them?" (American Foreign Policy website, and in Rick Atkinson, *An Army at Dawn*, 198).

A correspondent wrote, "The Allied marriage of convenience with the quisling Darlan was deemed a sordid betrayal of the fundamental Allied principles." Edward R. Murrow asked, "What the hell is this about? Are we fighting the Nazis or sleeping with them?" The British Foreign Office cabled its embassy in Washington, "We are fighting for international decency, and Darlan is the antithesis of this" (Rick Atkinson, *An Army at Dawn*, 198).

General de Gaulle, wanting to make known that he had nothing in common with the French Vichy government led by Darlan, officially sanctioned by the Americans, turned to the British, who allowed him to make an announcement on the BBC. It said: "General de Gaulle and the National Committee took no share and assumed no responsibility in the negotiations in progress in Algiers. An arrangement preserving the Vichy government in North Africa would obviously be unacceptable to Fighting France [name given to the Free French by de Gaulle]" (Charles de Gaulle, *Memoirs*, 363). As an unintended consequence of having kept de Gaulle at a distance, French public opinion shifted towards de Gaulle after the Darlan agreement.

French fleet in Toulon: When the Germans invaded the free zone of France they had allowed the fleet in the port of Toulon to remain neutral. The port admiral, who remained under Pétain's order, refused to sail for Africa, where he could have joined the Americans. The Germans, however, did not wait long before they ordered SS Panzer troops to storm the Toulon base gates.

Scuttled were three battleships, eight cruisers, seventeen destroyers, sixteen torpedo boats, sixteen submarines, seven dispatch vessels, three patrol boats, sixty transport ships, tankers, minesweepers, and tugs. Five submarines managed to leave and reach Algiers or Spanish ports (De Gaulle, *Memoirs*, 359).

Chapter 11
General de Gaulle prepares for the liberation of France (1943)

Formation of Provisional French Government: This was the culmination of six to seven months of political jockeying. After the occupation of the free zone by the Germans on 11 November 1942, the Vichy government of Marshall Pétain became a police state totally submissive to the Germans (they instituted a home grown Milice [repressive police], and agreed to the conscription of 600,000 young Frenchmen to work in Germany). The political future of France would now be decided in North Africa. The formation of a Provisionary Government in Algiers with General Giraud and General de Gaulle was the beginning of the end of a turbulent political evolution, which started in early 1943.

After Darlan's assassination in December 1942, the Americans named General Giraud to succeed him as Civil Administrator and Commander-in-Chief. He decided to continue the Vichy legal order established by Darlan. It meant that Pétain's National Revolution was still in force in North Africa, including the anti–Semitic laws that stripped the Jews of French citizenship (Christensen, *France During World War II*, 159). "North Africa effectively became an overseas Vichy regime under an American protectorate," wrote Dominique Lormier (Dominique Lormier, *C'est nous, les Africains*, 157).

Recognizing that General de Gaulle should be involved, President Roosevelt asked him to be part of the administration, but de Gaulle first refused to join a government, which effectively preserved the Vichy regime in North Africa. The Americans then proposed a triumvirate consisting of de Gaulle, Giraud, and an American General, but limited their jurisdiction to the administration of the colonies. De Gaulle again refused, arguing for a central government that included both metropolitan France and her colonies. "Everything would transpire as if France no longer existed as a state, at least until victory," he wrote, and added that he had "the highest consideration" for Roosevelt and Churchill, "without, however, recognizing in any respect their authority to deal with questions of sovereignty within the French Empire" (Charles de Gaulle, *Memoirs*, 391). He added, "From the moment America entered the war, Roosevelt meant the peace to be an American peace, convinced that he must be the one to dictate its structure ... France was reviving as a sovereign and independent nation" (Charles De Gaulle, *Memoirs*, 392).

Roosevelt had planned to place France under the administration of the American military until the end of the war, "keeping her from having a government until the war's end" (Charles de Gaulle, *Memoirs*, 412). It was unacceptable to General de Gaulle that the American military would administer France. Noting that the resistance movements in France had already rallied to him, he remarked, "There is a need for an institution with a central authority, in order to unify the various forces. This central authority must condemn Vichy and proclaim that the armistice was null and void." He added, "Fighting France symbolizes resistance against the enemy, the upholding of the Republic, and the revival of the nation. It is to Fighting France that popular feeling naturally turns at the moment when the illusion that was Vichy is on the point of dissolution" (Charles De Gaulle, *Memoirs*, 395).

French Committee of National Liberation (CFLN Comité d'Alger): That clear call to national pride and honor resonated with the French, who began to rally around de Gaulle. After a few months, Giraud agreed to rescind the Vichy regime laws and reestablish republican law, paving the way for de Gaulle's acceptance. Moving his headquarters from London, de Gaulle arrived in Algiers at the end of May and created the French Committee of National Liberation (CFLN) (*le Comité d'Alger*). De Gaulle was President, Giraud, Commander in Chief, the Vichy colonial governors resigned or were replaced, and the committee exercised sovereignty over the colonies and metropolitan France. After the liberation of France de Gaulle was committed to turn the committee's powers over to a provisional government of the Republic, and pledged to re-establish all French liberties, the laws of the Republic, and the republican regime.

De Gaulle proceeded to prepare the legislative, judicial, and administrative measures to be taken in France at the time of the liberation (Charles De Gaulle, *Memoirs*, 440–445). He proclaimed that "it was a step in the resurrection of the French representative institutions upon which the future of our democracy depends." De Gaulle had created a government in exile. "The U.S. and Great Britain recognized the CFLN only after many countries had already done so" (M. Christofferson, *France During World War II*, 161). He pledged not to be a candidate for office. He was not, but ran for president ten years later.

As a military commander, Giraud led the liberation of Corsica, showing great military skills, but "could not resign himself to any form of subordination to civilian oversight, and he proceeded in an inadmissible fashion vis-à-vis the government" (Charles de Gaulle, *Memoirs*, 465–467). After repeated instances, removed from his command, he was offered a role as inspector general, but refused and retired in April 1944 (Charles De Gaulle, *Memoirs*, 429).

"De Gaulle prevailed because of his own strength and Giraud's weaknesses" (Christofferson, *France During World War II*, 159).

Chapter 12

The liberation of France (1944)

De Gaulle and Provisionary Government: In May, the Algiers Committee had declared itself the Provisional Government of France and was recognized in June by most European countries. General de Gaulle landed on Utah Beach with a Canadian Regiment on 14 June and immediately appointed a Commissioner of Normandy to indicate without delay that the authority now proceeded from his government everywhere that the enemy had retreated. Before D-Day de Gaulle had selected half of the departmental prefects, who would take over from Vichy, foiling the intentions of

President Roosevelt to place France under an Allied Military Government for Occupied Territories (AMGOT), which would have governed France for a year or two (T. Christofferson, 172, 167). After about one month of dispute between the appointed American administrators and the French appointed prefects, the Americans relented and let the French govern themselves. The U.S. and Great Britain recognized the Provisionary Government formally in October.

Liberation of Alsace: After rejoining General de Gaulle in Algiers in December 1943, General de Lattre, able to reconcile the French Colonial Army and the French Free Forces, took charge of about two hundred thirty thousand men, Army B, composed of an equal number of Christians and Muslims. De Gaulle recalled, "Our armies found themselves joyously re-established and rid of the oaths and incantations which had largely paralyzed or misled them" (Charles de Gaulle, *Memoirs*, 585).

The liberation of Alsace and Strasbourg were the ultimate goal of the French Army, the sacred ground, as General de Lattre called it. He regrouped to form what became the French First Army to begin the liberation of Alsace, the last region of France not yet liberated. (After landing in Toulon, many resistance groups and the men de Lattre had trained in 1942 responded to form a force close to three hundred thousand men, which was renamed the First Army.) Starting in October, de Lattre and the First Army battled relentlessly in Les Vosges reaching the Rhine River in mid-November, having liberated most of Alsace, except for a pocket in the south. In the north, General Leclerc entered Strasbourg on 25 November fulfilling "the oath of Koufra" (March 1941, see Chapter 7). Then, when General Leclerc rejoined the Third American Army of General Patton to reinforce the Bulge in December, de Lattre took charge of preventing Strasbourg from falling back into German hands.

General de Gaulle wrote in his memoirs: "General de Lattre de Tassigny (and General Juin, in Italy) emerged unscathed from the traps, which the disaster of 1940 and after it the armistice regime, had laid for their honor. They now offered themselves to wield the high command for which they had been made and of which they had always dreamed.... They restored the French military command to honor in the eyes of the nation, the Allies, and the enemy" (Charles de Gaulle, *Memoirs*, 603).

General de Lattre understood that, and the officers as prisoners had shown the same sense of honor by their actions and resistance in captivity. In the book *Alsace* published by my father, General de Lattre wrote a dedication addressed to the officer POWs. It said, "While our fighting troops kept their oath to liberate Alsace, their comrades, who endured the long wait of captivity, joined them in a common fervor and equal attachment toward the dearest of our provinces" (Paris: Editions Jacques Vautrain, 1947).

Chapter 13

End of the war (1945)

Signing of the German surrender: During the night of 8-9 May General de Lattre, representing France, signed the final capitulation of Germany, after being first pushed aside by the Allies. After arriving at Joukov's headquarters in Berlin, he insisted that the French flag be added and flown with the American, Russian, and British flags. Then, told that he would only witness without signing, he declared, "I have received the order of my government to sign and I must sign.... If I allow my country to be excluded from signing the capitulation of the Reich, I will be hanged." He eventually signed as a full witness, an important affirmation for the French that their "honor was safe." When the German Marshal, Commander in Chief of the German Army, saw the French flag, he exclaimed, "*Hach,* that is the last straw" (http://fresques.ina.fr/jalons/fiche-media/InaEdu00174/signature-de-l-acte-de-capitulation-de-l-allemagne-a-berlin.html, and http://www.cndp.fr/crdp-reims/memoire/enseigner/reims7mai/09reims_berlin.htm).

Chapter Notes

Preface

1. Jacques Vautrain, "Présentation du Bloc VI," in Jacques Vautrain, ed., *Escale à Nuremberg* (Paris: Editions Jacques Vautrain, 1945), 12.
2. Johannes Müllner, *Die Entweihte Heimat: Ein Stuck dass nure wenige kennen, Zwang ensiedelt, verwahrlost, zerstört* (Allentsteig: Verein Information, Waldviertel, 1998). A review of the story in English is available at http://www.viennareview.net/commentary/commentary-commentary/austrias-dark-spot.
3. Bernard Fernique, "La recherche spirituelle," in *Escale à Nuremberg*, Jacques Vautrain, ed. (Paris: Editions Jacques Vautrain, 1945), 78.
4. Jacques Vautrain, "Présentation," in *Escale*, 12.
5. Karl-Heinz Frieser, *The Blitzkrieg Legend: The 1940 Campaign in the West*, trans. by John T. Greenwood (Annapolis, Maryland: Naval Institute Press, 2005). Originally published as *Blitzkrieg-Legende: Der Westfeldzug 1940, Operationen des Zweiten Weltkrieg* (Munich: Oldenburg). These documents became the basis for a French historian's book, *Comme des Lions (Like Lions: The Heroic Sacrifice of the French Army)* by Dominique Lormier (Paris: Calmann-Lévy, 2005), in which Lormier describes in great detail the battles of 1940.
6. Jacques Vautrain, "Présentation du Bloc VI," 12.

Chapter 1

1. The Maginot Line was considered an impregnable barrier. It was an intricate, self-sustaining maze of tens of miles of underground galleries, connecting sleeping quarters, lavatories, kitchens, mess halls, and canteens. The only structures above ground were bunkers for the artillery and observation towers.
2. Julian Jackson, *The Fall of France: The Nazi Invasion of 1940* (New York: Oxford University Press, 2003), 145–146.
3. Yves Durand, *La vie quotidienne des prisonniers de guerre dans les stalags, les oflags et les Kommandos 1939–1945* (Paris: Hachette, 1987), 19.
4. Jackson, *Fall of France*, 152.
5. *Ibid.* 149.
6. Richard Vinen, *The Unfree French: Life Under the Occupation* (New Haven and London: Yale University Press, 2006), 17.
7. Jackson, *Fall of France*, 152–154.
8. Vinen, *Unfree French*, 17.
9. Jackson, *Fall of France*, 161.
10. *Ibid.*, 179.
11. *Ibid.*, 65.

12. *Ibid.*, 178.
13. Alsace and Lorraine: two French provinces. The Vosges, a range of mountains running parallel to the Rhine valley, are the mirror image of the Black Forest in Germany, a region of large forests of pines, beech trees, and abundant wildlife with Lorraine on the west side and Alsace in the east.
14. Vinen, *Unfree French*, 19.
15. Dominique Lormier, *Comme des lions*, 320.
16. *Ibid.*, 322–323.

Chapter 2

1. Durand, *La vie quotidienne*, 23, and Lormier, *Comme des lions*, 323.
2. Cdt. Marcel Dones, *Un Dragon dans les Tourmentes*, 63, accessed December 2008, http://www.megabaze.com/page_html/099-The%2014-18%20and%2049-45. (Megabaze has not archived this).
3. Jean-Louis Saconney, *Les années noires*, 13, accessed December 21, 2008. http://www.memoireetavenir.fr/doc/Les%20Années%20noires%202.pdf.
4. Robert Christophe, *Les années perdues: Journal de guerre et de captivité 1939–1945* (Parçay-sur-Vienne: Editions Anovi, 2008), 75.
5. For a full account see Lormier, 198.
6. For these last two weeks see Oliver Bishoff and Richard Klein, http://www.Maginot67.com/present_site.htm (accessed July 25, 2008 in another format).
7. Bishoff and Klein, Conclusion, accessed July 25, 2008, http://www.Maginot67.com/Maginot/conclusion/Maginot_c_concl.htm.
8. Christophe, *Les années perdues*, 78–81.
9. Dones, *Un dragon*, 64–65.
10. Marcel Poisot, *Prisonniers à Neuf-Brisach* (Paris: Editions Jacques Vautrain, 1945, rpt. Office du Tourisme des Bords de Rhin, 2008), 10, 16.
11. Neuf-Brisach, designed by Vauban, Louis XIV's chief military engineer, was constructed between 1698 and 1720. The town has one of the most sophisticated defensive designs of the period: It is surrounded by star-shaped fortifications intended to prevent enemy artillery from reaching the inside. It survives today, untouched, despite numerous attacks. Great picture on Google Earth.
12. Poisot, *Neuf-Brisach*, 66–88.
13. Lormier, *Comme des lions*, 268.
14. Marshal Pétain's speech is available at http://pages.livresdeguerre.net/pages/sujet.php?id=docddp&su=48&np=97.
15. Alan Sheridan, *André Gide: Life in the Present* (Cambridge: Harvard University Press, 1999), 542.

Chapter 3

1. *Sélestat* is an ancient town, which traces its beginning to the Neolithic times, attributing its name, *Sladistat*, meaning the place of swamps, to the Germanic invasion of the fifth century. It grew as a major crossroads, encircled by fortifications in the thirteenth century. In the fifteenth and sixteenth centuries, its humanist school became a thriving center of scholarship. Today, its humanist library is recognized as one of the three treasures of Alsace.
2. Saconney, *Les années noires*, 14.
3. *Ibid.*, 4.
4. Donès, *Un Dragon*, 70.
5. In 1936 Hitler declared, "If France had then marched into the Rhineland, we would have had to withdraw with our tails between our legs," http://www.historylearningsite.co.uk/Rhineland_1936.htm.

Notes. Chapters 4 and 5   243

6. Raymond Gangloff, *Cinq ans d'oflag: La captivité des officiers français en Allemagne 1940–45* (Paris: Editions Albatros, 1989), 53.
7. Ibid., 36.
8. Frieser, *The Blitzkrieg Legend*, 216. For the French detailed description of the 1940 Campaign, see Lormier, *Comme des Lions*.
9. Winston Churchill, *Memoirs of the Second World War* (Boston: Houghton Mifflin, 1987), 283.
10. Conférence du Commandant Even, *La plus grande èvasion de la guerre* (Service historique de l'armée de terre), 6, Musée virtuel, Oflag XVIIA, http://www.memoireetavenir.fr, accessed in 2008.
11. Saconney, *Les années noires*, 18.

Chapter 4

1. Saconney, *Les annéed noires*, 16.
2. Articles 9–10–11 of the Geneva Convention.
3. Jackson, *The Fall of France*, 228.
4. Bernard Fernique, "la recherche spirituelle," in *Escale*, 78.
5. Vautrain, "Présentation du Bloc VI," in *Escale*, 13.
6. Dr. Andreas Küsternig and Ernst Bezenek, ed., *Allentsteig im 19. Und 20. Jahrhundert: Die Grosse Flucht und die Lageruniversität Oflag XVIIA—Edelbach* (Allentsteig, 2002), 5. Trans. Henri Giraud, French translation.
7. Robert Christophe, *Les flammes du purgatoire: Histoire des prisonniers de 1940* (Paris: Editions France-Empire, 1979), 54.
8. Viktor Frankl, *Man's Search for Meaning: An Introduction to Logotherapy* (New York: Pocket, 1973), 164.
9. Jacques Vautrain, "Présentation du Bloc VI," in *Escale*, 12.
10. Robert Paxton, *Vichy France: Old Guard and New Order, 1940–1945* (New York: Columbia University Press, 2001), 34.

Chapter 5

1. Article 24 of the Geneva Convention specifies the amount of the officers' pay during their captivity, paid by France. They could transfer some portion of their salary to their families.
2. Articles 9–10 of the Geneva Convention cover the physical conditions of POW camps; the establishment of a canteen, which was supposed to sell local produce and clothes. As described in the diary, neither was provided, and the conditions in the Oflag did not come even close to the requirements.
3. Christophe, *Les flammes*, 51.
4. Roger Ikor, *Pour une fois écoute mon enfant* (Paris: Albin Michel, 1975), 263.
5. In July, the French National Assembly of the Third Republic (French government since 1871) was called to assemble in the free zone and invested Marshal Pétain with full constitutional power. For further comments see Background, Chapter 5, Marshal Pétain.
6. The speech can be heard at http://www.charles-de-gaulle.org/dossier/18juin/temoignages/son22j.htm. See Background, Chapter 5, General de Gaulle.
7. De Gaulle was promoted to general after distinguishing himself on the battlefield in May 1940.
8. Charles de Gaulle, *The Complete Memoirs*, trans. Jonathan Griffin and Richard Howard (New York: Carrol & Graf, 1998), 84.
9. H. Favard, *Les saints de France* (Paris: Éditions Jacques Vautrain, 1946), Preface.
10. Anna Maria Sigmund, Karl Sigmund, and Peter Michor, "Leray in Edelbach," in *Mathematical Tourist* 27, no. 2 (2005), 41.
11. Marcel Corre, *Défense de photographier* (Clermont Ferrand: Imprimerie de la Montagne, 1954).
12. Georges Lacassie, "No Prisons," in *Escale à Nuremberg*, 153.

13. Christophe, *Les flammes*, 86.
14. S.P. Mackenzie, *The Colditz Myth* (New York: Oxford University Press, 2006), 155.
15. *Ibid.*, 6.
16. Bernard Fernique, "la recherche," in *Escale*, 78.
17. Mackenzie, *Colditz*, 171.
18. *Le Canard en K.G., 1941* (camp newspaper, January 1942). An almost complete collection is in the Austrian National Library in Vienna. Some issues can be seen at Musée Virtuel, Oflag XVIIA, http://www.memoireetavenir.fr.
19. Christophe, *Les flammes*, 51.
20. Mackenzie, *Colditz*, 158.
21. Raymond Gangloff, *Cinq ans d'oflag* (Paris: Editions Albatgros, 1989), 119.
22. *Ibid.*
23. *Ibid.*, 54.
24. Irwin Kappes, *Mers-el-Kebir: A Battle Between Friends*, http://www.militaryhistoryonline.com/wwii/articles/merselkebir.aspx. See Background, Chapter 5, for details.
25. Philippe Burrin, *France Under the Germans: Collaboration and Compromise* (New York: New Press, 1995), 9.
26. Complete speech at http://pages.livresdeguerre.net/pages/sujet.php?id=docddp&su=48&np=102.
27. Thomas and Michael Christofferson, *France During World War II: From Defeat to Liberation* (New York: Fordham University Press, 2006), 71. .
28. Armistice Day in France, in remembrance of the armistice of 11 November 1918, signed at 11:00 a.m., in the eleventh month. In 1940, it was purely a celebration of 1918. Now, while the emphasis is on the armistice of 1918, it also commemorates the sacrifices of the soldiers of all wars.
29. Lormier, *Comme des lions*, 326.
30. General Gamelin cited as the cause of defeat as "their (officers and soldiers) lack of respect for authority, their soft daily life, and not having received the moral and patriotic education that would prepare them for the war." Jackson, *The Fall of France*, 145.
31. Lieutenant Ribaud as quoted in Lormier, *Comme des lions*. 19.
32. Bernard Fernique, "la recherche," in *Escale*, 78.

Chapter 6

1. Dones, *Un dragon*, 70.
2. Christophe, *Les années perdues*, 81.
3. Colonel Lacassie, cited in Christophe, *Les flammes*, 34.
4. Christophe, *Les années perdues*, 114.
5. Poisot, *Neuf-Brisach*, 121–123.
6. Vautrain, "Présentation du Bloc VI," in *Escale*, 12.
7. http://www.maginot67.com/present_site.htm.
8. Vautrain, "Présentation," in *Escale*,10.
9. Poisot, *Neuf-Brisach*, 166–174.
10. Donès, *Un Dragon*, 68.
11. Vautrain, "Présentation," in *Escale*, 12.
12. *Ibid.*, 10.
13. Dones, *Un Dragon*, 67.
14. For the entire voyage see Christophe, *Les années perdues*, 162.
15. René Pierrelée, "Les groupements," in *Escale*, 133.
16. "L'education physique," in *Escale*, 125.
17. *Ibid.*, 125.
18. André Cuny, "Les Courses," in *Escale*, 121.
19. "Dans le domaine des sons," in *Escale*, 131.
20. Vautrain, "Le théatre," in *Escale*, 95.
21. Le Lieutenant Satre, "Retour," in *Escale*, 61.

22. Marcel Crouzet, "La bibliothèque," in *Escale*, 112.
23. Vautrain, "Présentation du Bloc VI," in *Escale*, 10.
24. Fernique, "La recherche spirituelle," in *Escale*, 77.
25. Georges Lacassie, "Nos Prisons," in *Escale*, 153.
26. Vautrain, "Présentation," in *Escale*, 12.
27. Crouzet, "Les conférences littéraires," in *Escale*, 108.
28. *Ibid.*, 109.
29. Vautrain, "Présentation," in *Escale*, 12.
30. Crouzet, "Les Conférences," in *Escale*, 107.
31. "Le Ping-Pong," in *Escale*, 130.
32. My father published it again in 1945 and it was republished in 2008 by the Office de Tourisme des Bords du Rhin à Neuf-Brisach.
33. Georges Bouquet, "Foreword," in *Beaudelaire: Petits poèmes en prose* (Paris: Editions Jacques Vautrain, 1942).

Chapter 7

1. Raymond Gangloff, *Cinq ans d'oflag*, 116.
2. "Mesures de la solitude," *Le Canard*, 1 February 1941, no. 3.
3. Marcel Corre, *Défense de photographier: Reportage photographique clandestin sur la vie d'un camp de prisonniers français* (Clermont-Ferrand: Imprimeries de la montagne, 1954). This rare album can be seen on http://www.grosseric.com/OFLAG%20XVIIA%20Defense%20de%20Photographier.pdf . If no access, try http://www.collection-appareils.fr/phpBB3/viewtopic.php?f=33&t=6942 and scroll down to Défense de photographier.
4. René Paira, Transcript of a talk given in the Oflag in *Alsace* (Paris: Editions Jacques Vautrain, 1947), 70.
5. Gangloff, *Cinq ans d'oflag*, 56.
6. Vautrain, "Présentation," in *Escale*, 12, 13.
7. Paul Fournier, "le colis de France," *Le Canard*, 15 May 1941, no. 14.
8. Looking at collection of issues in the Austrian National Library in Vienna sixty-five years later was an unexpected amazing experience for the editor of this book.
9. Anna Maria Sigmund, Peter Michor, and Karl Sigmund, "Leray in Edelbach," in *The Mathematical Tourist* 27, no. 2 (2005), 42, http://www.mat.univie.ac.at/~michor/leray.pdf .
10. Colonel Robert, "le mot du colonel," *Le Canard*, 8 February, no. 1.
11. Maurice Morin, "Petite France," in *Le Canard*, no. 1.
12. The oath of Koufra: see Background, Chapter 7, The Free French Forces, for details.
13. Buridan's ass faced starvation when it was unable to choose between two equally appetizing piles of hay, a story that is used to illustrate the dilemma of having to make a decision between two equally attractive proposals.
14. Marche Lorraine: Vous n'aurez pas l'Alsace et la Lorraine/Et, malgré vous, nous resterons français/Vous avez pu germaniser la plaine/Mais notre cœur vous ne l'aurez jamais.
15. Gangloff, *Cinq ans d'oflag*, 92.
16. Ikor, *Pour une fois écoute mon enfant*, 228.
17. Küsternig, *Die Grosse Flucht*, 36.
18. Crouzet, "La recherche," in *Escale*, 114.
19. A good example of the need to read between the lines: How could the prisoners have obtained a crucifix from the church of the village? Surely, the villagers would not have given away the cross of their church. That line sent me on a map search of Edelbach, which I could not find anywhere, as if it had never existed. It was disconcerting, at first, but eventually that search led me to discover the story of the displacement of the population and emptying of the village, narrated by a parish minister. See Introduction, note 3. The POWs, who were working outside the camp, probably alerted the officer POWs of the existence of the cross.
20. Paul Fournier, "Une closhe et son clocher, " *Le Canard*, 1 May 1941, no. 13.
21. J. D. Lazemar de Fabreuges, "Companions de France," in *Le Canard*, 1 March 1941, no. 7.

22. "A nos lecteurs" in *Le Canard*, 1 May 1941, no. 13.
23. Maurice Renault, "A la Nationale du camp," *Le Canard*, 1 May 1941, no. 13.
24. Donès, *Un dragon*, 69.
25. René Marie, "Le mot du Représentant Général," *Le Canard*, 10–15 juin 1941, no. 15.

Chapter 8

1. Christophe, *Les flammes*, 75–76.
2. Marie Granet, *Défense de la France: Histoire d'un mouvement de résistance* (Paris: Presses Universitaires de France, 1960), 122.
3. Christophe, *Les années*, 212–215, 243. The Germans' treatment of the officers of Jewish origin and the response of their comrades are fortunately detailed in Robert Christophe's *Les années perdues*. The diary, more cautious, only mentions the change of barracks.
4. Granet, *Défense de la France*, 123.
5. Pierre Buchoud, "Notre organisation de résistance controlait l'Oflag XVIIA," *Revue: Les Années 40*, no. 150, 1537.
6. Granet, *Défense de la France*, 122.
7. Roger Bousseau, *Annales de Roger Bousseau*, Musée Virtuel, Oflag XVIIA, http://www.memoireetavenir.fr.
8. General de Gaulle, afraid that the British would appropriate Syria and Lebanon for themselves if they were to win in Syria, had sent General Catroux with an Expeditionary Corps of Free French forces to fight alongside the British. See Background, Chapter 8, Syria and Lebanon, for further details.
9. De Gaulle, *Memoirs*, 180.
10. Christophe, *Les flammes*, 107.
11. "Les Adieux du Capitaine de Vaisseau MARIE," *Le Canard*, 15 July–1 August 1941, no. 17.
12. Maurice Renault, "La Grande Semaine: un concours organisé par le Canard en K G," in *Le Canard*, 15 June 1941, no. 15.
13. "Une visite aux Sportifs," *Le Canard*, 25 March 1941, no. 9.
14. Robert Christophe, *Comment fut réalisé Sous le Manteau* (Paris: Editions Opta, 1949), 6.
15. Buchoud, "Notre organisation de résistance,"1533.
16. Georges Bouquet, "Avant-Propos," in *Beaudelaire: Petits poèmes en prose* (Paris: Éditions Jacques Vautrain, 1942), prepared in Nuremberg.
17. *Le Canard*, special edition, December 1941; also what follows about *La Semaine*.
18. "La France eternelle," *Le Canard*, December 1941.
19. *Le Folklore à la semaine de France* (Paris: Editions Jacques Vautrain, 1945). It documents the musical scores and the detailed steps of each of the dances for the twenty-seven provinces represented in La Semaine de France.
20. Christophe, *Les flammes*, 61.
21. "L'atelier de Santa," *Le Canard*, 20 January 1942, no. 21.
22. "Nos jouets a Vichy," *Le Canard*, 31 March 1941, no. 26, and for following paragraph.
23. The game of the goose was a popular game thought to be the prototype for many European racing board games. A track of consecutively numbered spaces is arranged in a spiral. Each player's piece moves according to throws of two dice with different adventures on the way.

Chapter 9

1. Christofferson, *France During World War II*, 38.
2. J.M Dunoyer, "Mystique et Politique," *Le Canard*, 15 June 1941, no. 15.
3. Gangloff, *Cinq ans d'oflag*, 140.
4. Christofferson, *France During World War II*, 39.
5. Fernique, "La recherche spirituelle," in *Escale*, 77.
6. Christophe, *Les flammes*, 80.

7. Christophe, *Les années*, 225.
8. Granet, *Défense de la France*, 123.
9. Vinen, *The Unfree French*, 207.
10. Gangloff, *Cinq ans d'oflag*, 140.
11. Paul Fournier, "In Memoriam," *Le Canard*, 20 January 1942, no. 21.
12. A. L., "La Volière," *Le Canard*, 20 January 1942, no. 21.
13. Anastasie, http://www.liberation.fr/culture/2011/08/20/censure-ciseaux-d-anastasie-communique_755891.
14. Vautrain, "Présentation," in *Escale*, 12.
15. Gangloff, *Cinq ans d'oflag*, 140.
16. All the information about the Pétain Center is from the insert in *Le Canard*, 20 January 1942, no. 21.
17. Christophe, *Les flammes*, 158.
18. *Sous le Manteau*, clandestine film made in the camp.
19. Christophe, *Sous le manteau*, 6.
20. Christophe, *Les années*, 233.
21. Gangloff, *Cinq ans d'oflag*, 103.
22. A. L., "La fin de la Volière," *Le Canard*, 31 March 1942, no. 26.
23. Christophe, *Les années*, 243.
24. Gangloff, *Cinq ans d'oflag*, 121.
25. Christophe, *Les années*, 245.
26. It was the perfect opportunity for Roosevelt and staunchly anti-Gaullist American diplomats to prevent General de Gaulle from gaining the upper hand. Christofferson, *France During World War II*, 158.
27. For this event see Christophe, *Les années*, 251, 261.
28. *Le Canard*, 31 March 1942, no. 26.
29. Christophe, *Les années*, 253–254.
30. Ibid., 258.
31. Buchoud, "Notre organisation," 1535.

Chapter 10

1. Paul Fournier, "Le colis de France," *Le Canard*, 15 May 1941, no. 14.
2. Ibid.
3. Christophe, *Les années*, 262.
4. Küsternig, *Die Grosse Flucht*, 36.
5. Buchoud, "Notre organisation," 1533,
6. Paxton, *Vichy France*, 304–305.
7. Churchill, *Memoirs*, 653.
8. Despite a decisive victory, Field Marshall Erwin Rommel's orderly retreat prolonged the North African war until mid-1943.
9. It is only when the French ran out of supplies that General Koenig evacuated the fort at night with four thousand able-bodied men and succeeded in reaching the British lines. Dominique Lormier, *C'est nous les africains: L'épopée de l'armée française d'Afrique, 1940–1945* (Paris: Calman-Levy, 2006), 132–135. See Background, Chapter 10, Bir Hakeim.
10. As quoted in de Gaulle, *Memoirs*, 491.
11. Buchoud, "Notre organisation," 1538.
12. Christophe, *Les flammes*, 158.
13. Rick Atkinson, *An Army at Dawn: The War in North Africa, 1942–1943* (New York: Henry Holt, 2002), 116–124, has an excellent detailed description. For see major points of Operation Torch and political maneuvers see Background, Chapter 10, Operation Torch and Political Maneuvers, Occupation of Free Zone, and Political Aftermath
14. Atkinson, *An Army at Dawn*, 217. See Background, Chapter 10, French Fleet.
15. For an account of Darlan's assassination, see Atkinson, *An Army at Dawn*, 252–253.

Chapter 11

1. Christophe, *Les Flammes*, 86.
2. *Ibid.*, 89.
3. The descriptions relative to the escape are a composite from "Prisonniers français en allemagne," *Revue: Les Années 40*, no. 61, and Conference du Commandant Even, *Revue Historique de l'Armée*, Nouvelle Serie, no. 2 (1969), originally published in *Revue of the Army Corps of Engineers*, 1949.
4. "L'Alsace, province de France," in *Alsace* (Paris: Éditions Jacques Vautrain, 1947), 53.
5. Christophe, *Les flammes*, 94.
6. Conférence of Cercle Shoah, http://www.cercleshoah.free.fr, brochure and notes.
7. Christophe, *Les flammes*, 62.
8. Marie Granet, *Revue Historique de la Seconde Guerre Mondiale*, no. 37, 1698.
9. The two-prong attack on Tunisia by the Allies started in December 1942 from the north (Americans, British, and colonial French) and south (British and Free French), and ended with the liberation of Tunis in May. It liberated the entire Mediterranean coast of North Africa, opening a direct way to the invasion of Italy, one of the Axis countries.
10. As quoted in de Gaulle, *Memoirs*, 415.
11. *Revue: Les Années 40*, no. 61,1684.
12. Buchoud, "Notre Organisation," 1534.
13. "Cercles Pédagogiques," in *Escale*, 135.
14. Maurice Dubesse, "L'Enfant," *Le Canard*, 1 July 1941, no. 16.
15. Pictures of Typhon II and the tunnel can be seen at http://www.grosseric.com/OFLAG%20XVIIA%20Defense%20de%20Photographier.pdf. If no access, try http://www.collection-appareils.fr/phpBB3/viewtopic.php?f=33&t=6942 and scroll down to Défense de photographier.
16. Bodaglio negotiated a secret armistice with the Allies, announced by Eisenhower in September. The Germans reacted so swiftly at the announcement of the surrender that the Allies were able to gain little advantage from their surprise invasion of the mainland. After invading from the south, the war continued in Italy until 1944.
17. Christophe, *Les flammes*, 53.
18. General de Gaulle established a French government in exile. For details, see Background, Chapter 11, Formation of Provisional French Government and Comite d'Alger.
19. *Revue: Les Années 40*, no. 61.
20. *Ibid.*

Chapter 12

1. Landmark conference in Tehran, the first time that Winston Churchill, President Franklin Roosevelt and Marshall Joseph Stalin met. The joined statement expressed a determination to work together and establish an enduring peace. The declaration ended: "We came here with hope and determination. We leave here, friends in fact, in spirit and in purpose."
2. *Sous le Manteau*, film.
3. Buchoud, "Notre organisation," 4.
4. Christophe, *Sous le Manteau*.
5. Gangloff, *Cinq ans d'oflag*, 114.
6. Buchoud, "Notre organisation," 5, 6, 8.
7. Adren Pommier, ed. "Champs de Bataille," in *Normandie* (Paris: Editions Jacques Vautrain, 1946), 283.
8. Vinen, *The Free French*, 328.
9. "Preface," *Normandie*, 14.
10. "Champs de Bataille," *Normadie*, 305.
11. Lormier, *C'est nous les Africains*, 210.
12. Marie Grenet, *Revue de l'histoire de la seconde guerre mondiale*, no. 37.
13. De Gaulle landed in Normandy on 14 June. For details see Background, Chapter 10, de Gaulle, and Chapter 11, Formation of Provisional French Government.

14. Lormier, *C'est nous les africains*, 215, and for the French Army's liberation of Alsace see Background, Chapter 12.

Chapter 13

1. The actual surrender was signed in Reims on 7 May 1945, but the Russians wanted the signature in Berlin. It was signed officially at midnight on 8 May, and a delayed announcement was broadcast in the afternoon. Then the Russians dated it as of 9 May, to account for the one day difference with the rest of Europe. For details of the signing of the German surrender see Background, Chapter 13, Signing of the German Surrender.
2. Buchoud, "Notre Organisation de Resistance," 8.
3. Armand Oldra's Journal.

Epilogue

1. Gangloff, *Cinq ans*, 241.
2. Oldra diary recollections.
3. Gangloff, *Cinq ans*, 241–244.
4. Bernard Fernique, "La rechercher," in *Escale*, 78.
5. Gangloff, *Cinq ans*, 251.
6. "Resistance: Revue du peuple français et de son armée," *Aux Armes*, December 1945, no. 14.
7. Gangloff, *Cinq ans*, 11.
8. Vautrain, "Présentation" in *Escale*, 14.
9. Dupont, "Un reportage sensationnel à l'Oflag XVIIA," in *Le lien*, October-November 1955, no. 38.
10. Gangloff, *cinq ans*, Chapter 35.
11. Armand Oldra, "Journal," diary, 2 December 1996, http://www.memoireetavenir.fr; France Berlioz, "Armand Oldra La malle aux souvenirs," *Journal l'Humanité*, 1999, http://www.humanite.fr/node/214000.
12. In order to establish the maneuver ground, Hitler expelled seven thousand Austrians from over thirty villages, making them refugees. The Russians kept it as a maneuver ground, followed by the Austrian Army. Twenty of the villages were never rebuilt, eradicating six hundred years of the history of the area.
13. One article relating the story of Oldra and the trunk noted that the book was Rabelais' classic *Gargantua et Pentagruel*, to be published by the Editions Jacques Vautrain. The book was never published. I noticed the footnote in the article, and in 2010, some six months before Oldra's death, I talked to Oldra over the phone. He remembered fondly coming to my apartment shortly after the war to see my father (I probably met him), and then he sent me a copy of one of his sketches. This is one example among many of how a small note or remark gave clues that allowed me to reconstruct the story.
14. This story follows the diary of Armand Oldra.
15. Newsletter of the Oflag XVIIA officers association, *Le Lien*, October-November 1955, no. 38.

Bibliography

Atkinson, Rick. *An Army at Dawn: The War in North Africa, 1942–1943*. Vol. 1 of the Liberation Trilogy. New York: Henry Holt, 2002.

Berlioz, France. "Armand Oldra: La malle aux souvenirs de l'ancien prisonnier de guerre." *Journal l'Humanité*, 17 septembre 1999, http://www.humanite.fr/node/214000.

Buchoud, Pierre, Jean Gautier, André Guérin, Raymond Laporte, René Paira, and Edmond Petit. "Notre organisation de résistance controlait l'Oflag XVIIA." *Revue: Les Années 40*, no. 150. http://www.memoireetavenir.fr/.

Burrin, Philippe. *France Under the Germans: Collaboration and Compromise*. New York: New Press, 1995.

Le Canard en...KG. Camp Newspaper of Oflag XVIIA. Archives, Austrian National Library.

Christofferson, Thomas, and Michael Christofferson. *France During World War II: From Defeat to Liberation*. New York: Fordham University Press, 2006.

Christophe, Robert. *Les années perdues: Journal de guerre et de captivité, 1939–1945*. Parçay-sur-Vienne: Editions Anovi, 2008.

_____. *Comment fut realisé Sous le Manteau*. Paris: Editions Opta, 1949.

_____. *Les flammes du purgatoire: Histoire des prisonniers de 1940*. Paris: Editions France-Empire, 1979.

Churchill, Winston. *Memoirs of the Second World War*. Abridgment of the six volumes of the Second World War. Boston: Houghton Mifflin, 1987.

Collins, Jacqueline Vautrain. "Top Secret: The Grand Escape." *World War II History Magazine*, October 2014.

_____. "A Trunk, the Keeper of Memories." *The Pedigru Review* 6, South Carolina Writers Workshop (2012).

Corre, Marcel. *Défense de photographier: Reportage photographique clandestin sur la vie d'un camp de prisonniers français, Oflag XVII A (Autriche)*. Clermont Ferrand: Imprimeries de la Montagne, 1954. The book of pictures can be seen at http://www.grosseric.com/OFLAG%20XVIIA%20Defense%20de%20Photographier.pdf. Some further information is at http://www.collection-appareils.fr/phpBB3/viewtopic.php?f=33&t=6942.

De Gaulle, Charles. *Mémoires de guerre: L'Appel, L'Unité, Salvation*. Librairie Plon, 1954–1959. *The Complete War Memoirs of Charles de Gaulle*, trans. Jonathan Griffin and Richard Howard, New York: Carroll and Graf, 1998.

De Lattre, Simonne. *Jean de Lattre: mon mari*. Paris: Presses de la Cité, 1972.

De Lattre de Tassigny, Jean. *Histoire de la première armée française: Rhin et Danube*. Paris: Presses de la Cité, 1971.

_____, Lucien Dollinger, Hans Haug, and René Paira. *Alsace*. Illustrations de J.M. Curutchet. Paris: Editions Jacques Vautrain, 1947.

Dones, Cdt. Marcel. *Un Dragon dans les Tourmentes*. Accessed December 2008, http://www.megabaze.com/page_html/099-The%2014-18%20and%2049-45. Megabaze has not archived this.

Doody, Richard. *The World War: French Empire Time Line, 1940–1945*. "The Second World War in the French Empire," http://worldatwar.net/timeline/france/empire40-45.html.

Durand, Yves. *La vie quotidienne des prisonniers de guerre dans les stalags, les oflags et les Kommandos, 1939–1945.* Paris: Hachette, 1987.
Ellenberger, François, Gabriel Gahau ed. "Hommage à François Ellenberger, fondateur du Comité français d'Histoire de la Géologie." 1997. http://www.annales.org/archives/cofrhigeo/francois-ellenberger.html.
Even, Commandant. "La plus grande èvasion de la guerre." Service historique de l'armée de terre, Musée virtuel, Oflag XVIIA, http://www.memoireetavenir.fr, accessed 2008.
Favard, H. *Les saints de France.* Illustrations de J. M. Curutchet. Paris: Editions Jacques Vautrain, 1946.
Flaud, Jacques, Pierre Hintzy, and Edmond Petit. "Prisonnier français en Allemagne." *Revue: Les Années 40*, no. 61 (January 1980), Musée virtuel, Oflag XVIIA, http://www.memoireetavenir.fr.
Frankl, Viktor. *Man's Search for Meaning: An Introduction to Logotherapy.* New York: Pocket, 1973.
Frieser, Karl-Heinz. *Blitzkrieg-Legende: Der Westfeldzug 1940, Operationen des Zweiten Weltkrieg.* Munich: Oldenburg. *The Blitzkrieg Legend: The 1940 Campaign in the West*, trans. John T. Greenwood. Annapolis, MD: Naval Institute, 2005.
Gangloff, Raymond. *Cinq ans d'oflag: la captivité des officiers français en Allemagne, 1940–45.* Paris: Editions Albatros, 1989.
"La grande évasion de l'Oflag XVII-A." Le blog de l'ULAC de Bagnolet, http://ufacbagnolet.over-blog.com/article-20732621.html.
Grenet, Marie. *Revue de l'histoire de la seconde guerre mondiale*, no. 37.
Ikor, Roger. *Pour une fois écoute mon enfant.* Paris: Albin Michel, 1975.
Jackson, Julian. *The Fall of France: The Nazi Invasion of 1940.* New York: Oxford University Press, 2003.
Kappes, Irwin, "Mers-el-Kebir: A Battle Between Friends," http://www.militaryhistoryonline.com/wwii/articles/merselkebir.aspx.
Lepeltier, Françoise. "Autriche: les secrets de la malle d'Edelbach." *Le Figaro*, 9 novembre 1996.
Leray, Jean. Société Mathématique de France, http://smf.emath.fr/content/jean-leray-1906-1998.
Lormier, Dominique. *C'est nous les africains: l'épopée de l'armée française d'Afrique 1940–1945.* Paris: Calman-Levy, 2006.
_____. *Comme des lions mai juin 1940: Le sacrifice heroïque de l'armée française.* Paris: Calmann-Lévy, 2005.
Mackenzie, S.P. *The Colditz Myth: The Real Story of POW Life in Nazi Germany.* New York: Oxford University Press, 2006.
Menasse, Eva. "Armand et Angela: Die unwahrscheinliche Geschichte eines Koffers, den ein französischer Offizier 1945 im Waldviertel stehenliess," *Profil* 52, 23 Dezember 1996, Musée virtuel, Oflag XVIIA, http://www.memoireetavenir.fr/.
Müllner, Johannes. Doellersheim post scriptum in "*Doellersheim*," 2002, http://www.doellersheim.at/doellersheim/post_scriptum/Der_Koffer/der-koffer.html.
_____. "Die Entweihte Heimat: Ein Stuck dass nure wenige kennen, Zwang ensiedelt, verwahrlost, zerstört." *Allentsteig: Verein Information*, Waldviertel, 1998.
Natter, H., and A. Réfrégier. *6000 à l'Oflag 17A: or five years of captivity day-by-day.* Paris: Editions Jacques Vautrain, 1946.
"En 1943, des prisonniers français ont réussi la plus grande évasion!" Télé loisirs, 1996, Musée virtuel, Oflag XVIIA, http://www.memoireetavenir.fr.
Oldra, Armand. "Epilogue: 2 décembre 1996." Musée virtuel, Oflag XVIIA, http://www.memoireetavenir.fr/.
Paxton, Robert. *Vichy France: Old Guard and New Order, 1940–1945.* New York: Columbia University Press, 2001.
Pétain, Philippe. "Discours et Messages." *Les pages de livres de guerre*, http://pages.livresdeguerre.net/pages/sujet.php?id=docddp&su=48.
Poisot, Marcel. *Prisonniers à Neuf-Brisach.* Paris: Editions Jacques Vautrain, 1945. Rpt. Office du Tourisme des Bords de Rhin, 2008.
Pommier, Adrien, ed. *Normandie.* Paris: Editions Jacques Vautrain, 1946.
Porch, Douglas. *The Path to Victory: The Mediterranean Theater in World War II.* New York: Farrar, Straus and Giroux, 2004.

Rousseau, Roger. "Annales: La captivité à l'Oflag XVIIA." Musée virtuel, Oflag XVIIA, http://www.memoireetavenir.fr/.
Roussel, Frédérique. "Censure Ciseaux d'Anastasie Communiqué." Libération, Culture, http://www.liberation.fr/culture/2011/08/20/censure-ciseaux-d-anastasie-communique_755891.
Saconney, Jean-Louis. "Les années noires." http://www.memoireetavenir.fr/doc/Les%20Annees%20noires%202.pdf, accessed December 21, 2008.
Sigmund, Anna Maria, Karl Sigmund, and Peter Michor. "Leray in Edelbach." *The Mathematical Tourist* 27, no. 2 (2005).
Vautrain, Jacques, ed. *Escale à Nuremberg*. Paris: Editions Jacques Vautrain, 1945.
———, and Felix Paillard, eds. *Le Folklore à la semaine de France*. Paris: Editions Jacques Vautrain, 1945.
Vinen, Richard. *The Unfree French: Life Under the Occupation*. New Haven and London: Yale University Press, 2006.
Wolff, Etienne, and Nicole Le Douarin. "Un pionnier de l'Embryologie et de la Tératologie Expérimentales." Collège de France, http://www.college-de-france.fr/media/professeurs-disparus/UPL54027_necrowolf1.pdf.

Index

Numbers in *bold italics* indicate pages with illustrations.

Algiers (landing) 147
Allied forces 143, 147, 157, 162, 171, 172, 175, 176, 181, 187, 199, 201, 213
Alsace 13, 16, 19, 21, 23, 24, 27, 28, 29, 32, 66, 79, 135, 153, 162, 183, 185, 242*ch*3*n*1
Alsatians 22, 26, 28, 29, 78, 79, 85, 115, 134, 153, 155, 158, 162, 166, 178, 190, 216, 223
American Air Force 210
American troops 205, 214
American zone 215, 216, 217
Anastasie 122, *123*, 161
Appel (appeal) 50, 51, 231
armistice 16, 18, 19, 21, 23, 24, 28, 53, 63, 104, 147
armistice army 235
art studio 89, 91, 141
Austria 5, 7, 32, 35, 168, 196, 208, 224
Austrian guards 127, 158, 171, 175, 189

barracks, furniture 37–39, 40, 43, 51, 75, 78, 100, 171
Basque dances 48
beehives 98
Belgium 13, 15, 24, 69, 182
Benghazi 86, 87, 233
Bir Hakeim 144, 151, 234
birds 9, 67, 81, 121, 122, 129, 138, 198
bombing 31, 66, 175, 186, 204
bookbinding 88, 91, 135
books 14, 55, 71, 72, 90, 97, 100, 110, 121, 134, 154, 223, 228; *see also* bookbinding
boxing 108, 141, 162
British Expeditionary Force 13, 15, 32
British officers (POWs) 77
Bulge, battle of the 184, 239

Cabaret: *le Refuge* 156, 160; *la Volière* 121, 122, 129
cage 9, 33, 61, 77, 81, 88, 121, 122, 129, 156, 161
camera 26, 39, 110, 127, 156, 171, 172
camp layout 37, *52*, 106; *see also* central alley; open air theater; Petite France; *Vorlager*
le Canard en ... KG 82, *83*–84, 87, 88, 95, 96, 97, 106, 108, 118, 119, 124, 126, 131, 136
le Canard enchaîné 83, 123
canteen 47, 47*ch*5*n*2, *49*, 51, 59, 99
cape 127, 164, 171, 172
capture: Loire 18, 21; Nantes 19, 20, *see also* Haguenau
carjacking 26, 208
cartography 163
Cassecroute 126
cathedral 29, 82, 111, *112*, 113
Cavalry School (Saumur) 19
cease-fire (call) 16, 18, 45
cemetery 13, 120, 126, 192, 214, 224, 225
censorship 56, 68, 83, 88, 90, 92, 110, 152
central alley 35, 38, 79, 96, 105, 106, 118, 128, 137, 147, 150, 154, 175, 178, 189, 228
Centre Pétain 124, 129, 136, 137
Cercle Sportif 108
les Champs Elysées 16, 42, 150, 182
chapel 45, 53, 77, 80, 93, *94*, 95, 129, 146, 151, 152, 213
Le Chef 131
children 75, 79, 93, 95, 106, 115–117, 159, 182; upon return 211, 220; *see also* families
Churchill, Prime Minister Winston S. 31, 144, 232, 233, 234, 235, 237

253

Index

cigarettes 27, 33, 47, 51, 80, 128, 178, 185, 193, 201; tobacco 33, 48, 51, 61, 120
clandestine film 110, 171–172; pictures 55, 58, 78, 126, 127, 136, 145, 146, 171
classes 43, 54, 57, 70, 84, *85*, 87, 121, 158
clothes 40, 41, 58, 59, 79, 93, 115, 129, 181, 201, 208, 219
le colis de France 81, 82, 139, 140
colonial troops 135, 151, 233, 234, 239
comité d'Alger 161, 238
Commandant 41, 43, 45, 65, 91, 99, 101, 104, 115, 120, 157, 160, 175, 185, 186, 189, 195, 204, 205, 208, 214; sent to reprisal camp 107, 141
communiqués 41, 44, 105, 131, 133, 146, 162, 178, 179, 180, 181, 184, 186, 187, 191, 199, 202, 204, 205, 206
community 11, 17, 41, 43, 44, 53, 54, 60, 65, 70, 72, 73, 81, 82, 121, 137, 151, 175, 186
compass 90, 92, 156, 163, 166
control 9, 27, 28, 44, 50, 82, 87, 95, 111, 129, 151, 188
cooperation 41, 101, 155, 235; *see also* colis de France
Coupe-racine 126
courage 10, 28, 31, 69, 87, 119, 127, 183, 225; will 10, 46, 72
cross 42, 45, 93, 95, 129, 134, 179, 226
crowded 9, 10, 21, 27, 41, 58, 78, 82
crucifix 93, 99, 115, 120, 136, 192
le cubilo 130, 131
Czechoslovakia 14, 32, 165, 197, 200

Darlan, Admiral, Jean 86, 98, 104, 147, 148, 232, 234, 235, 236, 237
Défense de la France 142, 175
de Gaulle, General Charles 8, 49, 50, 51, 101, 104, 146, 161, 169, 181, 182, 231–232, 233, 234, 235, 236, 239
de Lattre de Tassigny, General Jean 8, 180, 183, 185, 235, 239
demobilization 18, 20, 21, 23, 63, 65, 219, 220, 235
detention camp 60
Dieppe, Operation Jubilee 142
dignity 6, 41, 44, 72, 125, 128, 129, 229
diplomatic pouch 141, 155
discussions 61, 62, 63, 101, 11, 124, 165, 178
doctors 69, 143, 185, 213
Dudule 130, 134, 162
Dunkirk 16, 31
Durs (Tough Guys) 96, 107, 108

Edelbach 7, 32, 35, 88
Eisenhower, General Dwight D. 182, 225, 234, 248

El Alamein 143, 144, 147, 151, 234
electricity 50, 58, 89, 96, 140, 146, 152, 184, 189, 192
Ellenberger, François 139, 223
enlisted men, French (orderlies) 35, 44, 80, 82, 93, 106, 122, 131, 152, 212
Equatorial Africa 233
equipment (made by officer POWs) 50, 60, 82, 183, 192, 193; *see also* stoves
escapes 63, 95, 102, 103, 118, 126, 128, 131, 132, 133, 141, 163; tunnels 89, 102, 130, 139, 140, 153, 157, 160, 170, 178
Ethiopia 100
exhibitions 59, 106, 111, 134, 136, 144, 145, 159
exile 9, 29, 74, 81, 82, 95, 117, 152, 210, 221, 224

families 9, 13, 29, 26, 44, 47, 50, 59, 66, 67, 70, 73, 74, 79, 109, 110, 122, 131, 140, 152, 153, 161, 175, 180, 210, 219, 221, 223; *see also* children
farandole 80
fields 37, 41, 124, 164, 186, 191
films 14, 110, 115, 125, 127, 134, 155, 156, 159
fleas 58, 161
Flying Fortress Bomber B-17 210, *211, 212*
folkloric dances 106; fandango, Yan petit 142; Languedoc *113*
food 10, 20, 21, 27, 33, 38, 44, 53, 54, 57, 59, 65, 66, 69, 80, 93, 124, 131, 173, 182, 185, 189, 195, 199, 202, 204, 207, 213, 214, 216; dreaming of 43; ingredients 38, 130, 148, 155, 173, 175, 205; meals 39, 58, 59
Frankl, Viktor Emil 45
Free French Forces 102–104, 144, 146, 151, 157, 232, 233, 234, 235, 239
freedom 38, 39, 45, 67, 68, 73, 81, 97, 104, 109, 122, 124, 132, 141, 166, 191, 192, 198, 206, 226, 229; *see also* spiritual life
Freistadt 299, 200
French First Army 183, 235
French town 5, 53, 82, 83, 84, 93, 94, 105, 106, 111
Frieser, Karl-Heinz 31, 64, 241*n*5

games: board games 59, 70, 77, 86, 97, 117; cards 14, 66, 84, 151; other 158
garden 98, 106, 145, 155, 158, 161, 175, 177, 183
Geneva Convention 9, 18, 38, 44, 200, 243*ch*5*n*1, 243*ch*5*n*2
German Administration 37, 39, 44, 48, 75, 90, 94, 106, 115, 120, 157, 160, 213; surrender 205; *see also* Mr. Loyal

Index

German reports 10, 31, 60, 78, 96, 126
German surrender 213, 240
Gestapo 44, 47, 89, 98, 134
Giraud, General Henri 133, 134, 135, 147, 148, 161, 234, 235, 236, 237, 238
gniouf 93, 106, 132, 133, 139, 174, 183
Göpfritz 34, 35, 109, 138, 187, 213, 214
Gratzen (Nove Hrady) 197, 216
Groupe Francs 208
groups 20, 22, 57, 60, 70, 74, 77, 146, 155, 175, 239; hobbies 53, 97, 121; *see also Centre Pétain*; temporary camps
guards 22, 28, 33, 36, 39, 62, 69, 86, 90, 91, 127, 128, 146, 158, 165, 167, 172, 174, 189, 194, 196, 200, 202, 204

Haguenau 19, 20, 22, 23, 52, 66, 67, *68*
Hess, Rudolf 98
hiding 127, 128, 157, 158, 171, 172
Hitler 7, 14, 15, 28, 35, 56, 61, 62, 79, 88, 98, 105, 118, 147, 153, 178, 200, 203
homeland 42, 56, 84, 93, 111, 117
honor 6, 10, 14, 23, 24, 40, 41, 63, 67, 73, 82, 88, 101, 104, 108, 113, 120, 125, 128, 131, 153, 203, 225, 229
horseracing 70
humiliation 9, 20, 29, 40, 65, 46; *see also* physical conditions

idleness 5, 41, 43, 45
infirmary 37, 136, 191
instruments 139; compass 90, 92, 156, 163, 166
isolation 38, 40, 77, 95, 222, 227, 231

Je suis partout (newspaper) 50
jeeps 207, 208, 215
Jews 181

Kaplitz (Kaplice) 200, 201
Koufra 87, 233, 239

Lager-marks 103, 114, 182
landings: Algiers 147; Dieppe 142, 143; Normandy 174, 175, 176; Toulon 180
landscaping 10, 106, 158, 175
language, foreign 40, 74, 77, 85, 146
latrines 38, 55, 173
Laval, Pierre 62, 80, 135
lavatory 38, 39, 58, 139, 173
Lebanon, Syria 103, 104, 233
Leclerc de Hauteclocque, General Philippe 150, 151, 182, 183, 233, 239
lectures 20, 43, 45, 54, 73, 74, 81, 87, 114, 178
Leray, Jean 54, 139, 223

letters 10, 26, 47, 48, 52, 70, 74, 88, 90, 109, 122, 141, 153, 184
liberation , 205, 210, 214, 215, 217
library 20, 66, 72, 73, 91, 97, 100, 121, 124, 134, 224
Linz 33, 199, 206, 209
Lormier, Dominique 237
Loyal, Mr. 34, 38, 39, 55, 57, 60; roll call 41, 63, 77, 89, 95, 97, 105, 118, 128, 139, 141, 145
Lübeck 181, 182
La Maffia 102, 110, 120, 127, 137, 141, 142, 155, 158, 171, 175, 182, 186, 189, 208, 222

Maginot Line 13, 14, 16, 19–20; *see also* Haguenau
mailroom 91, 110, 127
Mainz 30–33
La Marche Lorraine 88, 162
Marie, Capitaine de Vaisseau René 74, 99, 101, 104, 105
Mers-el-Kébir 60, 232
misery 9, 26, 36, 41, 110, 176, 223
Mitterand, François Maurice 40
morale 1, 13, 14, 15, 16, 20, 106, 110, 153, 214
motto 9, 229
movie camera 171
movie theater 114, 115
music 61, 62, 63, 71, 106, 115, 136, 178, 183; choir 9, 51, 53, 58, 77, 93, 147; orchestra 63, 71, 82, 88, 106, 120
Mussolini, Benito 14, 61, 160, 203

Neuf-Brisach 21–22, 52, 66, 67, *68*
news service 10, 146, 147
newspaper, French 142
night officer 61
nights 81, 96, 103, 107, 109, 118, 130, 146, 156, 171, 173, 197, 200, 205
Normand officers 175, 178, 179
North Africa 8, 14, 135, 147, 148, 151, 157, 233, 235, 236, 237

officer of the day 39, 56–58, 61
officer pay 47, 140, 182, 222
open air theater 114, 125, 153, 157, 161, 163
organization, formal 41, 188

packages 10, 56, 59, 60, 80, 88, 159, 173, 184, 187; censorship of 90; diplomatic pouch 141; diverting of 109, 110, 126, 127
Pelote basque 115, 142
Pétain, Marshal Philippe 16, 17, 19, 24, 53, 62, 103, 119, 120, 125, 135, 137, 147, 148, 223, 231, 235, 236

Index

Pétainists 101, 125
Petite France 84, 103, 144
physical conditions 35, 37–39
physical education 57, 70, 82, 87, 108, 158, 164
ping-pong 74, 87
poisson d'avril 131
Polish officers (POWs) 55, 57, 129
popotes 81, 170, 131, 183
powerlessness 27, 36, 44, 95; *see also* control
printing press 82, 83, 135
punishment 60, 96, 141

radio broadcasts 50, 103, 137, 143, 146, 147, 205, 214, 235
radios 10, 103, 126, 127, 141, 146, 147, 152, 179, 197, 235
rats 58, 185
Red Cross 14, 21, 41, 59, 60, 66, 69, 97, 120, 121, 128, 131, 173, 185, 199, 203
Régénération (group) 102; *see also* stool pigeons
Das Reich (movie) 139
Reims 233
repatriation 63, 78, 89, 104, 109, 136, 214
reprisal 17, 118, 133, 134, 142, 143, 185
reprisal camp 44, 107, 132, 141; Lübeck 181, 182
resistance 69, 93, 101, 142, 153, 156, 168, 182, 232; in the camp 137, 138, 169, 172, 175; *see also* La Maffia
respect 6, 10, 22, 44, 56, 120, 229, 244*ch*5*n*30
retaliation 63, 89, 96, 103, 126, 128, 233
La Révolution Nationale 119, 231
roll calls 6, 41, 45, 49, 58, 63, 95, 96, 130, 141, 145, 151, 152, 165, 174, 181
Rommel, Erwin Johannes Eugen (Desert Fox) 87, 144, 234
Roosevelt, President Franklin D. 189, 225, 235, 236, 237, 239, 247*ch*9*n*26
Russians 190, 215–217

saints 51, 53, 77, 120, 129
Santa Claus workshop 115, *116*
Sartre, Jean Paul 15
Scapini, Georges 56, 57, 87, 151
searches 26, 36, 39, 40, 68, 98, 102, 126, 127, 128, 139, 158, 160
seasons 59, 100, 130, 134, 136, 142, 155, 158, 161, 175, 185, 189, 207; *see also* winter
Sélestat 26, 27, 28, 242*ch*3*n*1
La Semaine de France 106, 110, 111, *113–114*
sentinels 27, 33, 35
shame 137, 222
shoes 39, 59, 66, 86, 92, 129, 141, 171

showers 10, 39, 58, 68
singe 173
snake 161
soccer 52, 66, 96, 135
solitude 77, 78
spanking 155
spiritual life 9, 38, 45, 81, 229
sports 52, 82, 87, 106, 141, 143, 162, 164, 178, 180
stadium 106, *107*, 108, 111, 115, 143, 162
stalags 5, 35, 64, 139
Stalingrad 145, 146, 148, 152
"sticky fingers" 126–127
stool pigeons 89, 102, 131, 140
stoves *(cupola)* 152, 154, 171, 172, 184, 225
supplies 90
surrender 19, 20, 23, 25, 40, 87, 100, 213, 239, 239
survival 41, 73, 82, 131, 221; *see also* spiritual life

teachers 74, 108, 121, 139
teams (sports) 52, 115, 135
temporary camps 20, 22, 65, 69
theater 71, 76, 77, 84, 85, 97, 108, 123, 130, 134, 157, 159, 183
tin cans (canned food containers) 60, 82, 89, 90, 106, 130, 136, 173
Todt, organisation 29
tools 40, 76, 106, 157, 162, 192, 215; pliers 63, 92, 96, 107, 126, 132
Tour de France 114
toys *116*, 117, 144, 207
le Trait d'Union 49–50
trunk 191, 215, 227
Tunisia 148, 151, 157, 248
typhon 160, 248

Université de Captivité Oflag XVIIA 54, 55, 84, 87, 91, 97, 99, 115, 121, 139, 151, 186
unrest 96, 128, 138, 145, 174

Veterans Day, *le 11 novembre* 63
Vichy regime 50, 103, 104, 123, 124, 125, 135
Vienna, Austria 7, 12, 35, 82, 95, 96, 97, 110, 126, 145, 160, 166, 167, 185, 189, 214, 216
Volkischer Beobachter 49, 50, 61, 80, 98, 120, 133, 136, 139, 184
Vorlager (administration building) 58, 88, 90–91
Vosges Mountains 16, 18, 19, 21, 25, 26, 68, 239

waiting (emotional state) 18, 37, 59, 81, 98, 145, 149, 164, 176, 184, 191, 203, 206, 207, 210, 220

Der Waldviertel 7, 223, 227
will 10, 46, 110
winter 14, 61, 63, 78, 79, 81, 100, 118, 120, 126, 150, 172, 185
Wolff, M. Étienne 48, 139, 223

women 41, 71, 76, 82, 113, 122, 161, 172, 194, 197, 220, 221
work for Germans 5, 44, 54, 82, 91, 126, 133, 134, 135, 138, 145
World War I veterans 70, 105, 107, 109, 110, 222

www.ingramcontent.com/pod-product-compliance
Ingram Content Group UK Ltd.
Pitfield, Milton Keynes, MK11 3LW, UK
UKHW041934140426
5217IPUK00014B/471